Temple Smith • London

First published in Great Britain 1972
by Maurice Temple Smith Ltd
Jubilee House, Chapel Road, Hounslow, Middlesex TW3 1XT

Reprinted 1972, 1974

Second edition 1975

First paper edition 1979

Reprinted 1983

© 1975 C. H. BARRY and F. TYE

Printed and bound in Great Britain by
Billing and Sons Limited Worcester

ISBN 0 85117 190 7

We acknowledge an immense debt of gratitude to a great many heads, deputy heads, inspectors, advisers and lecturers, who have shared their philosophy and experience with us, as well as to a number of administrators, reviewers and personal and professional friends, who have offered us constructive criticisms and comments upon the text.

Contents

Introduction

Running a School was written under compulsion. When we began to work together, in 1969, we quickly became aware that our general outlook and experience were corroborative and complementary. It was also clear that we shared a deep concern and anxiety for the welfare of secondary education, at a time of rapid change and growing uncertainty. The significance of these two factors was then massively reinforced for us, over the next five years, by the experience of working closely and continuously with groups of heads and deputy heads, in a series of working parties and study-conferences. These study-conferences began at the University of Manchester, and in 1972, were transferred to the Educational Management Centre at Padgate College of Education (near Warrington, in Cheshire). In concept and content they have been concerned with what can be broadly summarised as the philosophy and management of secondary education. Their impact upon us has been to strengthen and deepen our own convictions and attitudes, to make us re-examine our own beliefs and practices and to identify particular areas of stress and controversy in the running of secondary schools today. They have also revealed a widespread search and longing for some theoretical and practical help, which was expressed by a very large number of heads and deputy heads. They felt the need for something which might loosely be described as 'training', so long as it included reassurance, on the one hand, and the acquisition of new skills and management techniques, on the other, which would be applicable to the running of what have now generally become much larger and more complex secondary schools.

As the first draft of the book began to take shape, our own conviction grew that secondary education was passing through a period of crisis. Traditional beliefs and practices, educational as well as social, were no longer accepted without question. The basic foundations upon which secondary education had been developed were the subject of vehement and even acrimonious debate. Authority itself, together with many of the values, standards, assumptions and practices which had become closely woven into the whole fabric of secondary education, was now open to vigorous and often cynical attack. Society has rejected, in practice, many of the moral, cultural and educational aims upon which secondary education has been based, but still expects the schools to uphold them in their teaching and in the behaviour of their pupils. At the same time there has been thrust upon the schools responsibility for confronting and overcoming the inequalities, deprivations and ugly manifestations of contemporary society (from truancy and the disruptive pupil, to violence, vandalism and soccer hooliganism), and all this despite the fact that society itself is patently unable or unwilling to tackle the task itself. In consequence, schools have become subject to a degree of external pressure and publicity hitherto unknown. Moreover, this has occurred at a time when the schools are engaged in a determined attempt to assimilate the new ideas and techniques which size and reorganisation have imposed upon them, and are striving to reassess what they are trying to do, and how they might best hope to achieve it, within the resources available to them.

In this situation, we set out to conduct a pragmatic examination of many of the issues which face secondary schools today. We were concerned to apply theoretical concepts and principles to the solution of everyday questions and situations. We wanted to develop, if it were possible, a coherent philosphy of secondary education embracing purposes, convictions and values, which would (at the same time) sustain a consistent code of 'best practice', applicable to most of the professional, organisational and administrative problems with which all secondary schools are now confronted.

Running a School is not a handbook, although it is essentially about running schools. Most of its examples, illustrations and case-studies have been drawn from the practice of secondary education. It is directed particularly to the heads and deputy heads of secondary schools, and to all their colleagues, particularly those who are closely associated with them in the processes of framing policies and taking decisions. Throughout, our concern has been to identify fundamental principles and over-riding priorities. We have deliberately eschewed solutions, except in the most general terms. No attempt has been made to match every problem with a pat resolution of it : for we firmly believe that identifying the right questions is just as important, and often more difficult, than finding acceptable answers. Effective solutions can only be evolved in the light of all the personalities and circumstances involved, and of all the resources available in any one school at any one time. Nevertheless, we hope that the range of concepts and situations which we have explored is sufficiently varied to furnish readers with a strong incentive and a firm basis for reassessment of their own beliefs, practices and traditions. For our purpose has been to provide not a precise itinerary but a reliable map, upon which each reader can plot his own journey as he explores the ideas, the principles and the priorities which we have investigated, and then applies them to his own particular circumstances.

We have been most gratified by the response to the first edition. This has confirmed our own experience that there is an almost desperate search for professional support, technical skills and some degree of confidence and security, on the part of those who carry the burden and heat of the day in secondary education. The prospect of a second edition has given us an opportunity of re-examining and re-affirming our main thesis, of updating our material, and of revealing the extent to which our own philosophy has developed, in several important respects, in the light of experience gained since the first edition went to press. We still hope that the book may be of interest not only to the staffs of secondary schools, but to all who are responsible for the welfare of secondary education: that is to say to local authority administrators; chairmen and members of education committees; governors of schools; inspectors, advisers, and organisers (by whatever name our educational consultants are known in different areas), education lecturers in colleges, polytechnics and universities; student-teachers in training; and last, but by no means least, parents with children of secondary school age. While we have written in the general context of schools maintained by local education authorities, we believe that the principles which are discussed can apply, with equal force and relevance, to voluntary, direct-grant and independent schools. Indeed, much of our general argument should be of interest to all who carry managerial responsibility for education in general, not only in secondary but in primary schools and in colleges of all kinds.

Two further words of explanation are necessary. First, the case-studies and simulations included in the text are all drawn from genuine school situations, although they have been appropriately disguised. Any similarity to particular individuals or to identifiable schools is unintended. Secondly, although it is quite clear, in our context, that the term 'head' includes headmistresses as well as headmasters, our consistent use of the masculine gender is simply intended to avoid tedious circumlocution and repetition.

C.H.B.   F.T.

October, 1974

I PRINCIPLES

1 Robert Walton

You are Headmaster of Greenbank School, Easthampton, in the county of Radford. Greenbank is a 4-form entry secondary school for boys and girls. It serves one half of the small but ancient town of Easthampton, together with the adjoining areas of the county. You have been Head of Greenbank for rather more than four years.

Mr Robert Walton, your music specialist, and only teacher of music, is a friendly, willing but now ineffectual colleague of 49. He is completely incapable of maintaining discipline in any class, owing to his extreme diffidence, much of which is believed to stem from a severe mental illness from which he suffered, several years ago, before you came to the school. He is paid a Scale 2 salary (a probable indication of his capability as a music teacher before his illness), but the present standard of music teaching is very poor. Much inconvenience has been caused by noise and indiscipline in the music room, and by the difficulty of persuading classes to settle down for their next period, when they have come from a music lesson.

Mr Walton is very much in your mind, today, because you have not only had, this morning, through your deputy, the latest of a long series of complaints from the staff, but also a letter from the Principal of the neighbouring College of Education asking if you could accept a good music student for her five-week final teaching practice next term. By the same post you have also heard from the Director of Education of a neighbouring county, to whom Mr Walton has applied for a post in a junior school. You are asked for a confidential reference, and are told that the post for which Mr Walton has applied will include music throughout the school (8 classes) plus general subjects with one class, and that it carries a salary on Scale I.

Now this is a familiar enough situation with which, in broad general terms, every head is confronted, at some time or other in his career. It has been chosen for examination and discussion quite

deliberately, because its everyday, run-of-the-mill characteristics reveal
and illustrate many of the basic principles which underlie the running of a secondary school. It is, indeed, the purpose of this book to
suggest that, in such a situation as this, it is first necessary to identify
these principles, and then to put them into some order of priority.

To begin with, you are bound to be concerned for Mr Walton
himself. He has been teaching for nearly thirty years, and he was
clearly, at one time, a competent teacher of music. His present in-
ability to maintain even a modicum of discipline is evidently, at
least in part, a consequence of a nervous breakdown which he suffered
several years ago. He is, therefore, fully entitled not only to your
sympathy and concern, but to your professional support and protection. Confronted with the difficult situation arising from today's
complications, you are bound, first, to re-examine your professional
conscience as a headmaster. Have Mr Walton's difficulties with class
control been allowed to develop, and to become a habit, until they
have been accepted as inevitable, and are regarded as a cross to be
borne with what patience you and your colleagues can muster? Have
you yourself, and have senior members of your staff, at your instiga-
tion, done everything possible to help Mr Walton in the classroom
situation, by identifying, with him, the exact nature of his problems,
by offering him continuous support, encouragement and advice, and
by making him feel that you were all genuinely trying to help him to
overcome his difficulties? Has he obtained medical advice about his
state of health, and his general fitness to continue teaching, and have
you called upon all the available professional help from your local
HMI, his specialist music colleague, and the county music adviser?
In the course of all these discussions you have probably considered
whether Mr Walton's best interests would be served by transfer to
another secondary school, or whether he might be happier and more
successful if he were to teach younger children; indeed, you have
almost certainly asked yourself whether he might be well advised to
give up teaching altogether, by taking a breakdown pension, and by
making use of his musical skills in some other direction. In all these
anxious deliberations you will, of course, have been in continuous
consultation with Mr Walton himself, advising him to consult his
professional association, and leaving him in no doubt that you were
anxious, so far as lay in your power, to protect both his personal

interests and welfare as well as his professional status and position.

The more closely you have identified yourself with Mr Walton and his problems, however, the more forcefully you have been reminded that you cannot consider his difficulties in isolation. You have a concurrent responsibility for all his colleagues, whose work is being continuously disrupted, as well as for the children in the school, whose discipline is being undermined, and who are being almost entirely deprived of the contribution which music should make to their general education. The staff have 'carried' Mr Walton for a long time; although they have grumbled and complained, with good reason, several of them with musical interests have rallied round to rehearse the school choir, and to put together a modest, face-saving music programme on a number of special occasions. Some of the children, too, have shown their enthusiasm by starting spontaneous recorder, disc-jockey and pop groups, to foster their own musical interests. But these circumstances, although encouraging in themselves, have done little to ease your painful awareness that the balance of your curriculum is upset, and its content impoverished, by the failure of music to fulfil its proper function in the overall pattern of education which the school sets out to provide.

Inside the school, therefore, it is clear that Mr Walton and his personal and professional problems arouse many conflicting interests and loyalties. But, however you may wish that it could be so, these loyalties cannot be confined to the internal running of the school. For instance, your governing body is inevitably involved, and must be anxious to offer you effective guidance and support in establishing some order of priority among the interests which you and they have been appointed to serve and protect. Moreover, your local education authority is confronted with ultimate responsibility, not only for the employment of Mr Walton, but, through you, for the effective organisation and administration of Greenbank School. In addition, you are continually aware that you have a major responsibility towards the parents of your children. Indeed, the more closely you wish to involve your parents in understanding and participation, the more pressing is the need to take them into your confidence over the present state of music teaching in the school, and so to enlist their sympathy and patience. Neither you nor they can accept with equanimity a situation in which a whole generation of children is being deprived of musical experience, under skilled direction, and in which their curriculum embodies a significant imbalance of which you and they are fully aware.

Nor has the position been made any easier by the Principal's letter this morning. In one sense it would be a relief to have a skilful music student in the school for a period of five weeks, which might arouse fresh interest in music among the children and even, perhaps, ease Mr Walton's difficulties thereafter. Moreover, it is one of your basic tenets that Greenbank ought to make its maximum contribution to the education and training of teachers by offering to the college not only practice facilities but also close and continuous professional collaboration. On the other hand, would the situation be fair either to the student, however promising, or to the Principal, however fully you take him into your confidence, and however carefully you reveal the exact position to him? A really able student might, of course, not only arouse fresh musical interest in the school, but gain for herself some invaluable professional experience into the bargain. Equally, however, she might find herself defeated by the circumstances and so be unable to do herself full justice in a situation of crucial significance for her future career. This is a dilemma in which, quite clearly, a hunch decision or a snap judgement would be wholly inappropriate.

Again, the position is further complicated by the fact that you are under a powerful moral obligation, both to the Director of Education, who has asked for your help and advice, and to the head of any school to whom Mr Walton may apply for an appointment, now or in the future. You yourself have suffered from circumstances in which some of your fellow heads have developed a Nelsonian blind eye, and in which you have been expected, without warning from them, to discover the hidden truth from within the lines of their references. You are now convinced that you cannot avoid telling the whole truth about Mr Walton, as you see and know it, however embarrassing the circumstances or the consequences. This is no comfort, however, except to your conscience, for it merely aggravates the situation with which you are confronted. You and Mr Walton are, without question, most uncomfortably hooked.

This chapter began with a situation familiar in its general outlines and content to every head and to every school, one which it would

have been only too easy to dismiss with a gesture of confident familiarity, without laying bare the skeleton of principle locked away in
the decision cupboard. In this situation, however, you have been
compelled to recognise a great many interests, each with a perfectly
legitimate claim upon your support and protection, some complementary and some competitive, and you have found yourself uneasily
walking a tightrope of decision. How, then, do you begin to resolve
the problem for yourself, and to fulfil the inescapable responsibility
of reaching a decision, or a series of decisions, even if your decision
is the negative one, for the moment at any rate, that you will bear
with Mr Walton for another year? In such circumstances, it may
help to clarify your thoughts and intentions by reassessing in your
own mind the aims and objectives which you want to attain at Greenbank and by putting them in order of priority. Is a trusting, united
and contented staff your main concern, for example, or are you
convinced that your obligation to the children in the school overrides
all other considerations? Whichever you put first, how will you fit
into the jigsaw of conflicting loyalties your concern for good relations
with your parents, your governors and local authority, the college
principal, and your professional advisers and consultants both within
and outside the school?

Clearly there can be no one 'right' answer to this complex series
of questions, and we suggest that principles are the most stable and
significant of the factors which influence decisions. If, for example,
having weighed all the conflicting claims upon your compassion and
your judgement, you should decide that your obligation to the children,
and to their parents, is your first priority, then, inevitably, your concern
for Mr Walton will have to come second or even lower in the list.
The message of this chapter, then, is that the identification of
principles is an essential step towards the successful solution of any
problem which it might be tempting to solve either by hunch, by
yielding to pressures, or by taking the easiest way out. In this case,
concern for various interests has been analysed, priorities have been
established, and resources have been examined. Since many of the
factors, including personalities and circumstances, will vary from
school to school, solutions are bound to differ. If, however, the
analysis of a problem always follows the sequence of first identifying
objectives, determining priorities, and assessing resources, before

taking action, then the ultimate answer is more likely to be acceptable than one reached on any other basis or by any other process.

Let us examine this general thesis in the context of another school situation, this time concerned with academic organisation.

2   Hindsight

In the previous chapter we were trying to identify some of the basic principles and priorities which lie behind important decisions in the ordinary work of a head. In order to take this a stage further, we ask you to exercise your patience and to imagine yourself in an entirely different situation. You are now Head of Russell Grove Secondary School. Russell Grove is a 9-form entry, mixed, 11-16, comprehensive school, in the metropolitan city of Churchill. It serves a fairly prosperous neighbourhood area, with a majority of skilled artisans, for the most part employed in various aspects of engineering, and a minority of semi-skilled and unskilled workers, most of whom are in regular employment.

You were appointed head just fifteen months after your predecessor (who is now a principal lecturer in a nearby college of education) had made a major organisational change, by 'unstreaming' the school, and adopting instead a system of mixed-ability grouping in all subjects. Presumably, by philosophy and outlook, you were not unsympathetic towards this change of policy or you would not have accepted the post, but you are now, eighteen months later, beginning to have grave doubts about the way in which it was (apparently) accomplished.

You are already convinced that there must have been inadequate preparation, consultation and training, and that insufficient steps had been taken to secure the necessary staff adjustments in attitudes, record-keeping and teaching techniques. As the school approaches the end of three academic years of unstreaming, you have accumulated substantial evidence that all is not well. In the third-year forms, with whom the change was introduced in their first year, the staff are almost unanimous in detecting a falling-off in academic standards, and in work-rate and behaviour patterns, compared with previous third years. Among themselves the staff are divided in their attitudes, and many of them are as uncertain about their professional loyalties as they are about their teaching methods and performance. Indeed, you now believe that a substantial majority in the staff-room is unconvinced of the wisdom of mixed-ability grouping; of those senior members of the staff who have revealed to you that they were originally in favour of it, two heads of major departments (English and Mathematics) now *insist* that, from September, they must be allowed to set by ability in their own subjects.

It is clear, therefore, that you find yourself in an awkward predicament. It would seem to be an emergency, calling for swift and positive action, and yet any such action, in a particularly sensitive area of school administration, is beset by booby traps. Clearly something must be done, and done quickly, or the morale and standards not only of the third year but of the whole school, will begin to deteriorate. But in which direction should you act? Is it more important to safeguard the immediate situation, and to devise palliative steps, which will halt the decline in morale, without taking any fundamental decision either to confirm or to abandon mixed-ability grouping in the long-term? Or, should you return (temporarily) to a streamed organisation in September, and simultaneously set about the long process of staff induction, preparation and training, which ought to have preceded the original change?

As in the case of Mr Robert Walton your professional rectitude and skill are directly challenged and you are confronted with many competing priorities. On the face of it, there is probably no clear-cut, incisive decision which would safeguard your own aims for the school and also bring about an immediate and dramatic change in the attitude of the staff, and in the morale and performance of the school. So it is apparent that (as with Mr Robert Walton) you will have to make a choice: but what are the factors and principles upon which that choice must ultimately be based? To begin with, you yourself are somewhat inhibited by loyalty to your predecessor, whose regime at Russell Grove was regarded as markedly successful and who enjoys an enviable professional reputation. For most of your colleagues in the common-room, who served under him for many years, this is certainly a powerful factor; they are torn between loyalty and regard for him, and concern for their own professional inadequacy in the face of class-room situations in which they now recognise that they are out of their depth. You yourself are acutely aware that your long-term success at Russell Grove may well depend, to a very significant extent, upon the way in which you handle this prickly situation. Certainly your colleagues in the staff-room are relying upon your wisdom, expertise and guidance; they are not only anxious to resolve their own difficulties in the class-room, but they depend upon you to avoid another period of chopping and changing, and to revive, in them, a corporate sense of moving together towards an agreed end. The children, and particularly those in the third year, who have been the guinea-pigs in what turns out to have been an unsuccessful experiment, look to you for protection and security, while their parents need reassurance and confidence that the school is safe in your hands and that they can trust your judgement. Equally, your governors and your local authority will be looking to you for professional advice and expertise in a situation which they are bound to recognise as crucial for the school's welfare. Now it will certainly not have escaped your notice that most of these factors were equally relevant when you were trying to resolve the problems confronting Greenbank School and Mr Walton; and this repetition emphasises the conclusion which we drew from the Robert Walton exercise, namely that decisions must be based, first, not upon personalities and circumstances, but upon fundamental principles and considerations.

Well, what are the principles lying behind the difficult problem of academic organisation at Russell Grove? The first is, surely, the question of your own philosophy and intentions, what it is that you are hoping to achieve during your headship, and what immediate tactics, in relation to the organisation of the school, you are willing to adopt, within your overall strategy. For, unless you are intellectually and emotionally committed to what you are trying to accomplish, and unless you can harmonise your immediate goals with your long-term aims, then you may find yourself in danger of paying undue attention to the latest, or to the most persuasive, word in your ear, or of seeking to find the easiest way out of the impasse without regard to long-term consequences. As you consider each of the alternative solutions which you might adopt, it is bound to be a great source of strength if you can keep in your mind's eye what you are seeking to achieve, and so can weigh each tactical solution against the only kind of long-term strategy which you find acceptable. Anything less than this must be in danger of being a hunch or *ad hoc* decision, and of buying off present troubles at the price of continued instability and confusion.

Next you would be wise to recall and reconsider the purposes for which schools adopt any particular pattern of curricular organisation. A concern for the general welfare must be harmonised with responsibility for the intellectual progress of each individual; a desire to maximise the potential capacities of the staff, and to trust the judgement of heads of department, must be offset against the resources which the school commands in terms of professional skills, accommodation, teaching aids and equipment; and the contribution of each subject to the curriculum must be assessed in the context of a balanced education which is effective for individual and community alike. In choosing any particular form of organisation, the existing patterns of public examinations, and of university and college entrance requirements must be taken into account, while the general climate of opinion, both of experts and of employers as well as of the general public, must be not overlooked. At this stage in your consideration of the problem you may well feel that it would need the wisdom of Solomon to resolve such a tangled web of conflicting claims, and so you may turn, for distraction, to some of the other basic principles which are involved in your decision.

Again, they are many. For you cannot disguise from yourself that what are involved here are not only your aims and plans for the school—all the hopes and dreams which led you to accept the offer of appointment—but also the kind of head you are, and would like to become. If you believe in maximum consultation and participation, then you will not wish to reach a decision of this importance without the fullest advice of all those who can contribute to your resources of wisdom and experience. If, on the other hand, you believe that the head himself must accept responsibility for judgements of this order, then you will wish to make sure that your 'verdict', and the reasons for it, are clearly understood and appreciated by all concerned, and that they are communicated in such a form that they can be readily translated into action.

Whatever kind of head you may consider yourself to be, you will need to have at the back of your mind a series of principles for bringing about major changes of any kind, and for securing their acceptance; you will also need to have worked out ways and means whereby new ideas and perceptions can be ventilated and discussed, and new policies can be adopted. Any such machinery for discussion is bound to include channels of communication,.if not of consultation, as well as systems of 'training', so that new concepts and techniques, at first unwelcome to many, can be transmuted into practices which are acceptable to most. And, since you are wise and experienced enough to have been appointed to Russell Grove, you must also have clearly in your mind standards and methods of assessment which will enable you to check the success or failure of any experiment which you may decide to undertake, and of any change which you may resolve to introduce.

Whatever your philosophy and views you will still have to go through the process of weighing up all the relevant considerations, and then—ultimately—of reaching a decision, and of putting it into practice. Whether you are a fanatical believer in mixed-ability grouping, a convinced exponent of broad-banding, an unrepentant disciple of setting by ability, or a liberal middle-of-the-roader, 'open to conviction', you will still have to go through the mill of considering first principles and of weighing priorities against each other. For, only so will you reach a decision which will stand up to rigorous examination, and which will carry conviction as an integral part of your policy for the school.

Let us now summarise your experience so far. For the second time, and in quite different circumstances, you have found yourself considering a familiar and comparatively straightforward situation, and yet being driven back to first principles in order to achieve an acceptable solution. So it begins to look as though there may be a pattern behind all major decisions, that running a secondary school involves the exercise of analytical skills and of professional expertise— each of no mean order—and that there is a framework of principles within which all school organisation and administration takes place. In the next chapter we shall seek to identify these principles, to consider the processes involved, and to indicate the framework within which they operate.

3 Tackling the job

Is it possible, in fact, to detect a system or pattern behind the processes which we have been following in the exercises on 'Robert Walton' and 'Hindsight'? If so, can the characteristics of such a system be identified, and can they be shown to have general relevance in the context of education? In essence, both situations were of a kind often encountered in secondary school experience, but we found, on examination, nevertheless, that they involved many different groups of people (staff, children, parents, governors, local authority), and many different interests and concerns (the balance of the curriculum, the quality of the teaching, the security and effectiveness of the staff, the morale and welfare of the children, and the general reputation of the school — to mention only the most important of them). In both exercises, too, we were obliged to re-examine our aims and objectives, both long- and short-term, in order to find a genuine solution which did not merely blur, defer, or exacerbate the problems involved. Moreover, we were compelled to recognise that there were complicating factors in trying to establish an order of action priorities. First, there was the choice of which objective, among many, to pursue, as a matter of immediate priority, because of its intrinsic importance. Secondly, it was necessary to reach a decision about which objective to tackle in relation to its urgency in the time-scale, and to the possibility of putting it into immediate effect.

These two considerations may, of course, be incompatible with each other, in which case it will be necessary either to choose between them or to reach a satisfactory compromise. Such a compromise, although not ideal, must still be acceptable in relation to the assessment of priorities, and be capable of being put into immediate operation. It is salutary to remember, however, that while compromise is often inevitable, there are compromises and compromises: some will continue to have the best of two or more worlds, while others will only achieve the worst and will create no lasting satisfaction.

Over and over again similar dilemmas are experienced. In the first exercise, as we saw, it was necessary to decide whether the personal and professional welfare of Mr Walton should take precedence over the welfare of the children and the state of music teaching in the school. In 'Hindsight' there was the possibility of stark conflict between long-range policy in respect of school organisation, and the very natural wish to find a quick way out of a difficult situation. There was, in fact, no satisfactory way of avoiding a choice, in order of immediate priority, between the interests of the third-year forms, who were suffering from the experiment, and the morale and teaching effectiveness of the staff. Yet, even when it may be possible to establish a clear order of priorities, on grounds of significance alone, the time factor often enters into the calculation and so affects the final decision. The action which is recognised as coming nearest to offering an acceptable solution may, for example, be impossible to take, at that moment, for a whole host of reasons. The very urgency of a problem may brook no delay, and so may deny the opportunity for mature consideration of its implications; or a decision taken now may have serious consequences two or three years hence, and these consequences may be even more intractable than the problem which the original decision was designed to solve! Indeed, the truth must be faced not only that immediate objectives may often be in conflict with long-term aims, but that one objective may be in conflict with another.

In a dream world it would be exciting to press a button which would solve all the problems at once. But in the world of reality it would be a most unusual coincidence if a single decision could achieve a number of different results, simultaneously, however closely they were associated with each other. So choice becomes an integral part of the decision-making process, whether it is a choice between degrees of importance and significance (answering the question, 'Which is the most important objective at the moment?'), or a choice between action today, next week, next term—or never (answering the question 'When?').

It begins to look, therefore, as if we have now identified two basic factors in the solution of any problem. Before reaching a conclusion on any issue of substance it is suggested that the head should:

1   Make a critical appraisal of the exact situation by which he is confronted, and undertake a realistic assessment of the constraints to which he is subject, and of the resources which are available to him; and

2   Re-examine in his own mind exactly what it is that he is hoping to accomplish for the school—tomorrow, next term and ten years hence—so that general aims and explicit objectives can be considered in relation to any particular problem or set of circumstances.

These two stages should precede the reaching of decisions or the planning of policy, and we believe them to be of such importance that they will be examined in much greater detail in Chapters 4, 5 and 6.

When these two preliminary but essential steps before considering the solution of a problem have been taken, it is then, and only then, sensible to move on to making a decision, which will take full account of present circumstances and of future consequences, but which will also be in accord with long-term policy. However, in reaching a decision there are, again, limiting factors and restraints, and the cards may be stacked against good intentions. More often than not a decision is restricted by the nature and extent of the resources which are available for carrying it out. In Mr Robert Walton's case, for example, a particular difficulty was created by the fact that he was the only teacher of music on the staff, and the head was bound to rely, to a large extent, upon the quality and realism of the professional help and advice which were available to him from outside the school. In the same way, in the exercise on mixed-ability grouping, resources of space, time and man-power all have to be taken into account. It would be of little use to reach what might seem to be an ideal solution, if it could not be put into operation because (1) the teaching accommodation immediately available was inadequate or unsuitable, or (2) the necessary funds and materials were not at the school's disposal, or (3) the implementation of such a decision would demand greater time for preparation and execution than the circumstances afforded, or 4) it would strain the goodwill and expertise of the staff (and perhaps of children, parents and governors, too!) beyond reasonable expectation. So, for a head, as for an industrialist, a politician or a general, a realistic knowledge and appreciation of the resources available to him, at any one moment in time, is an essential prerequisite for effective action.

But, to be fully effective, this appreciation of present circumstances must be combined with a realistic forecast of the probable consequences which will follow any chosen course of action. This sounds fairly simple but experience suggests that it is easy enough to be caught out. For example, the introduction of a new subject or option into the curriculum, however courageous and justifiable, at the moment, will almost certainly involve additional teaching strength and additional teaching accommodation several years later. In addition, it may also damage or destroy the future status of another subject or option, already well established in the curriculum, and so not only adversely affect the prospects of the members of staff directly concerned, but even make specialist accommodation and equipment redundant. So, an imaginative calculation of consequences, by identifying and following through the probable repercussions of a decision on different groups of people, and on different sectors of a school's life, is yet another source of strength in the development of a decision or policy. Such consequences cannot always be foreseen in advance, however, and the process of forecasting is not as straightforward as it may appear at first sight. We shall be having another look at this procedure in Part II (Chapter 10), while the use of resources will be examined in some depth in Part III (Chapters 13-16).

A further element in the process of decision-making is the capacity to assess the consequences, both direct and indirect, which have actually followed a previous course of action. Earlier in this chapter we argued the need for assessing the immediate present, and for looking objectively at things as they are, and not as a head would like them to be, or as he assumes, without proof or confirmation, that they must be. Happy is the head who knows exactly what goes on in every classroom in his school! Yet, the capacity to look critically not only at what the consequences of an action may be, but also at what they actually have been, in practice, is an essential stage in the process of planning, a vital link in the machinery of decision-making. For, in a secondary school, as in so many other areas of major executive responsibility, this process and this machinery are in continuous operation; the calculation of how things may work out, followed by an assessment of how they have actually worked out in practice, will not only strengthen knowledge of the present, but will materially affect all new decisions about the future. So assessment becomes an essential element in every long-term policy or plan, and we shall return to this factor of assessment in Part IV (Chapters 17-19).

So we have now identified two more basic factors. These suggest that, before reaching a decision of any significance, the head should:

3 Estimate the probable results of all the actions which might be taken and then, having chosen one of them, use the appropriate resources and organisation to give effect to it; and

4 Pursue a policy of continuous assessment of any measures which he has put into operation.

However skilfully they are operated, of course, the four factors which we have now identified will not, by themselves, produce a solution. They are not, in themselves, a policy for action, but only a means whereby an effective decision may be taken. They will only indicate the balance of advantages and disadvantages, the pros and cons of each decision, having regard to existing priorities and resources and probable future consequences. They do not relieve the head of responsibility, nor take his decisions for him. They do not make the decisions any easier to take: indeed, they may sometimes appear to make them more difficult, by revealing underlying complexities, some of which he might otherwise have overlooked. The decisions will still be the head's, and this is surely right, not only in principle but in fact. For there can be no single answer or solution applicable to all schools which happen to be faced with a similar or common problem. Aims, objectives, priorities, personalities, resources, circumstances and styles of headship are all bound to vary from school to school. It is this which gives the British secondary school system one of its distinguishing characteristics and enables each school to maintain its own particular ethos, quality and purpose.

These four factors, then, offer a planned and systematic approach to the solution of any problem of educational organisation or administration. Problems vary in size and complexity, of course, and the practised head will resolve some of them quickly, by a combination of experience and intuition; but, even so, however unconsciously, he will probably have followed a thought-process which can be summarised in the following terms:

1 Analysing, precisely, the situation in which he finds himself.
2 Identifying his aims and objectives and establishing an order of priority among them.
3 Devising and putting into operation the means of achieving his aims and objectives. He will do this, first, by considering the full range of alternative decisions open to him and, then, by carrying out his chosen course of action, making the best use of his resources and of his organisation.
4 Devising and putting into operation the means of assessing the extent to which his aims and objectives are being fulfilled. This he will accomplish by establishing criteria and methods of evaluation, and by keeping them in continuous action.

For purpose of summary these four functions have been listed in linear form, but it would be more realistic to show them as a circle, the fourth function leading directly back to the first, and so keeping the whole process continuously in motion. Sometimes, the results of his assessment will cause the head to modify his aims or his methods, or both. Sometimes the results will show him that his objectives were unrealistic, his resources inadequate or his aims too modest and unambitious. In all of these circumstances, further decisions must follow. Too much complacency, or an over-developed sense of disappointment and failure, are equally disastrous. For success and failure, alike, have consequences, both immediate and long-term, and the whole cycle of decision-making must remain in continuous operation. New targets must be set, new methods adopted, new resources acquired and new criteria of assessment adopted.

It is implicit in all that we have so far said that despite his ultimate, individual responsibility, the head does not work in isolation, but that he will always be in close consultation, at all stages, with those who are in a position to offer him advice and to influence his judgement. By this means continuous consultation by the head becomes the hub of the school's decision-making process, as we shall see in Chapters 10 and 11. The head's example also inspires members of the staff to engage in consultation with each other, whether in upper, middle or lower school, within a subject department, within a house or year organisation devised for the exercise of pastoral care, or within many other levels and ranges of staff concern and responsibility.

At this stage, before we develop our thesis further, it may be appropriate to emphasise that there is nothing about this process which is peculiar to the practice of education. Indeed, these four factors would apply with equal force and relevance to anyone in a position of managerial responsibility — to the director of a company or the captain of a liner, to the commodore of an air force or the governor of a prison, to the secretary of a hospital group or the permanent secretary of a government department, to the chief education officer of a local authority or the vice-chancellor of a university. What we have defined in general terms are, in fact, basic principles of management in a host of different circumstances and situations. But there is much more to successful management than the recognition and operation of these four factors, as we hope to show in the course of this book. Yet we believe that the four factors can be seen to apply to the basic processes of planning and decision-making in the running of a school, and that they also get somewhere near to revealing the skeleton of management itself, as a general process. But it *is* only a skeleton. It will be brought to life by the head, with the flesh and blood of organisation which he imposes upon it.

We must, of course, be wary of claiming too much. It would be naive to pretend that this fourfold thought-process will apply exactly in every educational context. At the same time it would be unrealistic to suggest that a head will always be able to answer the questions in their strict chronological order. Circumstances and pressures beyond his control will frequently confront him with the questions 'upside down' or 'inside out'. Nevertheless, we are convinced that they provide a helpful framework on which to build our further examination of managerial skills. So we now propose to re-state our analysis in the simplest terms and, in the rest of the book, to explore these four direct questions:

> *Where are you?*
> *Where are you going?*
> *How do you intend to get there?*
> *How will you know when you have got there?*

4   Constraints

The scene changes yet again as the discussion leads us on to face and answer the first of these four questions, *Where are you?* and, with the change of scene, circumstances change too. Forget for the moment your association with Greenbank and Russell Grove Schools, and be prepared to find yourself in an entirely new situation.

For you are now the newly-appointed Head of Meadowvale School. It is the first day of the summer term, and your first working day in the school. Meadowvale is also your first headship. It is a well-established 4-form entry, mixed, secondary modern school, of a pretty traditional kind, which is destined to become part of a much larger comprehensive school (by amalgamation) at some unknown date in the future. This date is so uncertain, however, that you have received from your governors and the local authority positive assurances, which enabled you not only to accept the appointment, but to feel that you have an opportunity of making a real impact upon the school, and of preparing it to take part in its new and more complex role.

You are no stranger to Meadowvale, of course. Not only did you visit the school at the time of your selection and appointment, but you have been back on a number of informal occasions since, to consult with the retiring head and to make sure that necessary steps have been taken to guarantee the smooth running of the school at the beginning of the summer term. You recognise, however, that your impressions are only fragmentary, and you are resolved that you will use your first few weeks at Meadowvale to conduct an unobtrusive 'stocktaking', so that you may learn precisely where you and the school stand. Indeed you are for a short time in an unusually favourable position. Immediate decisions affecting the summer term's programme have already been taken, and you can rest assured that, apart from the inevitable quota of minor crises and problems, the school will go on quietly ticking over without you being continuously involved. This means that you have the chance to concentrate, for a few precious weeks, upon a subjective assessment of the whole school, a chance that is unlikely to recur, for it cannot be long before next year's time-table and current and future problems claim their full share of your attention and concentration. This being so, you explain to your generally sympathetic and receptive staff your determination to take full advantage of this opportunity, and to set about deciding just what it is you want to know, exactly what sort of a job it is that you have taken on, and what are the strengths and weaknesses of the school for which you have now accepted responsibility.

During this survey, you will collect and collate a great deal of factual information about staff and children, the organisation, the administration, the channels of communication and the degree of consultation and delegation, the school's recent record and achievements, and its external relations and commitments. You will also, of course, need to grasp the nature of the school's disciplinary system and the use of sanctions, its curriculum pattern, and the degree of choice available in optional subjects and courses. You will need to be informed about the number and size of contributory primary schools, and to comprehend the pattern of the school's contribution to higher and further education and to the employment market. LEA regulations and procedures must be assimilated, the role of the school's governing body must be studied, and you will need a working knowledge of the main political, economic and social factors which influence the life of the local community. If you are wise you will also make sure that you have some elementary knowledge of the common law, as it is interpreted by the courts, in respect of those problems which are particularly familiar to heads of secondary schools—accidents, misbehaviour, truancy, delinquency and vandalism. These areas all contribute to the complicated pattern of the school's internal characteristics and practices, and to its external image. All this information is, in essence, routine and factual. Nevertheless, it should not be decried or belittled on that account. Indeed, it is an essential part of your professional equipment. At the moment much of it provides an understanding of how the school operates, internally and externally, and a great deal of it can be stored away in your memory and your filing cabinet, so that it can be readily available to you when the need arises. At every stage, however, you will need to test the validity of the information which has been fed to you; and, eventually, it will furnish material for the assessment of those imponderable and immeasurable factors which illuminate— and ultimately govern—the nature, character and mood of a school's life and work. These include the quality of relationships, the orientation of attitudes, and the spirit which informs the views, habits, practices, customs and traditions which give the school its own particular flavour, and distinguish it from any other school. It is here that your work moves into top gear, as you begin to make those qualitative and subjective judgements which influence all your thinking and policy, and affect all your decisions. For your assessment of information, and of the circumstances and persons to whom that information relates, will reveal the system of constraints within which the school operates, and of which you must always be aware. Some of these constraints are flexible and can be modified or realigned; some are immutable, and just have to be accepted, while others offer freedom of action and development. You have to decide which constraint is in which category.

It is, in fact, within these constraints that the head identifies his room for manoeuvre. Not all the constraints are restrictions, of course: compact size, for example, despite its obvious limitations, may in some ways be a source of strength; a narrow range of academic ability and potential within a school, while limiting the variety of courses, options and subjects, may, nevertheless, have positive advantages in making it possible to focus the school's resources in a concentrated way upon its realistic needs. As we have seen in the earlier chapters, it would be an unpractical head who would dream his dreams and marshal his plans without a realistic appreciation of the resources available to him—resources of relationships and goodwill, just as much as resources of manpower, money and buildings. For these constraints and resources provide the map upon which he can plan his journey and plot his course.

It is still only the first day of term. On that day, and for the first few days thereafter, almost certainly you will decide to take morning assembly yourself. A perfectly natural nervousness, and a preoccupation with creating an agreeable atmosphere and image, will probably limit the range of impressions arising from the assembly which you will store away in your mind on these first few days. Your personal radar system is bound to be hard at work, however, relaying incidents, circumstances, and impressions to your brain. Towards the end of the first week, and probably on certain days in the weeks immediately ahead, you may decide to ask your deputy, or some other senior member of staff, to take assembly, leaving you without responsibilities or duties to perform. In this way you will be free to plan the beginning of the day to suit your own purposes. How then will you set about trying to discover 'where you are', and what are you likely to discover?

As you cross the playground in the morning, perhaps twenty or thirty minutes before the school officially opens, you are bound to notice whether any member of the staff is on duty, whether the school is already crowded with children and humming with activity, or whether the children are expected to wait until a bell or whistle tells them that they are free to enter. And, if they do wait, you will watch with interest to see whether they are then free to move into the school under their own steam. At assembly—particularly if you stand at the side or back of the hall—you will detect if the keynote is that of a community at worship, or whether the service is a routine exercise, to be scrambled through as expeditiously and painlessly as possible. Does the assembly begin with appropriate music from a piano, orchestra or record-player, and do the staff sing the hymns and join in the prayers? Do the children themselves sing cheerfully and with obvious pleasure (the grunters and growlers as well as the choir and the first year); have they taken any meaningful part in the planning or conduct of the service, or is it just an adult ritual which they must passively endure? When 'the Grace' has been said, do the notices about cricket or tennis results or swimming galas, a coming visit to Austria or a rehearsal for the school play, indicate the real purpose and value of the occasion? And then, as the school moves to the first period of the day, do the children leave the hall by forms or by houses, or do they move out independently to background music; and can the music which is being played be identified from a programme on the notice board?

During the first two or three weeks you are likely to give priority to personal, face-to-face contacts with all members of the staff, including the ancillary and non-academic staff, and to talk to them about their concerns and their careers. Perhaps above all else you will wish to establish a friendly working relationship with your deputy head, to understand how he has operated in the past, what his hopes and fears are for the future, and how your respective strengths and weaknesses can complement and support each other. For it is clearly absolutely essential that you and he should both know how each stands in relation to the other, and should work out together an agreed basis of consultation and collaboration. During the course of your chats with him you will, incidentally, learn a very great deal about the school and about the way in which it is run. You will naturally wish all your conversations with members of the staff to be as relaxed and informal as possible, but you will be storing away in your memory (and subsequently in your records!) little bits of information about their personal and domestic life and interests, and about their professional skills and concerns, their particular hopes and difficulties. Moreover, you will certainly make time, in these early days, to talk to some of the boys and girls, particularly members of the fourth and fifth years, for they are just as anxious to be reassured about their new head as you are to assess their maturity, their sense of responsibility, and their attitude to authority and to the school. In all these contacts you will be building up impressions and tentative judgements, uncoordinated and incomplete, and often unsubstantiated by anything more reliable than hunch or intuition, in the first instance, but, nevertheless, the very stuff of which headship is made, and by which the happiness and success of your school are secured.

While these informal 'interviews' are taking place you are also pretty sure to want to familiarise yourself with the school's daily life and routine, and this can be done, very unostentatiously, by wandering about the school, talking to those whom you meet, and quietly observing, without interrupting, what goes on. All this time your antennae will be hard at work, scanning the school's bustling life, and suggesting to you, among many other things, what sort of impact is made upon members of the school, and upon visitors, by the entrance hall, the corridors, the staircases and the notice boards. You will observe whether there are flowers, plants and pictures in evidence, and whether the impact of the art and craft department is immediately and excitingly apparent. The condition of windows, furniture, equipment and surroundings will create a positive impression:

is the school cherished and well kept, or is it slatternly and untidy, or somewhere in between? Do the classrooms strike you as stark, impersonal boxes, or are they subject workshops, full of books, illustrations and children's work in which there is an obvious incentive to teach and to learn? Is the staff common-room the most uncomfortable (and the untidiest!) room in the school, and what about the general state of the cloakrooms and lavatories? The answers to all these, and to many other similar questions, will add to your cumulative knowledge of the school, which will be continuously reinforced every day, and will grow by compound interest as your impressions mature. You will be learning a great deal about the school's philosophy, about its priorities, about the quality of its relationships between members of staff, and between staff and children, about the extent to which visitors are made welcome and about the school's attitude to parents, about the tempo of the school's learning, the nature of its discipline, its prevailing conception of and response to authority, and the range of its social and community life.

Much of this you can achieve quite incidentally, certainly with the maximum freedom and informality. But almost without knowing it, you will have been caught up in the subtle and delicate process of assessment, which is one of the head's most fundamental responsibilities and skills, not only on his first day, or in his first few weeks, but every hour of every day until his retirement. Not all assessment, however, can depend upon such comparatively slender and haphazard foundations; much of it will have to be planned with care and pursued with diligence. For example, you may well decide that a longish and rather more formal interview with a senior head of department would tell you not only a great deal about the organisation of the curriculum and time-table, but about the school's attitude to change and innovation, and many other factors as well. So you choose an occasion convenient to Mr Bond, the head of the mathematics department, and ask him to tell you about the organisation and work of his department. You will be particularly interested to hear about his general outlook on the subject (is it 'traditional' or 'modern'?), about the way in which mathematics classes are organised (in forms, sets, or house groups), and why. You will listen with particular interest to what he has to tell you about the number and quality of his colleagues in the department, the impact of mathematics upon the curriculum and upon the life of the school as a whole, the range of options available and the numbers who opt for them, the maintenance of standards, the external examinations taken and the degree of success achieved in them.

You will also be concerned to discover whether Mr Bond, in his turn, ever asks himself where *he* is, and how he exercises his responsibility for the content of the syllabus, the teaching methods used in his department, the purchase of books and equipment, and the classroom performance of all those who teach the subject. Does he know how his scheme of work fits in with other, related subjects? Are concepts and techniques taught by the mathematics department, for instance, at the point when they are needed by scientists or geographers in their work? What is Mr Bond's attitude to students on practice, to young teachers on first appointment, and to older colleagues whose academic foundations and habits are threatened by new concepts and new techniques? Does he himself teach any of the youngest or the less able children? Has he taken part in the selection and appointment of recruits to his department? If not, would he like to do so? How often does he hold departmental meetings to discuss academic ideas and problems, and not merely administrative procedures, and has he ever talked to the whole staff about the place of mathematics in the curriculum? How does he keep himself and his colleagues abreast of new knowledge, trends and developments, and new examination requirements? Are they responsive to these pressures, or are they simply defenders of traditional practice? A discussion ranging over topics such as these will tell you a great deal, not only about Mr Bond, his maths colleagues, and the teaching of mathematics, but also about the thinking behind many of the school's established practices in organisation, external examinations, internal assessment, and the degree to which there is any collaboration or integration between subject disciplines. It will also reveal staff attitudes and relationships, and indicate whether learning is regarded as a passive or as an active and cooperative process.

The school's concern with knowledge and with teaching and learning, however, is only one aspect of your overall responsibility, even though it is a major one. Of equal importance is the school's concern for pastoral care, and so you arrange to have a similar chat with Mr Houseman, who is responsible for coordinating the school's pastoral care organisation. From him you will be anxious to discover exactly what

it is that his organisation is intended to achieve, and how far it is successful in achieving it. Is it, for instance, possible to concentrate the school's
knowledge and concern quickly, and to focus it upon the welfare of a
particular boy or girl? Is every individual child known, in some depth,
to at least one member of staff? Who keeps the records of individual
progress and development, and who has access to them? Who deals
with correspondence from parents, and who sees parents about their
children in ordinary routine circumstances? What is the staff's attitude
to parental interest and concern, and how far do members of the staff
find difficulty in wearing their two hats, academic and pastoral? Is
there, in fact, any effective coordination between these two parallel
organisations and areas of concern?

As head you do not need to be reminded that there are still, of course,
vast areas of the school which you have not yet specifically investigated,
such as the library, all the remaining subject departments, the ancillary
staff (including secretaries, caretaker and cleaners, cooks and meals
helpers, technicians and groundsmen), the school's extra-curricular
programme, its care for the children's general physical welfare, and
all the host of varied interests, clubs, societies and activities which
enrich the life of a vigorous and well-balanced community. So you are
going to have a busy first term!

Enough has probably now been said, however, to emphasise that
there is no easy answer to the question 'Where are you?' There are,
however, three major sign-posts which point in that direction. They
are:

1 a willing acceptance of the validity and significance of the
   question;
2 a patient preparedness to collect the evidence, however subtle,
   fragmentary or insubstantial; and
3 a determination to set your impressions against all the evidence
   available.

Only so can you hope to reach firm conclusions, and to frame sound
judgements, in the continuous and critical process of deciding, not
where you think you are, nor where you would like to be, but *exactly
where you are.* For only when you know where you are, can you even
begin to think effectively about where you want to go.

Where *do* you want to go?

5 Aims and objectives I

In the previous chapter we were considering the first of our four questions — 'Where are you?' — in relation to Meadowvale School, and we found it necessary to assess the resources, the priorities, the relationships, the opportunities and the constraints upon which our answer to that question must always depend. We are now in a position to move on, and to tackle the second question: 'Where do you want to go?'

Looking ahead, taking decisions about future policy, and choosing between competing alternatives, these have always been accepted as a traditional part of the head's role; and this tradition still holds good today, although the decisions which all heads, and secondary heads in particular, now have to take are far more complex, and much more uncompromising, than they were in previous generations. Schools now have to come to terms not only with an unprecedented rate of growth in knowledge and in technology, but with fundamental changes in the structure of society, as well as in current beliefs, values, standards, customs, practices and behaviour. This is bound to make the definition of an acceptable philosophy, for any school, enormously more difficult than it has ever been in the past. Contrast, for example, the task of establishing aims and objectives for secondary modern schools between 1947 and, say, 1965, or for comprehensive schools in the late 1950s and early 1960s, with the aims and objectives of established grammar schools during this whole period. For the grammar schools' philosophy had been comparatively stable, their goals clearly defined, their objectives known and accepted, so that their success or failure was reasonably easy to assess, in relation to their own expectations and those of society.

Although, in a general sense, society expects schools to know where they are going, and what they are trying to do, as a nation we have always been more than a little reluctant to tie ourselves down too much, in advance. In an era of rapid innovation there is, of course, good cautionary sense in not determining precise objectives (e.g. particular skills) too far ahead, when technological and other changes may have made them invalid before they have been achieved. This in no way diminishes the importance of looking ahead, however, and of deciding where we are going; yet we tend to distrust the man and the organisation that know precisely where they are going, who say so in explicit terms, and who are confident of fulfilling their predictions. There is something almost indecent, we feel, and a kind of bragging about such assurance. So we shrug our shoulders in self-righteous distrust, expecting that, sooner or later, fate will intervene to prick the bubble of their over-confidence, and to confirm our own smug judgement that it does not pay to tempt providence too far ahead. Not only as a nation but as a profession, too, we are by nature cautious and pragmatic. We are happy to be left in peace to deduce our aims and objectives from our experience: in other words, to build up our experience first, and then to define our policy afterwards. This is a characteristic which Professor T. E. Chester of Manchester calls 'the British genius for retrospective planning', and there is a surprising degree of truth in his amusing paradox.

Nevertheless, however deep this characteristic may lie in our national and professional genes, it is most unwise to allow ourselves to become complacent about its consequences. It can so easily lead to a blunting of our awareness, and to a decline in our sensitivity, so that we either cease to be aware of what is actually happening, or (worse still) we fall into the trap of assuming that what *should* be happening is what *is* happening, or vice versa. Any hesitation in deciding what we are trying to accomplish also weakens an important factor in the process of decision-making. For without a reliable compass and a clear contoured map it is almost impossible to know whether any decision we take is a move in the right or in the wrong direction — confidently towards, or diametrically away from, our ultimate destination.

More dangerous still, we are sometimes tempted to justify our reluctance to say precisely where we are going by sheltering behind the excuse that many of our aims and objectives are, in any case, bound to be qualitative and, therefore, unmeasurable. This is true enough, but it is no reason at all why they should not be stated in terms as precise as we can manage; for although it is true that qualitative factors cannot be measured with accuracy, in practice we never hesitate to make such judgements, and to draw conclusions about them ('the worst fourth-year we've ever had', 'a good 1st XI', 'a brilliant girl', 'a poor concert', or 'an easy examination paper'). So, in all honesty, we cannot use this excuse for our reluctance to frame qualitative aims and objectives.

Moreover, unless the school community, in the widest sense, knows what the school is trying to achieve, and how that achievement is being planned and organised, there is an obvious risk that individuals and groups will pull in opposite directions, and so produce confusion, cross-purposes and lack of drive and momentum. How can you delegate effectively, for example, if you do not know what you are delegating for, and why a particular pattern of delegation fits into your strategic policy? How can your consultation achieve its full purpose unless you have a clear framework against which the fruits of consultation can be assessed? Unless you know the purposes for which your resources are deployed, and the objectives and priorities which they are intended to achieve, how can you tell whether those resources are being used economically and to maximum effect? These are questions which many schools, and many schoolmasters and mistresses, prefer to answer in the most general and innocuous terms — through fluffy rose-tinted clouds of verbiage — *or not at all*!

But there is another reason still, much more potent and pragmatic, why we must not shirk the unfamiliar task of articulating the values to which we adhere and of formulating our aims and objectives, of deciding where we want to go, and of making them known to our colleagues, and to all those among whom and for whom we are working. Quite simply the reason is this: if we do not make this definition for ourselves, then others will do it for us. Our philosophy will then become established, not by us ourselves, after full consultation, but by case-law and by default. Almost any member of a staff-room or, for that matter, anyone in an LEA office, could produce a spontaneous, off-the-cuff summary of the head's or the CEO's objectives, which is likely to be amusing and irreverent at the same time, though probably fairly accurate. But this assessment will be based not so much, if at all, upon what the head or the CEO says, as upon what he does, and woe betide him if there is a gap between the two! For every head and every CEO (indeed, anyone in a position of authority and responsibility) reveals a particular character and quality in the performance of his daily work which, in other spheres, would be called his 'style of management'. Every one of his actions, each one of his decisions conveys a message; it indicates an attitude and reveals a degree of priority, however subtly this may be disguised. For example, the head may constantly emphasise the virtues of tidiness, punctuality, orthodox dress, precise length of hair or the prompt submission of mark lists, although these are, in relation to other major and much more significant issues, still only of comparatively minor importance; or he may frequently comment upon the academic successes of the ablest boys and girls, or upon 1st XI and 1st XV results, but fail to mention other less distinguished individuals or teams, or those who have helped to catalogue the library, or looked after the livestock in the biology laboratory during the vacations, or performed other acts of valuable but unobtrusive social service to the school. If he does this kind of thing consistently, then his colleagues and his pupils will conclude that *these* are the observances and the achievements which he values most, whatever splendid theory he may propound on ceremonial occasions. We cannot, in fact, escape from defining our aims and objectives, whether we do it explicitly or unconsciously; and, if we do not do it for ourselves, it will be done for us. The quality of our relationships, the way in which we do things, the emphasis we put upon them, indeed the very tone of voice in which we speak to different people on different occasions — all these will inevitably convey a message about us, and others will interpret this message, however inaccurately and unfairly, as illustrating our real aims and objectives. How much better, then, to grasp the nettle for ourselves, and to explain our intentions, in unmistakable terms, so that we can share with others a knowledge of just where it is that we are striving to go.

At this point we should pause for a moment, to remind ourselves (although it must be obvious enough) that there can be no standard pattern of aims and objectives, no established regulations by which heads can 'work to rule'. This is due partly to the remarkable independence and autonomy enjoyed by schools in the UK, and partly to the different circumstances and resources of individual schools. There is bound to be some difference in aims, and probably a much greater difference in objectives, for example, between a brand new school and one which has been in existence for 5 or for 50 years, between a rural and an urban school, or between a 3-FE suburban grammar school and a 10-FE neighbourhood comprehensive. So there is bound to be variety and diversity in the philosophy, goals, priorities and practices of individual schools. In the long run this is a source of strength, embedded in British educational traditions, and it is a matter for congratulation: but it imposes a tremendous responsibility upon each individual head.

If our aims and principles are founded upon a firm base of realism and purpose, then it should be possible to assess any particular proposal, idea, change, suggestion or problem with which we are confronted, by reference to our overall philosophy. For our philosophy represents, for us, nothing less than a summary of our most deeply cherished beliefs and hopes about the purposes and practices of education. What we are attempting to identify is a set of principles which will motivate and govern the whole life of the school, as much through its organisation and administration as through the behaviour, attitudes and achievements of individuals. But there is bound to be a distinction between aims and objectives, between philosophy and practice, between what we should like to do and what is practicable at any one moment. Our aims are strategic concepts and principles; they govern all our thinking and planning, and identify our horizons. Our objectives, on the other hand, are the immediate tactical targets which we must define, as we seek to translate principles and priorities into practice, according to the varying circumstances of each week, each year and each generation.

Moreover, we must remember that the translation of aims — first into objectives and then into practice — cannot always be a rapid process. There is seldom a motorway to the fulfilment of objectives. Indeed, it may not always be possible to move without interruption towards the achievement of any particular set of objectives. Nevertheless, our aims will always provide us with a point of reference, by which to assess every decision we intend to take, however minor and unimportant that decision may be in itself. By their very nature and purpose our objectives must always be determined by resources, opportunities, circumstances and priorities. We may often, for example, for severely practical reasons, have to defer one specific target, and substitute another; sometimes, in an emergency, we may have to suspend a long-term aim, in favour of a short-term objective, or even to move, temporarily, in an opposite direction. But, in these circumstances, we should be aware of what we are doing, and should be prepared, as soon as the opportunity occurs, to get back on course again.

In one sense, it is true, the identification of objectives, in the day-to-day business of management, is an easier task than defining our philosophy. For with objectives we are concerned with practical decisions, and most of us are more at ease in the business of getting on with the job, than in identifying ourselves with theoretical concepts and abstract values, however genuinely we recognise their importance and their relevance. Defining our objectives, then, is likely to be a good deal easier than defining our aims. For while aims will certainly change, over a longish period, in response to changes in educational philosophy and techniques, and in step with changes in society, objectives are likely to be much less uncompromising and much less permanent; indeed, they may vary from year to year, and even (sometimes) from week to week. They are also likely to vary for different groups of children (e.g., fifth-form leavers and A-level university candidates), and they are bound to depend upon a complex of limiting and constraining factors — manpower, financial and physical resources, time, and the climate of opinion inside and outside the school. But whenever we reach a decision, in pursuit of an immediate objective, it is important that we should assess that objective against our ultimate aims, and satisfy ourselves that we are moving in the right direction, or (if not) that there are very good reasons for a temporary diversion.

Two riders must be added to this general thesis, however. First it may not always be possible to know precisely where one is going, before setting out. Indeed, just as a walker can usefully explore unknown country, without any precise objective, so can a head take an intuitive step, provided that he does it with his eyes open, feeling in his bones that it is in the right direction. Indeed, it has been said (perhaps cynically) that the best decision, in any circumstances, may well be that which an experienced manager suggests even before examination of all the options available. Secondly, it may not always be wise to adopt a plan aimed at the exact centre of the target. This would apply, for example, if the plan were susceptible to complete failure as a result of a change in a single factor, such as the loss of a particular member of staff. In those circumstances it might be sensible to settle for a slightly less acceptable but more robust plan, capable of absorbing unforeseen circumstances. In other words risks must be calculated and balanced, which emphasises why the art of judgement is such an important weapon in the head's armoury.

6   Aims and objectives II

In the previous chapter, we were trying to decide whether the question 'Where do you want to go?' is one which *should* be answered. We must now decide whether it is a question which *can* be answered. There can be no doubt that it is difficult to tackle, and particularly so in this book. For while aims, on the whole, can be generalised and stated in round terms, objectives only carry conviction in the specific and detailed context of a particular school with all its circumstances and resources; and, for us, in this chapter, there can be no such precise starting-point.

In consequence, we shall often have to be far more vague and indeterminate than we would wish. We can only hope that we shall be able to offer enough examples to show, in general terms, how aims *can* be translated into practice. Our aims may sound idealistic, and we are content that they should be so; but we are aware that our objectives may sound equally imprecise, and they may be dismissed on the grounds that they would need an archangel as head, and a common-room of angels, if they were to be put into practice in any particular school. Nevertheless, the establishment of aims and objectives, leading to the identification of priorities, is an essential task for every head, involving policy, planning and precision. Though it would be idle to deny that the result is always likely to be imperfect, it would be equally unsatisfactory if the attempt were abandoned on the grounds that it is too difficult. So let us see what kind of an answer can be devised to the insidious question 'Where do you want to go?' What, in fact, are we running a school *for?*

In order that our definitions may be easy to assess, and to examine in detail, we propose to arrange them systematically, under three separate headings:

Social and general aims

The aims of the curriculum

Pastoral aims

For ease of reference, 'Aims' are printed in italics, and numbered, with some relevant 'Objectives' immediately below them.

SOCIAL AND GENERAL AIMS AND OBJECTIVES

> *1   To develop, in the school, a caring community, exercising concern and respect for the welfare of others, and emphasising the overriding importance of good human relations, based upon sensitivity, tolerance and good will.*

1   To seize every opportunity of illustrating and practising the school's concern for others (both internally and externally) by inculcating an interest in service to the community, by furnishing opportunities of putting this interest to practical use, and by recognising such service when it is achieved.

In a particular school, the objectives of community service would be far more precise, of course. They might, for example, prescribe the following steps:

To nominate a member of staff to be responsible for organising and directing community service.

To carry out a survey of opportunities for such service in the locality, to be completed by a specified date.

To devise a programme of projects to be put into operation, by stages, within a definite period.

> *2   To encourage children to appreciate the virtues of collaboration, to foster habits of responsibility and self-discipline, and to promote initiative, endeavour and the exercise of individual judgement.*

2(a)   By using the school's resources to the full, to provide a rich variety of activities, which would enable children to plan, work and play together, and to accept meaningful duties, responsibilities and obligations. Such activities would include games, matches, plays, concerts, socials, clubs, societies, journeys, visits and expeditions, in all of which children would be expected to accept responsibility, within a system of supervision and guidance. (The precise form which these activities would take, would obviously depend upon the skills and enthusiasms available among staff and children, at any particular time.)

(b) By setting up a School Council, or by other appropriate means, to introduce children to the conduct of formal business meetings, and of simple financial procedures, to provide opportunities of learning from experience, by making mistakes under supervision, and to encourage a robust yet responsible attitude to authority.

> 3 *To project the school as the servant of the local community, and to accept its appropriate share of responsibility for equipping each child to find his own niche in his occupation and in society.*

3(a) To devise effective ways of discussing the welfare of children with their parents, and of reporting to them, at regular intervals, simply and cogently, on the progress of individual children, in the firm belief that the children 'belong' to them, and not to the school.
 This might be accomplished by:

Setting up a staff working party to devise an acceptable system of reporting on children to their parents.
Appointing a member of staff to be the school's adviser on its relationships with parents.
Arranging a regular series of occasions when parents could meet individual members of staff for meaningful discussions about the progress of their children.

(b) To establish an effective system of vocational guidance within the school, acting, internally, in close collaboration with the school's pastoral care organisation and, externally, with the LEA's Careers Advisory Service, with all other agencies in this field, and with employers, parents and governors who possess knowledge and experience which is particularly relevant to choice of career.

> 4 *To secure the active cooperation of the staff, and all others concerned for the school's welfare, in the continuous re-assessment of its aims and objectives.*

4(a) To establish close and effective working relations with:

The governing body of the school
The local education authority
Inspectors, advisers and educational consultants

These objectives might be achieved by some such means as the following:

Arranging, in turn, for heads of departments, and others holding responsibility for major aspects of school policy, to explain to the governors the philosophy and practice of the school in its various aspects.

Inviting governors with a specialist knowledge and experience to visit the school, in order to see work in which they are particularly interested, and to help wherever appropriate (for example, by conducting practice interviews with children).

Instituting a continuous dialogue with senior officers of the local authority, with inspectors, advisers and educational consultants, and with local employers, so that the school's objectives, purposes, successes and difficulties may be appreciated by all those who share a professional concern for its welfare.

(b) To secure the understanding and support of parents in the achievement of particular objectives for the school.

This might involve the establishment of an Association of Parents, which would not only assist with general support and material provision, but would be specifically invited to assess the school's philosophy and practices, with particular emphasis on the welfare of the children.

(c) Within the school, to establish a pattern of communication and consultation with members of staff, to ensure that they are continually in possession of relevant information, and that they have an opportunity of contributing to the formation and execution of school policy.

> 5   *To encourage an attitude of positive response to the persistent demands of a changing society, yet firmly upholding a belief in basic values and standards.*

5(a)   To arrange a continuing programme of discussion with governors, staff, parents and senior children, in order to reach general agreement on those personal standards and values which the school will seek to uphold in practice, because they are enduring rather than transitory or conventional.

(b) To invite the views of parents on the balance of responsibility, between the school and themselves, for those objectives which society finds it difficult to achieve, of itself, without the help of the school (such as sex education or racial harmony). This survey should also include those objectives for which there is a measure of overlap of responsibility between home and school, such as preparation for parenthood, understanding of domestic budgeting, house purchase, mortgages, insurance, and hire purchase, or the objective assessment of mass media. Where a sufficient degree of agreement is reached in respect of the school's share of responsibility, then every attempt should be made to use all the resources available to the school (internal and external), and to provide specific courses at appropriate stages in the curriculum. Physical development is clearly a joint responsibility, and the school should play its part not only through physical education within the curriculum, but by the organisation of clubs and societies for physical activities (such as sailing or mountaineering), as well as through medical and dental inspection, welfare services and school meals.

THE AIMS AND OBJECTIVES OF THE CURRICULUM

1 In so far as it lies within the resources of the school, to illustrate the inter-relationship of all human knowledge, to foster an appreciation of man's creative skills, and to stimulate a conception of learning as a life-long process.

1(a) By appropriate design of the curriculum, and of subject syllabuses, and by courses of general studies for senior pupils, to furnish some understanding and knowledge of the physical universe, together with some appreciation of man's achievements in the arts and in science, and of the importance of preserving the heritage of our environment.

(b) To encourage cooperation between subjects, and to develop cross-fertilisation and integrated courses between subject disciplines. This might involve team-teaching, sponsored reading from a staff library, inter-departmental meetings and study groups, and staff attendance at courses and conferences.

(c) So to design the curriculum and time-table that, throughout his school career, every child shall spend a significant part of every week on a creative activity or pursuit appropriate to his interests and skills.

> *2   Since it is impossible for a school to cover the whole realm of knowledge, to be rigorously selective in the material presented to children, but always to pay particular attention to:*
>
> > *stimulating intellectual curiosity;*
> > *directing and exercising the emotions;*
> > *encouraging clear thinking and discrimination;*
> > *developing an interest in the processes and resources of learning, and in learning how to learn;*
> > *fostering a capacity to tackle a problem, and to follow and sustain an argument; and*
> > *emphasising the difference between truth and falsehood, and between fact and feeling.*

2(a)   To provide an adequate school library (and resource-centre), whenever possible under a professional librarian.

(b) To establish a library committee, representative of all ages and stages of the school community in order:

to encourage and support the use of the library and resource-centre;
to ensure that all subject syllabuses and courses take full advantage of its facilities;
to keep a record of all borrowing by staff and children, and to make effective use of the information so derived; and
to encourage active participation in the selection of books, records and source material.

(c) To provide an effective range of audio-visual teaching equipment, and to ensure that it is fully exploited and efficiently maintained.

> *3   To develop a curriculum which is flexible, relevant and meaningful to the children, at different ages and stages, and which will be responsive to their needs and interests, as well as to the demands of employers, colleges, universities and examining bodies.*

3(a)   To devise a balanced curriculum, which will provide a range of options and alternative courses with opportunities alike for the most able and for those who find learning difficult or are retarded, but which will not demand significant choices until 16 +.

(b)   So far as is practicable, to tailor all syllabuses to meet the school's internal needs and interests and, when choice is available, to select those external examining bodies which offer the most flexible arrangements, and are most sensitive to the wishes and requirements of individual schools.

(c)   To subject the curriculum, optional courses and teaching methods to continuous and critical review, and to ensure that practice corresponds as closely as possible with the school's declared aims and intentions.

(d)   To keep in touch with the movement for curriculum development and renewal, particularly through the publications of the Schools Council, and to adopt teaching methods and experiments relevant to the school's objectives, such as those which are based on the discovery approach and individual investigation.

> *4   To recognise and to encourage talent of all kinds, and of all degrees, and to endeavour to stretch the intellectual and creative capacity of individuals.*

4   To organise the teaching groups, and to plan the time-table, in order to support and encourage concern for the individual, and to provide opportunities for the maximum development of talent, by designing individual programmes and assignments of work, by teaching children to work independently, and by emphasising the importance of private study.

5   To seek to measure the extent of an individual's success in making maximum use of his endowments and opportunities.

5   To design a system of marks, grades, tests, internal examinations and reports which will sustain the school's basic curricular purposes and intentions, by assessing the performance of an individual not only against his contemporaries, but also against his own capacity and potential.

6   To enable children to acquire the tools and qualifications necessary for earning their living and, when appropriate, for entry into skilled occupations and the professions.

6   By means of visiting speakers, and by the attendance of staff and children at lectures, courses and conferences, to keep in touch with contemporary trends, developments and problems in the employment market, as well as in higher and further education.

7   To develop fluency in the use of the mother tongue, and to foster enjoyment of all the processes of communication, oral, written and visual.

7   To publish a school magazine, and to organise dramatic performances (including opera), concerts, play and poetry readings, and debating and discussion groups.

It is useful to remind ourselves that, since much the greater part of a child's life at school is spent in the classroom, not only the objectives of the curriculum, but social and pastoral objectives, as well, must be largely attained, if at all, in the classroom situation. While the curriculum and time-table are probably a school's most powerful instruments of policy, the ways in which the curriculum is operated, in which subjects are taught and evaluated, and by which classroom relationships are established, are all of vital importance. Assessment and encouragement, praise and stricture, attitudes of concern and understanding — all of these in the daily context from 9 a.m. to 4 p.m. — will ultimately determine whether the school achieves its objectives or not. Hence the crucial importance of a staff united in a common purpose and working towards agreed ends.

PASTORAL AIMS AND OBJECTIVES

> *I   Recognising and accepting differences in endowment and environment, to hold every individual in esteem in his own right.*

1   To ensure that every individual boy and girl is known, in depth, and that all the resources of the school can be brought to bear upon his total welfare, through purposeful organisation, liaison with external social and welfare agencies, and the exercise of concern and responsibility by every member of the staff.

> *2   To accept responsibility for identifying the physical, intellectual, aesthetic, creative, emotional and social needs of each individual member of the school community, as an essential prerequisite to satisfying those needs.*

2   To develop a programme of regular appraisal for every member of the school community. In the case of a member of the staff, this would involve forwarding his career by identifying the need for further experience and training, and for acquiring fresh knowledge and skills, and by participating in the policies of the school through communication, consultation, delegation and administration.

Complete success and satisfaction are never likely to be achieved in any exercise of this kind; nor can it ever be a once-for-all operation, but it must always provide for repeated adjustment and reassessment in the light of experience. There can be little doubt, however, that, if undertaken in a spirit of determined exploration, much stimulus and profit are to be derived from the exercise itself, by concentrating thought upon fundamentals, and by compelling an assessment of how far aims and objectives are realistic and compatible, and to what extent cherished hopes and ideals can be translated into practice. The exercise also emphasises the supreme importance of guaranteeing that there is close correlation between 'Where do you want to go' and 'How do you intend to get there?'; and it is to this, the third of our four questions, that we must now turn.

II ORGANISATION

7 Principles

Part II will be mainly concerned with means, rather than with ends, although the two must always remain inextricably intertwined. So we now get to grips with the translation of purpose into practice, in response to the question: *How do you intend to get there?*

In any community, however simple, there is felt to be a need for some form of organisation. Decisions — of varying degrees of importance — must be taken, and it must be clearly understood who is to take them; appropriate information must be made available to all members of the community; tasks must be shared, in order that decisions can be translated into action; and the results of such actions must then be reviewed. Even in a two-teacher husband-and-wife primary school (which is as simple and enviable an educational organisation as can be devised), it must be decided who does what and when. There must be two-way provision for reaching and communicating decisions, for conveying information and instructions, for converting theoretical decisions into positive action, for securing a consensus of view in relation to both policy and practice, and for regularly assessing progress. In such a school, so happily placed in terms of management structure, these operations would all be personal and informal; but they would occur, nevertheless. At the other end of the spectrum, in large and complex schools, of which there are now so many examples, the organisation is bound to be more formidable and of greater critical importance. All schools, in fact, are organised in one way or another, for these purposes. It may, therefore, be helpful to discover, at this stage, whether there are any common principles which might be a guide in devising an organisation for schools to suit their own particular needs. Our own examination of the issues involved leads us to suggest that there are, in fact, eight principles.

First, (although it may seem at first sight to be too obvious to deserve more than momentary consideration), each school should plan its organisation to meet its own particular needs and circumstances. Its organisation, in other words, must be so designed that it will directly support and advance the aims and objectives which the school seeks to foster. This primary purpose is probably easiest to formulate in theory, and to express in practice, when starting a new school. In such a situation, the new school's aims and objectives are likely to be of greater clarity and lucidity than when, in later years, they have been overlaid by a patina of usage, custom and tradition. In general, however, experience shows that it is surprisingly easy to plan a school organisation which is, in some respects at least, in direct conflict with its declared policies. A sophisticated piece of machinery (such as the organisational structure of a large school) can be positively misleading if its effect is, in some measure, to direct the school's energies and enthusiasms away from the main stream of its announced intentions. There is often a significant difference between the stated aims of a school's organisation, and the message which that organisation conveys in practice.

For instance, a school may strive to exercise real concern for the welfare, progress and development of each individual in the school community; but, if the number of those with knowledge of any one individual is so large that they cannot regularly meet together, formally or informally, to pool their knowledge, or if the organisation does not clearly channel and direct that knowledge, then the school's purpose may be frustrated, and its concern for any one individual may be (as it often is) imperfectly fulfilled. Similarly, a school may wish to emphasise that the possession of talent, of whatever nature, earns no merit of itself, but becomes admirable and praiseworthy only when it has been exercised and developed. This intention, however, may be thwarted by an organisation of teaching-groups on a basis of selection and streaming, with prizes and rewards for academic achievement, but with no recognition of success in other fields, having regard to an individual's potential, however significant that success may be to the individual himself. Such recognition would, of course, be of particular significance in a remedial department or group where, of necessity, progress must be assessed against individual endeavour and potential. Again, a school may claim to be fundamentally unwilling to emphasise the differences between the abilities of individual children, and yet go out of its way to highlight such differences by the unbalanced and unfair allocation of teaching skills or other resources between one teaching-group and another (as, for example, between the first year and the sixth form, or between the most able and those of less than average ability). In yet another context, an avowed belief in the value of a general studies programme, as part of a balanced curriculum in the sixth form, is seen to have little or no validity when it succumbs to the first hint of time-table pressure. A school in which the declared aim is to make sure that one member of staff is in a position to know all about every child in a group for which he is responsible, makes that task more difficult for him if it organises the tutor-groups in a vertical pattern. Since his children, all of different ages, will be working in different teaching-groups, and also engaging in a variety of activities outside the classroom, the tutor will find it necessary to gather information from a very large number of colleagues, and this puts enormous strain upon the communications system.

A more subtle trap lies in the path of heads who set up an organisation which does not match their own styles or temperaments. For example, a naturally authoritarian head, who sets up an academic board, is likely to demonstrate through his relations with it, and his response to its recommendations, that it is no more than a face-saving operation.

The organisation, therefore, must serve as a constant reminder of the school's philosophy in daily operation and practice. It must foster an awareness not only of intent but of performance. This means, in practical terms, that those who carry responsibility should constantly ask themselves whether there is still a close correlation between organisation and purpose, between what they are striving to achieve and what they are actually achieving. They should be on the continual look-out for indicators, either that purpose and organisation are no longer in harmony, or that the organisation, in its daily operation, is obscuring or hindering the attainment of those ends which it was specifically designed to fulfil. So important is this process that responsibility for monitoring the way in which the organisation works, in day-to-day practice, should be assigned to a member of the top management team, in the same way that the sensitive head of a subject department keeps his syllabus under continual review, assesses the internal and external pressures to which it is constantly exposed, and decides upon the extent to which the syllabus should respond to them.

Secondly, the organisation of the school must ensure that the school's knowledge and concern can be focused effectively upon the needs and problems of individual children, not only in an emergency, but in daily practice. This knowledge must embrace not only the academic progress of individual boys and girls, but their total welfare, progress and development. Where such knowledge and concern are inevitably shared by many people (as in any large school), there must be a means of bringing this knowledge and concern to bear upon an individual problem, in a time of need, in the shortest possible time, and with maximum effect. This might vary, for example, from an application by a pupil for a job, or for a place in higher education, to some acute problem of maladjustment, social distress or parental anxiety. But, although such 'crisis' situations and urgent questions make themselves obvious, and impose immediate demands upon what has come to be known as the school's pastoral care organisation, they must not be allowed to divert the school from its central purpose, which is to care for the normal boy and girl. It is only too easy to concentrate upon the deviant, the distressed and the obstreperous, on the very bright and the least able, and so pay scant attention to the rest, despite the fact that they constitute, in any secondary school, a substantial majority of the children.

How then, can a school's concern for its children be translated into practice through appropriate organisation? For many years the system operated through the form master or form tutor, responsible for thirty or so children. At its best, it worked pretty well, but it suffered from a number of built-in handicaps. Good personal relationships are the foundation of such success, but no form master, however skilful and dedicated, can guarantee to be on equally flexible terms of intimacy and friendship with every child in his form; and where this happy relationship is lacking, then the child's interests will be less well served, particularly if (as often happens) the master moves up the school with his form. Moreover, not all form tutors will be equally skilful or equally concerned with individuals as individuals, either because of qualities of temperament or because some of them may see their role as subject teacher as being of greater importance.

Again, no form tutor can expect to know, and to be able to establish immediate contact with, all the resources (both internal and external) which are available to help with the welfare of any child who is the subject of particular concern. In addition, this system, which imposes almost total responsibility for a particular form upon one man tends, inevitably, to encourage a sense of isolation and of independence. Rarely if ever will the form master have additional non-teaching time made available to him, so that he can talk to individual children in his form during the day. Nor will he find it easy to talk to his many colleagues who know, in some significant way, each of his children, either in the classroom or outside it. In a small school it may be possible to tap such knowledge and advice fairly readily and informally, although the small school suffers from the disadvantage that its total pool of professional expertise is limited by the size of the staff. In a large school, on the other hand, although the total resources are enhanced, and may well include a counsellor or careers adviser, the difficulties encountered in cross-communication and cross-consultation are correspondingly greater. Many members of staff will know a particular boy or girl, but consultation of them all by the form master presents severe problems, particularly when the form master himself, on a staff of seventy-five or more, perhaps dispersed over several buildings, may not even know all the colleagues concerned!

In order to overcome these difficulties, a new practice has developed in recent years. This involves breaking down the organisation of pastoral care into manageable units, such as lower, middle and upper schools, houses, years, vertical groups, horizontal groups and combinations of all of these alternatives. For the sake of simplicity, and for the duration of this chapter, we propose to refer to all these alternatives under the general term of 'houses'. These 'houses' are then entrusted to heads of 'house' or 'housemasters'. This additional tier in the organisation, between the form tutor and the head or deputy head of the school, gives new status and authority to the pastoral care organisation, which is then seen by everyone to be an important feature of school policy. Moreover, the creation of such posts has enriched the careers of many teachers and has, indeed, provided a new pool of experience from which deputy heads and heads are now drawn (instead of, as formerly, mainly from among heads of academic departments).

Heads of 'houses' will usually have an allocation of non-teaching time for their work, which will enable them to talk to each other and to parents and to draw upon each other's specialist knowledge. The division of particular responsibilities then becomes possible, so that (for example) one of them can take on the work of liaison with the external social and welfare agencies, and can win their confidence, so that their help will be readily available, and they will be willing to take part in case-conferences, when particular difficulties arise. Moreover, since any one 'housemaster' will be responsible only for supervision of the work of a limited number of 'house' tutors, he can more easily help and support them, and coordinate their work. The tutors, in their turn, can claim a considerable share of his attention, and use him as a channel of communication with other members of staff and with parents.

It has become increasingly apparent, however, in the last few years, that all is not well with this new organisation of pastoral care, which has now been commonly adopted all over the country. At the time of re-organisation, when separate schools had to be cobbled together, and when the interests and status of individual masters had to be safe-guarded, it was justified in principle, and often worked well enough for a time. But although the pastoral care organisation opened up a new and welcome career structure and avenue of promotion, so it also engendered, in some schools, a feeling of jealousy between 'academic' and 'pastoral' staff, despite the fact that nearly all members of staff are deeply involved in both these spheres of responsibility! This sense of separatism was accentuated by the fact that the 'academic' and 'pastoral' organisations were often responsible to two different deputy heads (sometimes known as the Director of Studies and the Director of Pastoral Care), which almost seemed to imply that the welfare of children could be split into two distinct compartments ('academic' and 'pastoral'), which could then be safeguarded each in strict isolation from the other.

Thus an unhappy dichotomy has often developed between these two spheres of responsibility, 'academic' staff sometimes shrugging off their concern for the welfare and progress of individual children to their 'pastoral' colleagues, and vice versa. 'He is being paid for it: let him get on with it'. Experienced heads are well aware of this new development, which is a matter of very real concern to them and to us, not least because the growth of pastoral care responsibilities is one of the happiest features of secondary education since the Act of 1944. Perhaps the time has come, therefore, to reconsider the implications of the pastoral care structure within the organisation of the school as a whole.

We believe that the adjustments to the present system which we consider to be necessary lie in the realms of philosophy and attitudes (involving, in turn, a redefinition of roles and responsibilities) rather than through revolutionary changes in structure or organisation. Four convictions form the basis of our own proposals:

1 The primary reason for a child being in school is to learn, in the broadest sense of that word. This is confirmed by the fact that every child spends an overwhelming proportion of his school time in the classroom, laboratory or workshop, in the gym, on the playing field, or in a great variety of skill-learning situations.

2 A child is a person, one and indivisible and, in the last resort, his total welfare must be the responsibility of one member of staff, who can collect and collate all that is known about him, liaise with colleagues who are concerned for his welfare and with his parents, and accept responsibility for *all* the decisions which have to be taken in his interest, throughout his school career.

3 This member of staff must be the 'housemaster,' who is in the best position to build upon all that is known about his progress and development, including his progress in the classroom, and who alone can establish a complete picture of the child as an individual.

4 In order that the 'housemaster' may be able to fulfil this responsibility, there must be clear lines of staff inter-communication and inter-consultation, so that the school's knowledge of an individual child can be focused upon his needs and interests, and can be carefully recorded.

These four criteria suggest to us, therefore, that the separation between the 'academic' and the 'pastoral care' organisation of the school, which has become so common, is both indefensible and self-defeating. It is true, of course, that virtually all members of staff operate within both spheres (the head of mathematics as a house or year tutor, for example, or the head of 'house' as a member of the geography department). But the basic concept of their roles and responsibilities, as at present understood and practised, demands not only an extremely subtle and skilful marriage between them, but an overriding commitment to mutual support and collaboration; and these conditions are clearly not being fully achieved. For this reason we believe that the posts of 'housemaster' must, in the long-term, be held by members of the staff who are of high 'academic' standing and repute, so that the school's twin purposes of 'learning' and 'caring' can be seen to be united in their responsibilities. The 'housemasters' would also carry final responsibility for advising the head on the curriculum, since only they can know enough about individual children to ensure the appropriate curricular response to their needs. Furthermore, we suggest that the deputy head, to whom the 'housemasters', would 'report', should himself be qualified to hold the position of Director of Studies, and we recommend that this would be an appropriate title for him. There could then be no doubt about the essential 'academic' content of the school's 'caring' role.

We realise, of course, that the sudden acceptance and introduction of these ideas and suggestions would involve some initial staff dismay and concern, as roles and responsibilities, status and prestige, were subject to reassessment and adjustment. We assume, therefore, that the introduction of a fundamental change of this nature would be a gradual process, only being put into operation, by stages, as opportunities occurred. But we believe that much staff anxiety would be allayed if, alongside the post of Director of Studies (in the new context which we have just outlined) another member of the school's top management team were to be appointed as Staff Director. For the first time this would focus most welcome emphasis upon the school's equal responsibility and concern for the welfare and career development of every member of staff, and would ensure that adequate attention was continuously paid to staff recruitment, induction, in-service training and promotion.

Thirdly, we suggest that another most important principle, behind any school organisation, is to maximise the use of all its resources. In a particular context, a school time-table is a simple illustration of this principle in operation. For it is only by first identifying, and then harnessing, the rich potential of human and material resources at its disposal, that a school can hope to achieve its aims and objectives, whatever they may be. In other words, the organisation must recognise and respond to the wealth of skills, interests and enthusiasms of those who are available to operate it at any one time. This means that the organisation must be flexible and must be responsive to staff changes. It must never become rigid or formalised, so that individual assets have to be confined, constrained or imperfectly deployed, in order to meet its Procrustean demands. Like a school time-table, it must be sensitive to the changing pool of skills and experience, and adapt itself to them. At a time like the present, when a school's total resources are limited by many external factors, and may well become even more restricted in the immediate future, it needs no emphasis on our part to stress the significance of this principle in fashioning an organisation.

Let it not be supposed, however, that this process of identification and response is either easy or automatic. Experience reveals that, even in the most successful schools, there are undiscovered talents and hidden resources, which have never been harnessed because they have never been recognised. Yet the organisation of a school provides an ideal framework for staff training and development, and it offers an invaluable series of stages by which individual staff careers can be fostered and developed. Step by step, individual responsibilities can be stretched, broadened and changed around, thus greatly facilitating the objective of producing future generations of deputies and heads, as well as future leaders in such posts as heads of subject departments and heads of 'houses'. Not only is staff training and development an aspect of a head's responsibilities which is seldom given the importance and priority which it deserves, but the organisation of the school is seldom recognised as offering the admirably flexible opportunities for staff training which, in fact, it affords.

Fourthly, the organisation must be so designed that it ensures clear channels of communication (downwards, upwards and sideways), provides the necessary machinery for consultation of staff and pupils, and indicates the precise areas within which delegated responsibilities and authority are exercised. It must also denote the necessary administrative support, so that teachers are put in a position to teach most effectively and economically. What we are really considering here are ways of stimulating and directing a general flow of ideas within the school, of emphasising a pattern of responsibilities, and of underpinning the teacher's professional role as a teacher. These are all aspects of running a school which are clearly of the utmost importance, and they will all be discussed, in some depth, in the chapters which follow. At this stage in our thesis, it is only necessary to stress that they should not be left to whim, chance or afterthought, but should form an integral part of the school's pattern of organisation.

Fifthly, the organisation must ensure that the school will function smoothly in the absence of individuals, or even of groups. This is of far greater significance than it used to be. Absence of staff from school in working hours is now far more common than in the past. The demands, from outside the school, upon heads and members of the staff, either to serve on committees, to act as examiners or assessors, to take part in curricular experiments, or to attend professional and administrative meetings, are steadily increasing. In these circumstances it is essential to know upon whom responsibility directly devolves, when absence from school temporarily breaks the chain of command at any point.

The fulfilment of this principle would have another important consequence. It would enable the head, or one of his senior colleagues, to devote his whole attention to a particular problem, knowing that the school will continue to function efficiently and smoothly while he is so preoccupied. For example, the head would be free to deal with a sudden crisis, such as high-alumina-cement beams, or to devote virtually the whole of his time (for a few days or even perhaps, for a few weeks) to a programme of reading, to a major innovation under consideration, to an important change of policy or practice, or to the induction and training of new members of the common room. Equally, he could be engaged in identifying the principles on which next year's time-table will be based, or concentrate his attention, for a sustained period, upon a particular aspect of the school's life and work, such as discipline, or homework, or examinations policy, as part of his normal process of continuous assessment and review.

Sixthly, the organisation of a school should bear in mind the needs of those who have business with the school from outside its doors. Those who live and work within it have a pretty good idea how things happen, and to whom to go for advice or to lodge a complaint. But to parents and even to professional associates, such as

LEA administrators, exactly the reverse may be the case. For them there is only one obvious point of entry into the internal affairs of the school, namely the head himself. Yet, if the principles of organisation and delegation, which we have been discussing, have any significance at all they must surely mean that access from outside, either in person or by letter or telephone, can be made direct to the point at which relevant decisions are taken (such as the head of 'house', or the head of a subject department). Hundreds of telephone calls in both directions between schools and LEAs would be infinitely more productive, if only each knew more about the organisation of the other, and so could establish contact, instantaneously, at the precise point where the information or decision is most readily available. Similarly, the perplexed layman, baffled by a hierarchy and a pattern of organisation which he does not understand, and which are seldom explained to him, would welcome any indication of how best to establish communication with the school on any particular issue which he may wish to raise.

Next, another self-evident principle is that a school's pattern of organisation must take account of its physical circumstances. Nowadays, these may vary from school to school to a remarkable extent. No longer is it possible to envisage a school as occupying purpose-built premises, designed for its own needs. There are for example, simple amalgamations of adjoining premises (often, originally for boys and girls respectively, but now occupied by a mixed school). But premises may be adapted from their original purpose in even more significant ways, with a primary or a secondary school becoming a middle school, or a selective school becoming a comprehensive. A school may have been subject to a continuous series of changes involving the erection of additional accommodation, either in permanent or temporary form. A rash of 'temporary' classrooms has become a feature of our generation of secondary schools, as common as the huts, of varying degrees of unsuitability and permanence, which disfigured school sites after the First and Second World Wars. This unhappy repetition may well have indicated the response of schools to a rising birth-rate, to a longer school life for many pupils, and to constantly-changing educational policies and priorities. But, whatever the justification for them, there can be no doubt that such physical circumstances must be taken into account when planning a school's organisation. At the lowest level, they will clearly affect the quality and ease of the school's system of internal communication, and its patterns of internal movement, while they may well determine the size and pattern of teaching-groups which can be provided, and hamper the effective deployment of resources.

These major variations from a standard model, arising from expediency and from changes in educational philosophy and practice, are of comparatively minor significance, however, compared with new patterns of secondary schools. These have emerged from the recent processes of reorganisation, which are still continuing. To begin with, a great many secondary schools are substantially larger and, therefore, more complex and more difficult to run, than anything we have known before. A single school may now embrace two or more separate schools on the same site, with varying degrees of centralisation, common purpose and common facilities; or, it may involve the amalgamation of two or more schools, on completely different sites, often a considerable distance apart, and with a major road to negotiate in the inevitable traffic between the school's several sites. Such a 'school' may have few common facilities, or none at all. It may have a swimming bath of its own, with playing fields of its own on the spot, or it may have neither, with the obligation to provide intricate and time-wasting transport arrangements, in order that its children may take advantage of such provision elsewhere. Some of the worst examples of such planning expediency owe their existence to political and sociological enthusiasm, rather than to educational wisdom or practical common-sense. In such circumstances, making the best of a difficult job imposes immense new strains upon a school's organisation. It becomes necessary, for example, to appoint a head in each separate building and to allow time, and even to provide transport, for necessary movement between one building and another. The maintenance of a common philosophy, outlook and purpose becomes that much harder to attain, and the problems of cross-communication and cross-consultation are enormously intensified. Delegation, too, becomes far more complex since no one, whether the head of the whole school, the head of a subject department, or the master in charge of games or of external examinations, can be in more than one building at any one time; and effective administration becomes a crucial factor if chaos is to be avoided. In all these circumstances, skilful organisation, recognising the school's particular difficulties, and seeking to overcome them, become of paramount importance. In recent years, heads of secondary schools have shown very great resilience and ingenuity in responding to demands and situations such as these, of which their predecessors were mercifully unaware.

Finally, the organisation must be so designed that it makes possible the sharing of tasks and duties, and enables executive responsibility to be broken down into manageable units. For example, there is obviously far too much knowledge and professional expertise, within the curriculum of any school, for any one man to master it all. Most commonly, therefore, the devolution of curricular responsibility has been organised through heads of subject departments, who may vary in number from fifteen to twenty-five, or even more, in secondary schools. Such an organisation, however, immediately raises the question of how many staff (for whose work he is directly responsible) one man can effectively communicate with, supervise, control and support. This number, which is within his managerial grasp is known, technically, as his 'span of control', and it is a factor which will vary substantially from one individual to another, and from one particular set of circumstances to another. Some heads and deputies, indeed, insist that they can relate effectively and directly with all their heads of subject departments; but the situation must be judged from below as well as from above. Can all these fifteen to twenty-five heads of departments be sure of securing a reasonable share of the head's or deputy's time? 'I can rarely get in to see the head; he's always engaged' is a not uncommon cry. Would such control be more effective, for instance, if it were exercised not with heads of departments direct but, instead, through a small number of heads of grouped subjects or faculties?

Span of control is undoubtedly an important aspect of top management. Built into the school's organisation there must obviously be a convenient means whereby the wisdom and experience of the head and of his senior colleagues can be brought to bear, quickly and effectively, upon a very wide range of important decisions, both short- and long-term. This is likely to mean, in the interests of speed and economy, that the number of staff concerned at this level should be small; on the other hand it must be large enough to carry the respect and confidence of the common-room. Equally, those who share responsibility for school philosophy and policy, must be able to meet regularly, without interrupting the normal work of the school. At the same time, they must not be isolated but must, between them, continue to operate through all the channels of communication and consultation, by means of which the life and work of the school are directed.

For many years it was the practice in secondary schools to appoint a single deputy head and, in mixed schools, a senior master or mistress in addition. In the first edition of this book we advocated the appointment of a number of assistant heads, one of whom would be designated to deputise in the absence of the head. Such an arrangement has since become possible, under current Burnham regulations, and is now operating in many larger schools. We welcome this development, which is a tremendous step towards evolving a coherent top management structure. All of these assistant heads, as we see it, should be of deputy head status, and should have an appropriate allowance of non-teaching periods, but they should retain at least one foot in the common-room, and should continue to enjoy first-hand experience in the classroom. All should have assignments which offer both personal and professional satisfaction. We have already suggested that two of them might be the Director of Studies and the Director of Staff. Perhaps a Director of Resources and a Director of External Relations might complete the team. Such an organisation would provide the head with expert experience, knowledge and advice, across the whole range of the school's activities, and it would do so comfortably within his span of control. It would also provide his colleagues in the team with invaluable training in top management, within the full context of secondary school experience. Such a top management group or team would constitute what might be called a 'cabinet' or 'management box'.

The term 'management box' is taken from industrial practice, and may be suspect to schoolmasters on that account; equally, the idea of a school 'cabinet' is liable to mistrust and misconception because of its political overtones. Nevertheless, there are interesting parallels between a school organisation, such as we have described, and the established structure of cabinet government in the UK. One senior member of the cabinet may be designated as Deputy Prime Minister, but the practice varies from one government to another and, in any case, the constitution does not recognise the role of Deputy Premier. All ministers in the cabinet accept corporate responsibility for cabinet policy as a whole, but all carry their own departmental responsibilities in addition; and all of them have to compete for the allocation of resources. In these respects the comparison with school organisation is very close indeed. Moreover, not all ministers are in the cabinet, just as not all senior members of the staff would be in the school's top management team. Yet they, too, would all hold posts of major responsibility, and all would have substantial and satisfying roles to perform. As an additional advantage arising from this concept, there would be a strong incentive for the school's middle management (i.e. those below cabinet rank) to achieve a measure of collaboration; for all would need to present their case for staffing, finance and resources to the member of the top management team responsible for that section of the school within which their particular responsibilities lay.

One other important point remains. It is a fundamental tenet of our top management philosophy for schools that the head himself should always have direct responsibility for a specific area of school policy. Often there would be good reasons for suggesting that this should be external relations, which have traditionally been regarded as part of the head's own particular responsibilities. The choice, however, as we see it, should always depend upon the pool of experience and expertise within the top management team at any one time, and should respond to changing membership of that team, so that all the available strengths, skills and flair can always be used to best advantage.

Let us now quickly remind ourselves of the main burden and message of this chapter. We have been concerned with one answer to the question: *How do you intend to get there?* that is with the translation of aims and objectives into practice. This translation will not be automatic; it will not just happen. It will depend, first, upon a clear understanding of what is being attempted, secondly, upon an equally clear acceptance and commitment by all those who share responsibility for its fulfilment and, thirdly, upon the head's skill in devising a structure and pattern of organisation which will make it possible for policy to be achieved in practice, and that not just every now and then, but consistently from month to month and from year to year.

Successful organisation consists in nothing more profound, and nothing more important, than getting things done by other people. Accordingly, the organisation of a school must make it easy for members of the staff to play their part in getting things done. It is this which the organisation seeks to achieve, by providing channels of communication, consultation, and delegation, and of administrative support. Through skilful organisation it must ensure that the school's combined wisdom and expertise will be continuously involved in and directed towards the conduct of its life and work.

It must be apparent, however, that the organisation of a school will never be better than the quality of those who design and operate it. It will depend upon the head's style of management and his skill as an organiser and administrator, and upon the goodwill, concern, conviction and capacity of all his colleagues. For schools depend for their success entirely upon people, and upon the quality of human relationships which they establish. Inevitably, formal structures of organisation will be matched by informal structures, operated by both staff and children. The formal organisation, for example, may confer equal status upon two members of staff, but they may well be wholly unequal in the eyes of their colleagues. Advice will not necessarily be sought from those whose formal responsibility it is to give it; staff will often go to masters whom they trust and respect, whatever their position in the school's organisation. Children, too, develop their own patterns of communication and their own concepts of influence and authority. Boys and girls will cut across the established lines of communication, and seek help from sympathetic adults whom they trust and respect, whatever their position in the organisation of the school. To ignore these informal structures is unrealistic; to make use of them is common sense. For example, to appoint as head of a major subject department a master who has achieved academic distinction, but who exerts little influence in the common-room, would be to misinterpret the evidence. On the other hand, it would harness his own potential, and buttress the confidence of his colleagues, if a master known for his good standing in the common-room were assigned by the head to a post of particular responsibility (within his capacity) or were appointed to an important committee or working party. Similarly, in a staff discussion, it would be prudent to attach full weight to the views of a master who is generally held in high esteem and respect, whatever the importance of the post which he may hold; for, unless *he* can be persuaded or convinced, any decision which may be reached as a result of this debate is likely to be supported with a good deal less than whole-hearted conviction. In the same way, the appointment of a head boy must take account, not only of his undoubted merits, but of the influence and authority which he is known to exert among his peers. If 3C are known to have played the leading part in undermining and destroying a master's confidence, then it would be worth spending a good deal of time on winning their cooperation, since any change of heart or behaviour on their part is likely to make itself felt outside their particular group or classroom. Recognising these informal power structures and channels of information and authority which staff and children establish, and using them to the best advantage, will go a long way towards making the most effective use of a school's resources.

Informality and flexibility are among the happiest characteristics of small schools. In large schools, however, informality and flexibility will not be spontaneous. Paradoxically, informality has to be organised, and flexibility has to be planned. Neither neatness nor complexity of organisation have any particular merit in themselves, although it is probably true that the simpler an organisation the more likely it is to operate efficiently. It is how the organisation works which really matters; but, before we consider how the organisation of a school might support the essential processes of communication, consultation, delegation and administration, let us spend a morning in the head's room, and see what his life is really like.

8 Daily round

In the previous chapter, we stressed the importance of an effective organisation for many of the processes and purposes connected with the successful running of a school. Yet one of the first and most fundamental lessons derived from actually running a school is that things do not always happen as they are supposed or designed to happen. Moreover, the ordered pattern of life, which a precisely-structured organisation is intended to guarantee, is liable to be interrupted or overthrown not only by pressure of events but by the unforeseen and uncontrolled order in which those events arise.

Their unexpectedness and urgency, and the bewildering variety of questions awaiting the head's decision, will often mean that he is juggling with a dozen problems at the same time, with little or no chance to dispose safely of any one of them before the others, in turn, demand and concentrate his attention. It may be salutary and illuminating, therefore, to sit alongside a head at work. This will give us a chance to watch him in operation, wrestling with an uneasy pattern of smooth pre-arrangement and unexpected interruption. Joining the head of Crossfield Park School, as he goes about his work in November 1974, let us assume his identity for a few hours, the better to understand some aspects of what being a head really involves.

Crossfield Park is a new 7-form entry, mixed, 11-18 Comprehensive School. You were appointed head in April 1971. In September of that year the school opened with the first three years. A fourth year was added in September 1972, and a fifth year in September 1973. It is now the autumn term of 1974.

On the morning of Monday, 18 November 1974, Jeremy Painton stayed behind after assembly, and spoke to you about wanting to drop A-level mathematics from his curriculum in the lower sixth. Jeremy assured you that he had discussed the idea with Miss Lever, his maths teacher, who had raised no objection to his proposal since (according to Jeremy) she considered that his chances of success were 'virtually nil'. You remembered that his choice of mathematics at the end of his fifth year had been largely determined by his intention to become an industrial chemist, so you realised, immediately, that what he was now suggesting involved a major decision, affecting both his course of study and his career. Accordingly, you advised Jeremy to ask his parents if they would come and discuss the matter. On returning to your room, with someone already waiting to see you, you recorded a quick note on your memo pad to remind you to collect all the relevant information about Jeremy's maths performance, both in the fifth and in the lower sixth, before his parents telephoned or called.

On Wednesday morning, two days later, after dictating some urgent letters left over from yesterday (when you were away for the greater part of the day, attending a meeting at County Hall) you follow your usual daily practice of checking your memo pad, to remind yourself about jobs which still remain to be done. In this way you come across your note about Jeremy, and are reminded that you have not yet heard from his parents, nor have you collected the information about his mathematics which you will need when they come to see you. So you ask your secretary to invite Mr Pulley, the head of the department, to have a word with you, in your room, over morning coffee. Almost as soon as you open the subject of Jeremy and his maths course, Mr Pulley takes your breath away by revealing that Jeremy handed in his books, and stopped attending maths lessons, on Monday afternoon! Mr Pulley had been informed of this decision, he tells you, by Miss Lever, who had been assured by Jeremy that he 'had seen the Head about it'. You ask Mr Pulley to consult his departmental colleagues, and to let you have (if possible within the next twenty-four hours), a written assessment of Jeremy's work in mathematics in both the fifth and sixth forms. When Mr Pulley departs for his next lesson all kinds of anxious questions immediately begin to chase themselves through your mind. It would seem, at first sight, that Jeremy has 'pulled a fast one' on you all, although he had certainly spoken to Miss Lever and to you, and had truthfully told each of you that he had spoken to the other.

At this point, Mr Gainsford, a member of the English department, who joined the staff at the beginning of term, comes to see you by appointment. Bursting with enthusiasm, he quickly reveals that he wants to start a film society in school with (he hopes) the support of parents. Membership would be limited, and would be subject to the payment of a subscription. You are interested in his proposal, and make a note to sound your governors and the local authority, to get some very necessary legal advice and, when the time comes, to consult parents. You also decide to have a word with the manager of the local cinema, to forestall any objection or protest. Mr Gainsford tells you that he has calculated the initial sum which will be required to set the society on its feet. You jot down his rough estimate, but warn him that, in his enthusiasm, he mustn't jump the gun, that many enquiries will have to be made, and that you will have to check the balance available in the School Fund. You also hint that, even if all goes well with his proposal, some discreet scrutiny of film society programmes may be necessary. You applaud his initiative, however, and promise to talk to him again, when you have collected the necessary information and advice.

At this point your telephone rings and your secretary, apologising for interrupting, tells you that she thinks you ought to speak to Mrs Welsh, the mother of David Welsh in 2S. You ask Mr Gainsford to wait. because there is another matter you would like to raise with him. Mrs Welsh is very concerned because David fell off his bicycle last night and was taken to hospital, where his left arm was found to be fractured, and was put in plaster. He insists on coming to school after lunch because he has a school examination, so she proposes to bring him at 1.30 p.m. She wants you to know that he will be working under difficulties, and she is particularly anxious that the staff concerned should realise that he is left-handed; although he can hold a pen in his fingers, he will not find it at all easy to write. You promise that David will be 'looked after', make soothing comments and commend his courage.

You are about to resume the conversation with Mr Gainsford when, once again, you are interrupted by the telephone. Peter Bertram, the County Adviser responsible for your school, tells you that he has two Australian visitors with him, that their programme arranged for this afternoon has fallen through, and he knows you well enough to ask if he can bring his guests to your school after lunch to see something of the work, particularly in languages and science. You explain that you have to go out at 2.15 p.m. to take the chair at an important meeting of heads of schools in your area, but 'you don't want to leave your Adviser in a spot', and therefore you will make some arrangements for him, although you don't at this moment know what they will be.

At last, you turn back to Mr Gainsford and mention that Miss Sangster (Deputy Head) is worried about Sandra Wesley and is considering moving her into another English set, for purely personal and social reasons. As Sandra is in one of the fifth-year English sets which Mr Gainsford teaches, you wonder if he could tell you how Sandra's work compares with that of the other pupils in her set. To your surprise, Mr Gainsford indicates that he cannot answer your question precisely. He explains that he does not award marks or grades because he believes that, at best, they are unhelpful, and, at worst, they are positively discouraging. His policy, he explains, is to write critical but encouraging comments on each piece of written work, relating its content and quality to his assessment of the writer's capacity. Any absolute standard is, in his view, impossible to achieve. Warming to his convictions, Mr Gainsford implies that it would be arrogant for him to try to impose his own standards on a creative writer, and all his children are encouraged to be creative: 'So, please, headmaster, would you re-phrase your question?' Rather taken aback by this direct and pertinent exposition of his views (for which you believe that there is some theore-tical justification, and with which you have some sympathy), you explain to Mr Gainsford that selection of children for different subjects, courses and examination objectives has to take place at various stages in their progress through the school. In practice, there-fore, some comparisons are unavoidable and, in fact, in the summer of 1972, a system of assessment by grades had been agreed by the staff, after long discussion spread over many months. So you point out that, at the end of term, Mr Gainsford will be expected to provide information for form tutors and year masters. He then reminds you that this system was agreed upon before he joined the staff, which leaves you wonder-ing whether the procedure for acquainting new members of staff with established practices, and with school routines, has failed in this instance, and whether it is time for it to be reviewed and revised. So you send Mr Gainsford off to his next class, with a promise that you will look into this matter, as well as the proposed film society.

Now what have these events on the morning of 20 November revealed? It should not be supposed that there is anything unusual or special about them. Far from being exceptional or unduly harassing, it is (in fact) a perfectly ordinary morning in the life of a head, noticeable more for its ordinariness than for its particularity. But it clearly reveals that all organisations are subject to human frailty; that it can never be safely assumed that intentions will automatically be fulfilled, unless they are continuously monitored and nurtured; and that learning from experience is a continuous process, which only becomes effective if we are always willing to reassess (instead of believing, for example, that all is well with our systems of communication or delegation, and that no re-evaluation or change is called for).

It has also become apparent that a head's responsibilities extend far beyond the school: in the space of forty-eight hours the head of Crossfield Park has had two important meetings. This indication that a school cannot be isolated from the community which it serves is further borne out by the crucial importance of effective contact with parents, and of good external relationships, in general, here illustrated by the County Adviser and his Australian visitors. The important role of the head's secretary, and the need for adequate administrative support are also emphasised. At the same time the narrative indicates the value of systematic recording by the head of simple memoranda to himself (and to his colleagues) so that consequential actions are not forgotten and he and they are continuously reminded of problems which still await decision.

Finally, there is evidence of the danger of jumping to conclusions. It would be easy, for example, to decide that the head was initially at fault in his handling of Jeremy Painton and his mathematics. His close knowledge of Jeremy's choice of A-level subjects might suggest that the head was assuming direct responsibilities which really ought to have been delegated. Nevertheless, in a steadily-growing school it might be perfectly understandable for the head to deal himself with the school's first entries to the sixth form; and this would forcibly illustrate our thesis, put forward in the previous chapter, that all members of the top management team, including the head, should carry direct responsibility in accordance with their particular knowledge, experience and skills. At any rate, the lessons of this busy morning will certainly have caused the head to have another critical look at his patterns of communication, consultation, delegation and administration; and we now propose to explore these areas of management in the next four chapters.

9   Communication

To guarantee an effective flow of ideas and information presents a wide
range of complex problems. This is because the processes of internal
communication are inextricably involved with all aspects of running
a school. Let us begin, therefore, by looking at some of these problems
from three different angles.

The first major difficulty is to identify not only different categories
of information, but the optimum moment for their disclosure. When
new ideas or proposals are under consideration, for example, or when
changes of attitude or practice are being discussed, a decision has to be
taken about the best time for making an announcement to the whole
school. For there are as many dangers in partial or premature disclosure
as there are in withholding information altogether; and, if we probe
a little deeper, we shall find that the problems are legion. For instance,
there must be a firm policy on the delicate question about whether
every member of staff should have unlimited access to confidential
information about every child, or whether such information should
be confined to those who have ultimate responsibility for the child,
such as the house or year master. Again, there must be an understanding
about the amount of information which members of the staff should
have about each other. Obviously, all must understand the responsibilities which each carries, and the authority which each exercises,
but are staff salaries a matter of private concern to each individual?

Looked at from another standpoint, experience shows that few
policy decisions are more important than identifying, collating and
distributing the information and instructions which new members
of staff will need; and, in curriculum matters, the line must be drawn
between those aspects and decisions which all members of staff should
share, and those which can be reserved for staff who are directly concerned. Do the whole staff, for example, need to understand the
principles on which the curriculum is based, and to know the full

range of subject options and alternative courses which are available? Should heads of department be aware of the syllabuses and teaching methods of all other departments? How much ought every member of staff to know about experiments which may be going on in the school, whether in curriculum development, in subject integration, in the growth of a resources centre, in new teaching techniques (such as mixed-ability grouping or team teaching) or in the use of language laboratories, video tapes and computers? When someone has a bright idea, or a serious problem, whether it be the head or the newest recruit to the staff, who ought to know about it first? When information comes into the possession of a member of staff, which may be of importance and concern to the school, what action should he take?

In addition, looking outwards from the school, there must be a firm policy about how best to communicate with parents, and how little or how much to tell them. Much also depends upon a decision about how the school can best organise its use of radio and television programmes, and how it should maintain useful contact with the news media, as well as with a host of external bodies such as examining boards, colleges and universities, local industry and commerce, voluntary organisations, and the welfare and community services. It is only necessary to pose these questions to realise that precise answers are difficult to define, and still more difficult to put into operation.

Yet, although this may seem a wearisome series of intricate questions, involving policy decisions, they are all concerned with communication. In fact, they afford no more than a bare outline illustration of the multitude of similar questions, many of them involving fundamental issues of principle and of policy which have to be resolved. They all arise from asking the simple question: *Who ought to know what and when?* They are questions, moreover, which cannot be shirked. They must be answered, accurately and precisely, if the school's patterns and channels of communication are to function smoothly and effectively. For no organisation can be efficient, unless those who work within it have all the information which they need, when they need it, know how to act upon it when they've got it, and understand how to feed back the results of that action. Effective communication demands far more than that, however. The provision of accurate information, after all, ought to be a comparatively simple process; but deciding who ought to receive information, and when, and exactly what information they need, no more and no less, is a sensitive process, involving imagination and discrimination. For it is necessary to ensure not only that the right people get the right information at the right moment, but that (so far as is humanly possible) the information so provided is easy to understand, and difficult to *mis*understand. The recipient, moreover, must be mentally and emotionally committed to an appropriate course of action, if the information is to achieve its purpose. Finding the best answers to these and countless other similar questions demands skills of the highest order. Of them all, however. the art of judgement remains the most important, despite the immense technological advances in the processes and means of communication. The question: *Who ought to know what, and when?* is one which has to be asked many times every day. For example, after every interview or consultation, the head would be well advised to record a brief note for his own records, with enough copies for distribution to those who are immediately concerned. In the last resort, the answers will depend upon the head's philosophy and style of management, and upon the circumstances of each separate school. Nevertheless, it remains true that the answers will be crucial to the effectiveness of a school's system of communications which is, itself, at the very heart of the whole business of running a school.

Let us now look at the problem from the second angle. Anyone who has ever worked in a large organisation knows how desperately easy it is for even the most conscientious member to be unaware of information or instructions just at the very moment when awareness becomes vital, and when the lack of the information or instructions is not merely embarrassing to himself, but may be inhibiting to the whole organisation. By the time the unawareness becomes apparent, it is often already too late. A pattern of communication is, in fact, essential for a school, as for any organisation. The passing on of information or instructions is a comparatively simple process, and can be almost mechanical in operation, with established procedures to be followed. Even so, it can quickly go wrong, if the receipt of information or instructions remains an entirely passive process. By one means or another, the recipient of a communication should be expected to react in a positive way, either by accepting an appropriate degree of commitment (even if that commitment involves no more, at the moment, than a mental or written note to record the instructions, so that he can instantly recall them, when the need arises) or by taking whatever appropriate action is indicated.

Once again, discrimination and clarity are required, if communication is to be successful. In any community such as a school, it is a serious misjudgement, for instance, to impart a tit-bit of information or inside knowledge, which is of general interest or concern, either casually or on the spur of the moment, to an individual or group. Those who do not happen to be present at that moment of revelation, and who hear the news second-hand, will lose their confidence in the established channels of communication. Ideally, therefore, any piece of information which concerns more than one person should, so far as is practicable, be revealed to all those whom it concerns at the same time.

Discrimination is also required in deciding which method of communication to employ on any particular occasion. The question now at issue is: *How do they know?* Yet, however carefully the choice is made, there can be no guarantee of complete success. Oral notices, whether by word of mouth, or over the telephone or tannoy, will be misheard, misinterpreted or simply fall on deaf ears. Even when a communication is delivered, orally, in the presence of those for whom it is intended, for example at assembly or at a staff meeting or just before setting out on some school expedition, there is still no assurance that it will have been heard correctly. For most people only hear what they want to hear, or what they are able to absorb at a particular moment. Moreover, in our own experience, there is often a difference between what we actually said, what we thought we said, and what others thought we had said. Equally, written notices may fail to catch the eye of those for whom they are intended, or they may arrive at an awkward moment (most irritating of all — in the middle of a lesson), or their very frequency may dull the sensitivity of those upon whose responsiveness so many daily demands are made. Pigeon-holes, in-trays, and notice-boards become congested and untidy, while posters become dog-eared and tatty. Bulletins and information sheets, by their very frequency and familiarity, only too easily become a matter of routine; in consequence, expectation and awareness are diminished, and crucial items of news escape the attention of those for whom they were particularly intended.

To make matters even more difficult for the large school, the longer the line of communication, and the greater the number of those who are tuned to its particular wave-length, the greater will be the margin for error and disappointment. Difficulties arise not only from the simple corruption of a message in transit, but from a change of emphasis or interpretation, imparted to it (either consciously or unconsciously) by those associated with its transmission. Indeed, it is broadly true to say that the longer the line of communication, the more likely it is that the question at the end of the line will no longer be the question which was originally asked, and that the answer (when it finally reaches the top) will not be an answer to the original question.

If important decisions are reached at a staff meeting, a minority will disagree with them, and will adopt varying degrees of non-cooperation; those who are absent will have to be informed by specific means, calling for imagination and forethought. Even those who are present, and who indicate their support for any particular proposal, will vary in the extent of their understanding, and in the degree and accuracy of their immediate commitment and response. If sectional or group staff meetings are preferred, with the advantage of smaller numbers, or if attendance at most staff meetings is made voluntary, then there is the danger that some will hear of proposals while they are still only in the process of consideration, while others will be annoyed because they have only just heard of suggestions or decisions which seem to be common property.

Another important aspect of the communication process has still to be recognised, namely that communication is not a one-way street, operating only from the top to the bottom of the organisation; indeed, information or suggestions which rise from the bottom or middle reaches of the organisation to the top, may often be of supreme importance. They may present a new idea, reveal a bottle-neck or a cause of misunderstanding, or provide invaluable comment and feedback on a communication which came, originally perhaps, from the head. So important is upward communication, in fact, that it may be prudent to provide for it a separate and unfettered channel of its own, such as a common-room committee, 'under' its own elected chairman, or a school council. In the same way, the need for all members of an organisation to keep in touch with one another, and especially with their 'opposite numbers', means that communication sideways is of paramount importance. There are three directions in which communication operates — downwards, upwards and sideways — and the most difficult of these is sideways. The fact that the Crossfield Park maths department was content to accept Jeremy Painton's decision to give up mathematics, without reference or consultation. illustrates the importance of sideways communication. For it emphasises that any effective system of communication must rely upon the sense of responsibility and cooperation of every member of the organisation. Nothing approaching perfection will be achieved unless everyone dependent upon or affected by the system is willing to recognise that there are principles to be followed, practices to be established and obligations to be accepted. Everyone must be willing to play his part in seeing that the channels of communication are designed to achieve their purpose, that they are kept open, and that they are subject to continuous review.

This brings us to the third angle from which to consider the problems of communication. To support an oral communication with a written reminder (and vice versa), to repeat instructions on strategic occasions, to ask for evidence that communications have been received (by initialling a circular, or indicating receipt of a document in some positive and identifiable way), all these are likely to prove useful measures. To provide copies of documents for as many individuals as possible is often a prudent form of insurance but, even so, there is no guarantee of complete success. Paper proliferates, and one piece of paper begets another, until multiplication becomes a habit which defeats its own purpose. Much time, energy and indignation would be saved if every communicator would establish an effective kerb-drill for himself: 'Look right at why I am sending it, look left to the person to whom it is being sent, and then look right again to see if it is really necessary'. Ideally, the form and nature of a communication should be appropriate to its content. It should reach the person for whom it is intended at the moment when he is most receptive to it; it should be so clearly phrased as to eliminate misunderstanding, and should demand some form of individual response and commitment. Moreover, it must be remembered that, what is true for the head and for the school as a whole, is equally true, in principle, for the director of studies and all his heads of faculties, for the head of department and all his subject colleagues, for the head of year or house and all his tutors, and for the chairman of the common-room and all its members.

This raises the question of reminders. Perhaps the simplest way for a head to ensure that he is reminded of the need to follow up a previous action at the appropriate moment (maybe a few hours, a couple of days, or a fortnight later) is to put a note on an extra copy of the original document. This can then be placed in an 'action pending' tray, with a reminder date clearly marked upon it in bold figures, and with all the papers in that tray arranged in date order. Alternatively, his secretary can be asked to record, in her desk diary, the dates on which particular notes or papers should be automatically brought up again for reconsideration, in order that there may be an opportunity of deciding whether a reminder should be issued, or whether any other similar action is called for. If she then makes a habit of consulting the pending tray and/or her desk diary first thing every morning, the chances of overlooking or losing sight of a piece of un-concluded business will be substantially reduced. As a result of this process, recipients know that reminders will be regularly issued (in mounting degrees of urgency), and this will generally have a dramatic effect upon the speed with which answers are given or returns are submitted in the first instance. There is one inherent danger in this knowledge, however, in that it encourages a belief that initial instruc-tions or requests are no more than preliminary range-finders, and can be safely disregarded until reminders are issued. To discourage this attitude of mind it is essential that persistent back-sliders should be swiftly identified and be firmly brought to book.

Parallel with the importance of making sure that the issue of infor-mation, instructions, enquiries or requests is supported by a system of automatic reminders after a decent interval, is the need to remember that routine instructions, once issued, become progressively less effective as time elapses, unless they are constantly revised and re-issued. In the school situation the importance of this precaution is emphasised by the turn-over in staff appointments, which may vary from none to one or two in a primary school, to as many as fifteen or twenty or even more staff changes in a large secondary school in any one year. In the last chapter Mr Gainsford's apparent ignorance of the school's agreed marking and grading practices was an example of this difficulty.

There is a further aspect of efficient communication which is commonly experienced, namely the feeling of relief that, having polished off a difficult letter, an important report, or a long memorandum, it can be forgotten. This over-confidence relies upon the hope that others will leap into action, but it ignores the hazards to which all human communications are subject. It overlooks the fact that papers can easily be lost in transit, misplaced on receipt, put at the bottom of the pile 'for later consideration', deliberately ignored or even intemperately consigned to the waste-paper basket. Yet, in all these circumstances, further action will have to be taken. For this reason, it is seldom wise to 'put away' an important communication which calls for positive action by someone else, without first making a note about it. This note will guarantee that a reminder will be issued, if necessary, and so will begin the process of communication all over again. For here the crucial question is: *How do you know that they know?* It is, indeed, profoundly unsafe to assume, once and for all, that when a communication has been issued, it has been correctly received, correctly understood, and correctly acted upon. The message to Jeremy Painton's parents in the previous chapter is a good example of this danger. For of all the ills to which human flesh is heir, misunderstanding (or just simple failure to understand) is probably the commonest affliction, and gives rise to infinite frustration and waste of time. And for this, only too often, the author of the original communication has himself to blame, because he failed to achieve the necessary degree of precision and lucidity in the first instance.

Seen against the background of these three probing questions, communication within a school offers no fail-safe procedures such as those with which astronauts are familiar. But failures can be diminished if, every time a difficulty or breakdown occurs, it is noted, the reasons for failures are diagnosed, the individuals responsible are identified, and steps are taken to prevent a recurrence. It is not reasonable to expect perfection, considering the difficulty of securing absolute clarity of intent in any form of drafting, however expert. Many members of the legal profession would be wholly unemployed, for example, if parliamentary acts were held by the courts to mean what they were intended to mean, without any room for interpretation, disagreement or discrepancy. Whatever machinery for communication is devised, and however precisely it is subject to a constant system of checks and controls, it will still be dependent upon human skills and subject to human frailty. In the face of these factors, therefore, the best practice is to avoid complacency, and to be prepared to work untiringly for success, yet to probe with perspicacity and dogged determination every instance of failure. A significant degree of success will be achieved only when all concerned are prepared to carry their burden and share of responsibility. Many experienced heads agree that communication comes very near the top of their private list of difficult problems; there is abundant proof that it will tax even the most patient, the most ingenious and the most resourceful. Those who come nearest to success are likely to be those who day-in and day-out, with diligence, persistence and infinite patience, seek to find an answer to these three simple questions:

> *Who ought to know what, and when?*
> *How do they know?*
> *How do you know that they know?*

10   Consultation

The purpose of genuine consultation between the head and his staff is not to persuade those who are consulted to agree with him! The basic purpose of consultation is to enable the head to draw upon the knowledge, experience and judgement of his colleagues, while they (in turn) derive professional satisfaction from making their views known, and from putting their advice at his disposal. Through consultation they also acquire training for posts of greater responsibility by being involved in consideration of major issues of policy and planning. Every school, of whatever size, affords abundant opportunities for consultation, both formal and informal. In the small school, whether primary or secondary, specific points can be discussed, quite informally, and decisions reached, either before assembly or in the coffee break or during the dinner hour, or in the twenty or thirty minutes immediately after school. Practice will vary from informal discussion with one or more individuals, to an examination of a problem with a small group, or in a meeting of the whole staff. When it can operate naturally and effectively, such informality is a precious quality, to be retained at all costs; even so, it is an invaluable safeguard for the head to develop the practice of making a written note after each discussion or consultation, however brief, and however informal, as a useful record and reminder. This is the equivalent of the impersonal minutes of a meeting which are appropriate on more formal occasions.

In all secondary schools, there are obvious channels of consultation through departments, houses or years, and other clearly identifiable sectors of the school's organisation, such as form masters or house tutors; and these may be used for the consideration of a whole host of different issues and problems. They should not be so rigidly employed, however, as to exclude informal consultation of individuals or of groups, outside the organisational structure, as long as the head is careful not to cause offence by short-circuiting or excluding those who have a right to expect consultation. Nothing, in fact, should ever prevent the right of each individual member of the staff and, indeed, of every boy and girl in the school, to have direct access to the head, although it is obvious that this right must be used sparingly and with discretion. Members of the staff will always wish to discuss with their head strictly personal issues, such as illness in the family or other domestic difficulties, or the next stage in the development of their own career; and, despite the most careful provision of channels of communication and consultation, at each level, every member of the staff, and every boy and girl, should feel a sense of confidence in the head's accessibility, integrity and sympathetic concern. If, however, anyone (whether staff or pupil) should exercise his right of direct access on inadequate grounds, then it would probably be wise for the head to see him, on the first occasion, so that confidence may be retained; but the head should gently suggest that, in similar circumstances in future, it would be well if he were first to use the organisation provided, and to see the member of the staff directly and immediately concerned.

Formal staff meetings still have a useful part to play in the processes of consultation. Other things being equal, they should be arranged far enough ahead to avoid embarrassment or disappointment for those who find it difficult to attend meetings after school hours, but this must not preclude a spontaneous meeting, called at short notice, to discuss an issue of immediate importance. In large schools, the formal staff meeting, as a means of deliberation, presents many difficulties. Only a small minority of those present can speak, and it is difficult to prevent a monopoly of the discussion by a self-selected few. The skilful head will, of course, draw into the discussion those who have a particular contribution to make but who might otherwise be intimidated by colleagues who hold positions of major responsibility, or who have axes to grind! Even so, it is difficult to be certain that all those who originally wished to speak have done so, or that all those who have taken part in the discussion have been completely outspoken and candid; and this raises the question of whether it is wise to take a vote at staff meetings. Sometimes 'one man one vote' will be appropriate; sometimes it will not. The head of history may have an important contribution to make, but his opinion may not be of equal value to that of the games master on a question which concerns competing priorities between major games. The reverse may be the case if the problem under consideration concerns external examinations policy, or internal assessment of academic progress. Knowing his colleagues individually and collectively, the head will often be well advised to listen, to assess the weight of argument and opinion, and to reach his decision without a vote.

Full staff meetings, therefore, may be most effective mainly as a means of reaching a final decision, after a long process of consideration in groups or sectional meetings. Some schools, in fact, find it expedient to put staff meetings on a voluntary footing, so that only those who are directly concerned, and have a positive contribution to make, or who have a particular interest, will attend. But it must be recognised that those who choose not to be involved in such meetings may be sacrificing an important opportunity for their own professional development. At the same time, it may well mean that, when decisions are eventually reached and put into practice, they will not be either fully informed or wholly committed. This principle should not apply, however, to those occasions when a formal staff meeting is called in order to complete the final stages in a long process of consultation spread over many weeks or months: this should still be mandatory, even if it is difficult to guarantee one hundred per cent attendance. We do not accept the by-no-means uncommon argument that all staff meetings must be held in school hours, and that it is manifestly unreasonable to expect attendance at other times. This would seem to imply a wholly unprofessional attitude. Indeed, we hold it to be of very great importance that the staffs of all schools should meet regularly, as a body or in groups, out of school hours, in order to discuss major issues of philosophy, policy or practice, to examine new ideas or techniques, or to consider changes in the balance and structure of the curriculum. Such meetings might be held immediately before the opening of each term, or on the day after term is over, or in the evenings (say, between 4 and 6 or 6.30 p.m.). Whenever staff meetings of any length are held out of school hours, they would benefit from the provision of appropriate refreshments. Experience shows that the touch of social grace which such an arrangement affords also contributes to the quality of discussion and participation.

In many large schools it is now becoming common practice not only to hold regular group or sectional staff meetings, but to set up staff 'working parties' or 'task forces'. A staff working party, for example, might be set up 'To consider the school's methods of assessment of individual children'. In another context it might be appropriate to set up a working party of governors, staff, children and parents 'To consider the school's policy on the wearing of uniform'. All such working parties should clearly be temporary in nature and ad hoc in constitution. They should carry authority and conviction, succeed in generating far-ranging and detailed discussion, and feel sufficiently confident to put forward positive recommendations. They should be free to invite suggestions from all who are directly concerned, or who have contributions to make, but the recommendations of a working party should have no final authority, in themselves. Rather, their purpose is to identify and to examine all the aspects of any problem or proposal referred to them, and then to submit their conclusions to open debate. To this end, the reference of a problem to a working party should be as open-ended as possible. It should not invite comment upon one particular solution or on a straight choice between alternative solutions. Instead, it should encourage consultation on all aspects of the problem, so that every point of view, and many possible solutions, may be considered. In order that consultation shall be effective, and free from restriction. the head should never say: 'I am proposing to take such and such a step: what do you think of my proposal?' Rather, he should say: 'We are confronted by this problem, or by that situation: how do you recommend that we should act?' Or, again: 'It has been suggested that we should re-examine the purpose and operation of our prefect system. Please consider all the issues involved, and let me have your recommendations'.

It is equally important that adequate time should be allowed for these processes of consultation to take place. On a complex and contentious issue such discussion may well be spread over a whole term, or even longer. If consideration is likely to be prolonged, then the head's initial reference to the working party should be reinforced by the publication of interim statements, indicating the headway made towards finding an acceptable solution, and defining the aspects of the problems which have not yet been resolved. In this way interest is maintained, targets can be reassessed, and progress can be measured.

This whole process of consultation, however, must be used with moderation and discretion. It would not be sensible if the total consultative process were to be triggered off by every minor problem. Some schools have fallen into the trap of using consultative sledgehammers to crack pretty small nuts.

There is one situation in which consultation is of particular importance. In the pressures of accelerating innovation to which secondary schools are now subjected, it is essential not only to ensure adequate preparation for change, and to avoid the development of a bandwagon mentality, but also to retain staff confidence and to foresee, as far as possible, all the probable consequences of any changes which are under consideration. The aims and the methods, as well as the consequences, must be fully understood by all those who will be involved, before the first step is taken. Directed reading, discussion, courses, conferences and visits will all play their part. So the working party technique may be particularly effective when major changes of policy or practice are under consideration. This would apply, for example, to the proposed introduction of team-teaching, the adoption of mixed-ability grouping or the development of individual time-tables and private study in the middle school. In Chapter 8 we saw, by implication, that starting a school film society, or reaching agreement upon a common marking and grading system, were also matters calling for careful consideration and consultation.

Many issues raised by proposals of this kind illustrate the implacable law of infinite repercussions, and clearly demand a concerted effort of understanding and agreement, *before* the change can be smoothly and successfully implemented. In all such situations, as we saw in the 'Hindsight' exercise in Chapter 2, it is vitally necessary to retain the confidence and goodwill of the staff, and to protect their interests. While it is imperative that schools should be aware of social and educational changes, and should be responsive to them, so that they may keep abreast of current ideas and techniques, they will ignore, at their peril, the importance, at the same time, of protecting staff confidence and security. Any change in staff status or esteem, whether in their own eyes or in the eyes of others, and any new demands upon their professional skill and expertise, must involve patient, continuous consultation, over a long period. It would be nothing short of lunacy to introduce a major change, such as we have been considering, without the fullest opportunity for debate. Some members of the staff are likely to find themselves in a minority, and will be prickly on that account; those who are conservative and traditional in outlook may feel themselves threatened by a particular proposal, which destroys their confidence in themselves, seems to call in question the validity of their long experience, and leaves them with a sense of confusion and inadequacy. For all these reasons, quite apart from the basic necessity of thrashing out a proposal until all its implications have been understood, and a substantial measure of agreement has been reached about the right course to pursue, it is essential to move slowly and patiently, and to be particularly sensitive and sympathetic to those who seem to find themselves on the edge of a professional precipice.

To take this general argument a stage further, it may be illuminating to examine a specific proposal in this category. Let us suppose that the head of the mathematics department has asked for a special allocation of funds, so that he can buy a series of new textbooks in order to introduce modern mathematics into the curriculum next year. At once it is apparent that this is not simply a change affecting the mathematics department alone. First, there is the question of the best use of the school's limited financial resources: more money for the mathematics department inevitably means less for all the rest. Should the change be introduced gradually, one year at a time, beginning with the first year, or could it be introduced into the first and second years simultaneously? Then there is the question of how the change in the mathematics syllabus will affect other related subjects, such as physics, chemistry, engineering science and geography: will they accept the change, and adapt the content and pattern of their own syllabuses, or will they continue to base their work on traditional mathematics? Is a variety of textbooks on modern mathematics available, so that a suitable choice can be made; are there also some authoritative books on teaching methods and techniques, written by practising schoolmasters, which would offer relevant advice and experience in the introduction of modern mathematics? Then, is this a matter on which the views of governors, the local authority and of parents should be invited, or is it entirely within the school's competence to decide? Will new setting or grouping arrangements be necessary, and new teaching techniques be required; if so, will additional apparatus or teaching equipment be needed, in addition to new textbooks, either immediately or over a longer period? Moreover, are all the members of the mathematics department prepared to accept the change, and competent to put it into effect? Will additional mathematics staff be required either now, or in the foreseeable future, as a direct result of this change alone?

And then, looking outside the school, will the introduction of modern mathematics affect external examination courses and involve a change of external examination policy? Would it be wise to consult the professor of mathematics in the neighbouring university, and the principals of the local colleges of education and of further education? How would the change affect primary and middle schools in the catchment area, other secondary schools in the neighbourhood, and children moving into or out of the school, on transfer? What would be the reaction of employers in the area, especially engineering firms? Can other secondary schools be identified in which the change has already been made, so that staff visits can be planned in order to study the problems and advantages at first-hand? These are only some of the many issues raised by a proposal of this kind, which clearly call for a most careful examination of all the issues involved, before a final decision can be reached.

Moreover, in addition to staff consultation, it may often be appropriate to consult the children, in whose ultimate interest all major changes should be planned. In the first edition of this book we suggested, rather tentatively, that the organisation of a school should also recognise and provide for pupil consultation. Such an attitude, in the autumn of 1974, now seems to us to be pusillanimous. There are, in fact, two very good and robust reasons why a school should be prepared to face this issue without apprehension or condescension. The first is that the views, reaction and suggestions of pupils (given the appropriate machinery and integrity of purpose) constitute an invaluable source of assessment material. If there is one lesson more than another which teachers (including heads) need to learn, it is to talk less and to listen more, not only to pupils and parents, but to anyone who has something interesting and useful to say. It is pointless to invite opinions from pupils, however, if their freedom of speech is limited to the safe and unexciting, to school uniform and school meals, and other minor aspects of school rules and regulations. Since secondary school pupils are now invited, even at 12, 13 and 14, to associate themselves with academic and curricular choices which may affect their whole lives, it is illogical that they should not be free to discuss major aspects of school policy, such as curriculum, options, homework, examinations (internal and external), and the effectiveness of teaching techniques. The hoary professional belief, still practised though less often expressed in such blunt terms, that 'teacher knows best', is no longer acceptable either in theory or practice. The second reason for squarely facing this question is that in the current climate of participation, with adults in our sixth forms and pupils on our governing bodies, it is shortsighted to deny them, earlier in their school careers, the mental discipline which comes from unfettered but controlled discussion of issues which affect their lives and the welfare of the school.

Unfortunately, such experience as is available in this field, at present, is not very encouraging. Many formal structures of pupil consultation, such as School Councils, are often as self-fulfilling and restrictive as many teacher assessments of their pupils. To begin by building an impregnable perimeter fence, in the hope of containing discussion within it, is to destroy any hope of genuine pupil consultation. There must be a willingness, on the part of the staff, not to stand aloof on their professional dignity or to adopt attitudes of dismay and unbelief, but to welcome constructive suggestions and comments, including comments on their own teaching. Consultation must be encouraged to develop momentum so that it does not appear to the pupils as a process of meticulous sifting and straining, from which their deeply-felt convictions emerge only as meaningless generalities. Here, then, is an area of school policy in which, at the moment, honest endeavour is more important than any dividend which may be derived from it: to travel hopefully towards this goal, until we have a much greater body of experience upon which to rely.

At this stage in the development of our thesis, two other points must be made clear. The first is that we know, from experience, that not all members of staff wish to be involved in consultation. There are some (perhaps a majority?) who welcome consultation up to the point of decision, but prefer these decisions to be taken by others, and then communicated to them; others welcome the chance to carry consultation to the point of being associated with the final decision.

A few are content with their role as teachers (and may well be the salt of the earth on that account): they have no wish to become involved in the formation or execution of policy at all, except in so far as it concerns their work in the classroom. Reactions vary from school to school. But, while it may be perfectly legitimate to offer consultation to all, on a voluntary basis, the importance of professional training must never be overlooked. It may be wise, therefore, to attempt to persuade the reluctant that, by opting out of the thousand and one decisions affecting the running of the school, they may (in the long run) be adversely affecting the development of their own careers, and they are certainly diminishing the pool of the school's total resources. Moreover, we do not wish to imply, for one moment, that the setting up of committees or working parties involves any reduction in the status or independence of the head. It does not imply any abrogation of his authority, nor does it necessarily imply the acceptance of collective or collegiate responsibility. The heads of some very large schools, it is true, have chosen to exercise their authority as chairmen of committees. With men whose natural style of management this is, and whose colleagues are prepared to accept their full share of responsibility, it may work well enough. But, generally, our own philosophy is that, on any issue basic to the school's policies, the head must take the final decision, as well as carry the final responsibility: but when there is a balance of choice between decisions, all of which are in conformity with the school's declared aims and objectives, then it may sometimes be appropriate for a head to abide by a consensus of opinion, and to accept a majority decision.

One thing is certain, however. After consultation has taken place, it is essential that decisions should be reached as soon as possible, and should be made known to all those who contributed to the discussion. Where some delay between consultation and decision is unavoidable, then the reasons for delay should be revealed; and, when a final decision differs from the recommendations put forward, then the circumstances should be carefully explained, not only to justify the decision itself, but to confirm that it was reached only after mature consideration of all the issues and responsibilities involved. Sometimes, after all the discussion and argument is over, the head may very well say, in effect: 'Thank you all very much indeed for your help and advice. I shall now go into retreat, and let you know my decision next week'. Whichever way his decision goes, there can be no doubt whatever that the staff, after consultation in which they have taken part, will be better informed about the issues involved in this particular matter, as well as about the general principles and problems of good organisation and administration. In addition, they themselves will have grown in stature and experience. At the same time, the head's own judgement will have been substantially reinforced by the collective wisdom and advice of his colleagues; if, for example, he had referred the question of introducing modern mathematics to a staff working party, then his eventual reply to the head of the mathematics department would have been much more soundly and securely based than if he had trusted to his own appreciation of the problem, reinforced, perhaps, by the advice of one or two senior colleagues.

Consultation, as we see it, then, is a natural tool of good organisation, a matter of professional advice and involvement; it operates not by the undermining of authority, but by the pooling of experience and expertise. The quality of secondary education would surely be enriched if its policies and practices were to be continuously supported and sustained by the massed zeal and professional know-how which staff common rooms can command, more particularly if that consultation were courageous enough to aim at unfettered discussion, not concealing differences, and not aiming at conformity. There is an amusing story (however apocryphal) told about the famous Dr Jowett, of Balliol College, Oxford. Dr Jowett was anxious to introduce a major change in college policy. His proposal was discussed, at length, in a meeting of college Fellows, and was greeted with unanimous opposition. Dr Jowett was unmoved, however, and, in indicating his final determination to go ahead, his only concession to their vehement disagreement was to admit that he would adopt his proposal 'with the greater reluctance'! When there is a fundamental difference of opinion over a proposal, it may sometimes be wise for the head to prolong the discussion, rather than to support either the majority or minority view. In such situations discretion may often be the better part of valour. For if every head were to go through the processes of consultation, and were then invariably to ignore the advice given him, the staff would quickly see through the pretence, and consultation would become nothing more than a meaningless gesture. On the other hand, since he cannot shirk his final responsibility, if the head (after the fullest consultation) were never to exercise his own independent judgement, in a sense contrary to the advice which he has been given, then his own stature and authority would be seen to be diminished.

11   Delegation

'I don't believe in delegation.' 'I delegate only under compulsion.' 'I wish I could learn to delegate more.' 'I couldn't possibly run my school without a complete structure of delegation.' These, and other statements in the same vein, are all recognisable attitudes which are common among practising heads. But the truth is that every head delegates; even the most authoritarian head, who purports not to believe in delegation at all, delegates, in fact, the moment that he devises a time-table. Staff responsibilities are precisely defined (such as to teach English or mathematics to a particular form, class or set, at a particular time, in a particular room); members of the staff are then expected to carry these composite responsibilities, within the framework of the time-table. Moreover, the time-table assumes that every master will follow the prescribed syllabus, will use the appropriate books, stationery and equipment, and will cover the stipulated course for each class, by the end of the school year, which are all of them admirable examples of delegation in operation. Incidentally, the time-table also extends the principle of delegation to children since they, too, are expected to be where the time-table requires them to be, at the time which the time-table stipulates, largely without supervision, except perhaps with regard to their conduct as they move about the school, along the corridors or up and down the stairs. Again, the most authoritarian head will often maintain a prefect system: yet the appointment of prefects implies the devolution of authority, in specific areas and in precise terms, which is a basic principle of delegation. Even in a primary school, which may operate an integrated day without any formal time-table, responsibility is delegated to the staff, not only to use their day's programme of work to cover the different areas, aspects and activities of learning but, also, to be in particular places with their classes, at particular times, such as in the hall for assembly, or for physical education or music. Delegation, then, is an integral and unavoidable part of the process of organising and running a school.

This being so, and our thoughts being directed, throughout this part of the book, to *How do you intend to get there?* it is axiomatic that the purpose and practice of delegation should be to advance the aims, and to sustain the objectives, of the school. By skilful delegation the organisation is strengthened and diversified, so that aims and objectives will have the best possible chance of fulfilment. Each single strand or sector of delegation should have precise significance: it should relate not only to the individual to whom responsibility is delegated, but should also take the school a stage further along the road towards its destination. The responsibilities delegated to the head of the science department, for example, must not only indicate his status, his responsibilities and his authority for carrying them out, within the pattern of the school's curricular organisation, but must also include an acceptance of the agreed purposes of science teaching, within the school's long-term aims and objectives. It might have been agreed, for example, that science teaching should stimulate intellectual curiosity, provide opportunities for observation and discovery, and encourage the formation of tentative conclusions based upon those operations. These terms of delegation would then be wholly nullified if the teaching of science were to be directed by the head of the department in a way which made little or no use of practical periods, followed slavishly the chapters in the textbook, and devoted a considerable part of each lesson to the dictation of notes.

From this it follows that effective delegation must be in precise terms. These terms must be understood by the head, by the person to whom he delegates, and by all his colleagues, so that the staff, as a whole, may know exactly who is doing what, to whom they should turn for information or advice, and to whom they are themselves, in turn, responsible. The effective exercise of delegated responsibility, however, is dependent not only upon precise definition, but upon the possession of the necessary degree of authority. This measure of authority, too, must be exactly defined, and must be accepted by all the parties concerned. In this way, all should understand that delegated authority is authority exercised on the head's behalf. This principle used to be picturesquely illustrated at the opening of Assize Courts in provincial centres, by the performance of traditional ceremonies and formalities designed to make it plain that it was the Queen's justice — the Justice of the Realm — which was being administered. If the terms of responsibility and authority are to be precise, however, it is obvious enough that there must, first, be a degree of mutual confidence and trust between the head and the colleague to whom he is delegating. 'Delegate and forget' is, superficially, an attractive precept, because it suggests a degree of confidence in his colleagues which they will find heart-warming, and which will develop their growing maturity in the acceptance and exercise of responsibility. It also suggests that the head can lighten his load in this way. But the truth is that a man who delegates is now accountable, not only for his own actions, but for the actions of those who exercise responsibility on his behalf. Delegation may reduce the number of chores, but it augments the total load of responsibility! This is not to suggest that, having delegated, a head should continually look over the shoulders of his colleagues, or resume control at every crisis. But it does emphasise the high degree of sensitive judgement and skill demanded in the establishment of any successful pattern of delegation: on the head's part in deciding whom to trust and to what extent; and, on the part of the one who exercises delegated responsibility, in recognising when to act on his own initiative, when to ask for reassurance, and when to seek advice.

On a severely practical issue, for delegation to be effective it must be buttressed by the provision of the necessary resources. Delegation is in danger of becoming meaningless, unless it is feasible in terms of time, manpower, money, tools and equipment. Just as the appropriate number of teaching periods must be allotted in the time-table, in order to cope with responsibility for a particular subject, so an adequate allowance of non-teaching time must be made available for those responsible for pastoral care, for careers advice, and for other additional assignments. In some cases, clerical assistance, office space and suitable equipment will also be necessary. Nevertheless, under the pressures and constraints with which secondary schools are only too familiar, heads sometimes find themselves obliged to assign a substantial degree of additional responsibility to a colleague, yet knowing full well that his existing commitments cannot be reduced, nor his resources augmented. In such instances, however, it is not always the case that every alternative has been fully explored. Such problems constitute an exercise in the identification of priorities, and in the use of manpower resources, which will be explored in Chapters 13 and 14.

There is another aspect of delegation which is quite fundamental to its success, and that is the question of assessment. Whoever is charged with delegated duties must recognise that these duties include assessment of the extent to which his own delegated responsibilities are being satisfactorily discharged; among these duties he accepts a degree of accountability, not only for his own performance, but for the performance of all those who work 'under' him, within the sphere of his delegated assignment. This is the translation into organisational terms of the biblical concept: 'to whom much is given, of him much is expected'. He to whom responsibilities are assigned is manifestly accountable for the way in which those responsibilities are exercised; but he is also accountable in respect of all those to whom he, in turn, has delegated a share of *his* responsibilities. Through him they are answerable for the quality of operation achieved in that sector or aspect of the school's life which is immediately concerned. Effective delegation, in other words, must include a regular and systematic review of the way in which delegated powers are exercised, by him who delegates, in consultation with those to whom he has delegated. This will become apparent when we come to consider the role of a head of department in the second half of this chapter.

An inevitable — but not always readily accepted — consequence of delegation is that, sometimes, responsibilities will be fulfilled less well than they would have been by the head himself. One of us knew well the headmaster of a large and flourishing secondary school in Yorkshire, in the 1950s, who stoutly maintained that he could teach every subject in the curriculum better than those to whom this task was entrusted (including needlework and cookery!). He was a remarkable man and so, perhaps, he could have done, as long as he only had to teach one or two subjects at a time; but as soon as the number of subjects he was teaching expanded beyond a certain point, he would have been quite unable to do equal justice to them all, and would have found it extremely difficult to achieve an acceptable standard in any one of them. This is, in fact, a basic reason for adopting any pattern or system of delegation; often it would be quicker and easier to do a particular job oneself, at a particular time, rather than to delegate. But, once the range, variety and complexity of responsibilities pass beyond the grasp of one man, then delegation is inevitable, even though some, or even all, aspects of those responsibilities could be better performed, in isolation, by the head of the organisation. This is a fact of life which must be accepted, and it emphasises, yet again, the need for precision in delegating, the exercise of skilful but unobtrusive control over its operation, and the practice of regular review and assessment.

Another consequence of delegation arises from the practice of what may be called 'delegation in parallel'. This occurs, for example, when a similar degree of delegated responsibility is assigned to two or more housemasters. Some diversity of practice then becomes inevitable including, perhaps, even a measure of inconsistency. This is because those who exercise delegated responsibilities must be free to use their own judgement and initiative, and to derive job-satisfaction from so doing: for, if they are not so free, then they are in danger of becoming automata. This is seen particularly clearly in the classroom, where two men, teaching the same subject, to the same age-group, and according to the same syllabus, are pretty sure to adopt different methods and approaches, to develop different emphases, and to establish a different quality of personal relationships between teacher and taught. The exploitation of these personal enthusiasms and skills, which fire the imagination and arouse the curiosity of the taught, is what distinguishes a successful teacher from a reliable teaching-machine; and this is a notable area in which non-conformity may be a positive virtue. Similarly, a housemaster may establish a general pattern of attitudes, relationships and sanctions, which he expects his house tutors to follow: but each tutor must be free to exercise his own professional and individual judgement, and to interpret the housemaster's philosophy in his own particular way. This diversity of interpretation may even produce occasional embarrassment, for example in the exercise of discipline, and in the award of punishment; but this diversity must be accepted (within tolerable limits) if a school is to be a community of individuals, dependent upon the combined strengths and qualities of professional men and women. So long as all are fully aware of the school's purposes and philosophy, take good care to operate within them, and act in close consultation with each other, while seeking advice in every case of perplexity or doubt, then diversity can become a source of strength, and can contribute to the richness and variety of the school's corporate practice.

Indeed, it is one of the greatest advantages of delegation, and one of the soundest reasons for its adoption that, like consultation, it harnesses the full potential of a school's resources, and makes maximum use of the knowledge and experience which the school enjoys. In so doing, not only does it focus the totality of the school's professional expertise, both upon its purposes and upon the ways in which those purposes are fulfilled, but it affords stimulus and zest to all those who share in this process, offering them professional reward, with continually widening experience and personal satisfaction.

Let us now examine the practice of delegation in two contrasting areas of the life of a school. No one questions the extent of the caretaker's responsibilities, nor doubts that he is accountable, both for his own performance, and for that of all the members of his staff. If dissatisfied, for example, with the work of a particular cleaner, most heads and most teachers would automatically take up the matter with the caretaker direct, and expect him to take appropriate action. In their turn, the staff of cleaners see, in the caretaker, their natural channel of communication, in both directions; they expect to receive information and instructions through him, and they rely upon him to convey their wishes, anxieties and grievances to higher authority. They assume his right to allocate their duties, to fix their working hours, and to provide them with the necessary working tools, materials and resources. They accept, without question, their responsibility *to him* for the satisfactory performance of these duties. In many cases, moreover, the caretaker will recruit and appoint his own staff, subject to confirmation by the head; he will certainly sign their weekly time-sheets, and will often distribute to them their weekly wages. So it would seem that the caretaker's authority is based upon a precise understanding of his accountability to the head, and to the members of his staff, just as the head accepts his own accountability to his colleagues, his governors, his local authority and the community which the school serves.

The caretaker, then, in the exercise of his delegated responsibilities, and in the positive acceptance of accountability illustrates, in practice, many of the basic principles of delegation which we have been examining. Is this equally true of the head of a subject department? In some schools, certainly, it is, where the role of the head of department is fully developed and fully understood. His colleagues in the department accept his direction and guidance; they appreciate that the extent of his responsibilities includes assessment of their work as well as of his own, and that he carries total accountability for the welfare of their department. They regard him as a natural channel of communication and consultation, on curricular matters, in both directions. Often, a head of department will be consulted about, and be associated with, appointments to the staff of his department; often he will be expected to allocate the teaching periods in his subject among his colleagues; often he will take part in the discussions preliminary to the planning of the time-table, and may even be allotted 'block' periods which he can allocate at his discretion, with freedom to adopt appropriate teaching groups and patterns. Often, at regular departmental meetings, not only will routine and administrative matters be decided, but basic academic and professional questions will be discussed, including a review of the content and balance of the curriculum, the place and contribution of their subject in that curriculum, and liaison with other subject disciplines. Clear aims and objectives for the department will be defined, appropriate teaching methods, techniques and resource materials will be chosen and agreed systems of marking, and of assessing and reporting upon pupils will be adopted. There will also be discussion of in-service training and the planned provision, for the department's staff, of additional knowledge and experience through departmental and staff libraries, and through visits to other schools, and attendance at courses and conferences.

Where most or all of these things happen, then delegation to a head of department is comprehensive both in intent and in fulfilment; but it would be sheer delusion to assume that these practices are universally adopted. We have already seen how difficult it is, in current circumstances, to guarantee heads of department the necessary resources, particularly of adequate time; and, in our own direct experience, only a minority of departmental heads are yet willing, in practice, to accept full accountability, including responsibility for the supervision, guidance and assessment of their departmental colleagues. Presumably this is because the terms in which their delegated responsibilities were defined were not sufficiently detailed or precise. Moreover, by no means all heads, even if they contrive to spend a substantial portion of their time collaborating with the work of their colleagues in the classroom, will automatically refer, direct, to the head of a department, examples of excellence or of weakness, which they encounter in the course of their classroom visits, as well as discussing them with the master concerned. Many heads of department will be held responsible for a sector of external relations, and this may well include liaison with local primary and other secondary schools, with examining bodies, with the Schools Council, with university faculties and departments, with colleges of education and of further education, and with inspectors, advisers and educational consultants, in general, as well as with industry and commerce and the careers advisory service. But practice varies enormously, from school to school and, even within a school, from one department to another. The degree of autonomy and independence which a head of department will be expected and be willing to exercise will depend, to a large extent, upon the degree to which the philosophy of delegation in a secondary school has been carefully examined and assimilated, and its terms of operation have been precisely defined.

One of the factors of greatest significance in this situation is the isolationism engendered by the classroom teaching context. The notion that each classroom is a teacher's castle, autonomous and inviolate, has become a good deal less prevalent in recent years. A siege mentality is still fairly common, however, based upon the illusion that the professional independence of teachers is under attack; and it is unfortunate that this attitude should be unwittingly reinforced by heads who would not dream of hearing a colleague teach, although these heads are, often, among the most competent, experienced, respected and successful. Happily, there are unmistakable signs that a rapid thaw of this mentality has set in, encouraged by cooperation among teachers in the classroom, and by the growth of team-teaching. We investigate this problem further in Chapter 18.

Of course there are many other areas of school life in which delegation operates. We have looked at only two examples, in some detail, but running a school depends upon a complex system of delegated responsibilities, and the same principles apply in all of them. Most important, as we have seen, is the setting of boundaries, by precise definition of roles, responsibilities and authority: but there are two dangers here which must be mentioned. If the definition is too tight, then there is a risk that those who are not directly involved will opt out even of their general but indirect responsibility. ('It's his job, not mine; let him get on with it!') On the other hand, when these boundaries are too loosely defined, action may either not be taken at all ('All teachers are teachers of English'), or everyone will act simultaneously, so causing repetition and confusion. Take, for example, such areas of school life as behaviour, discipline, the wearing of uniform, tidiness or punctuality. If these are (rightly) regarded as the joint responsibility of the whole staff, then either they run the risk of becoming the responsibility of none, or everyone sticks to the letter of the law, so causing general irritation. Thus, a boy who has come to school improperly dressed, because he is not wearing a tie, may either escape notice altogether (because everyone assumes that someone else has spoken to him), or he is challenged in classroom and corridor twenty times a day, until legitimate rebuke turns into apparent victimisation! There is virtue, therefore, in setting boundaries as precisely as possible, even in such areas as those affecting general behaviour and appearance.

12   Administration

There are those who bridle at the very mention of 'administration', as though it were, somehow, an indecent or improper exercise of human endeavour; there are even those, within the teaching service, who fall into the habit of perpetuating a wholly false distinction between 'us' (the teachers) and 'them' (their colleagues, the educational administrators). This is particularly unfortunate for the general welfare of the education service as a whole, since the relationship between teachers and educational administrators should be (and often is) one of fruitful and continuous partnership. Moreover, it is not difficult to identify the basic purposes of efficient administration in a secondary school: for these purposes are not esoteric or imaginary, but they have their roots in the school situation, and can be analysed in simple, practical terms.

First, they are intended to provide services, and to establish a system of procedures, which will uphold and facilitate the school's professional objectives. This will involve the provision of appropriate forms, reports, returns and records, specifically designed for the purposes which they are intended to fulfil.

Secondly, they should be designed to put every teacher in a position to teach more effectively. To this end he must be provided with administrative support, which will avoid the misuse of time, skill and energy that occurs whenever teachers perform functions and provide services for which they are neither trained nor equipped. Ineffective and amateur administration by teachers inevitably detracts from the quality of their professional performance; and, since teachers are expensive, in the coldest economic terms it is a waste of money to expect them to perform clerical or administrative chores. These are tasks which can be carried out, more efficiently, by less expensive but trained administrative staff, thereby enabling teachers to devote the greater part of their time to their teaching role. The full implications of this claim are examined, more fully, later in the chapter.

Thirdly, established procedures enable each decision or situation to be dealt with as part of a coherent pattern, supported by past experience and precedent, rather than as an isolated, 'one-off' occurrence, with no accumulated wisdom or inherited expertise upon which to depend. Rationalisation of procedures does not (as is often alleged) involve standardisation of decisions. A well-designed school report form, for example, is an excellent illustration of a standardised procedure, but the comments on the report can be highly personal, diagnostic and particular. It is simply not true that the laying down of standard procedures converts members of the staff into puppets, and involves action which becomes purely mechanical; this is a misconception. It is always within the discretion of a responsible individual to abandon or vary an agreed procedure; indeed, there is a positive obligation on all concerned to use their discretion, and to recognise the occasional circumstance which calls for special treatment. At the same time, the fulfilment of any agreed procedure will still allow for flexibility and tolerance, since it will always be subject to the infinite and subtle variety of practice involved in any pattern of human relationships. The most meticulous administrative framework, in fact, can still permit infinite variety in the nature and quality of decisions, and in the methods by which they are implemented. A taut administration simply guarantees that decisions are taken, and that they are based upon all the information available. It does not indicate what those decisions shall be.

Fourthly, a well-designed administrative organisation will seek to spread the total load of work over a stipulated period, such as a term or a year, by fixing important dates well in advance, by reducing the number of peaks and troughs in the work load, by establishing an even distribution of pressures, by avoiding bottlenecks, and by staggering repetitive events such as staff meetings, meetings with parents, internal examinations, the issue of reports or the holding of school camps and field study outings — to mention only a few. Some schools, indeed, have found it useful to present their school calendar in pictorial form as a flow-chart or critical-path diagram, clearly revealing the points at which acute pressures arise while spreading, as far as possible, the flow of work at an even pace throughout the year.

Fifthly, sound administration establishes clear channels of communication and of consultation. By-passing these established links, by cutting corners, will sometimes be justified but, in general, it is likely to cause only confusion and irritation. Knowing when to ignore an established procedure is, in fact, an exercise in the art of judgement, which should prove the validity of the rule by the infrequency and urgency of the exception.

Sixthly, the larger the school, the more important is the quality of its administrative procedures and services; for size emphasises the need for an efficient professional organisation and (as we have seen) that organisation, in turn, must be nurtured and sustained by an efficient administration.

Finally, it is a fundamental characteristic of good administration, which is of particular importance to secondary schools, that it should be flexible, unobtrusive and unfussy, yet capable of rising to occasions, of coping with emergencies and of adapting to change.

Before these purposes can be fulfilled in practice, however, there must be a convinced recognition of need, together with a cogent understanding of the advantages which can be expected to accrue to the school from the support of an effective administrative machine. As with communication, there must be willing and total belief on the part of every member of the organisation (in this case the whole staff) in the need for administrative services, and in the extent to which competent administration will support and sustain their work. Half-hearted commitment, or patent unbelief, will result only in patchy and ineffective administrative operations. This means, therefore, that good administration, like good management (of which it is an integral part), is dependent upon explicit principles as part of a coherent philosophy, and in furtherance of agreed aims and objectives. Accordingly, a new school must adopt a positive attitude to administration, from the beginning, and must weave this attitude into the general pattern of its relationships and its working practices. A school already in operation, with only a skeleton administrative structure (which is still the common pattern), on the other hand, cannot hope to achieve efficiency by just 'tacking on' administrative resources and procedures: unless they form part of a consistent design of beliefs and intentions, they will be in danger of becoming little more than limpets on the surface of the organisation, neither drawing sustenance from nor contributing strength to the main-stream life of the organisation as a whole.

The development of an efficient administrative organisation, in other words, must be a dynamic process. It must proceed from an exact identification of need to a precise method of satisfying that need: it must be realistic, in terms both of money and manpower, and it must lead to greater professional productivity by teachers. This latter requirement is one which will be accepted by all teachers and by many administrators; but teachers are handicapped in pressing their claims for adequate administrative support by the fact that the effects of a failure to recognise their need are not apparent outside the school, particularly to lay members of education committees. A teacher, especially if he holds a responsible position, has many claims upon his time. Among them he is bound to give priority to what may be called systems-maintenance, just keeping things going, for unless these basic chores are done the school will grind to a halt. In these circumstances, what is then in grave danger of being crowded out is the higher level of professional administration, involving such processes as curriculum planning and reform, syllabus revision and staff development. Providing an extra clerk or technician, another telephone or a piece of duplicating equipment would relieve a teacher of elementary tasks such as writing letters in longhand, typing and duplicating examination papers or teaching materials, preparing apparatus, checking stock and equipment, compiling requisitions, passing invoices for payment, or cataloguing and repairing library books. It would offer no immediate or measurable return, however, which can be assessed in pounds and pence; nor, at first sight, does it furnish an argument likely to convince those who control the LEA purse-strings. Yet it is an argument which must prevail. As schools become larger and more complex, and as claims upon teachers' time mount inexorably, it is essential that they should be set free to concentrate upon the professional job for which they were trained, and for which they are paid. And this remains true, despite the fact that some administrative chores involve the exercise of professional judgement (such as choosing books or equipment) while others offer a welcome degree of relief and variety in a teacher's working day.

Happily, there are signs of the acceptance of this principle by quite a large and growing number of LEAs. Many large schools now have administrative officers, often called bursars or registrars; some have matrons responsible for domestic matters such as school meals, hos-

pitality and first-aid; some have both. At the same time, more technicians, more telephones and more clerical help are being provided,
and rigid financial control is being relaxed in favour of more delegated
responsibility, and greater autonomy. The right of virement (an ugly
term used by accountants to describe the transfer of expenditure from
one approved budget heading to another) is being more readily offered to schools. In consequence some schools can choose, within an
agreed budget, between different kinds of appointment to the staff
(teaching, technical, clerical or administrative) on the one hand, and
spending the same amount of money, instead, on some form of duplicating equipment or technical aid, on the other. Flexibility, however,
is all-important. Uniform or blanket provision for all schools in an
area (although still very common) is certain to be wasteful and extra-
vagant. Schools need to become cost- and efficiency-conscious, and
they must be prepared to state a case, convincing to an accountant, in
support of the administrative services which they need, in order that
their resources may be efficiently and effectively deployed. But,
unless professional productivity really is increased — with teachers
devoting more time to reading, thinking and discussion and more
attention to philosophy, purpose and technique, thus enabling better
preparation and monitoring of lessons together with more sensitive
and effective care of individual children—the provision of adequate
administrative services in secondary schools will be very difficult, if
not impossible, to justify.

Having examined the general theoretical purposes and objectives
of administration in the secondary school, and having considered the
general question 'why?' we must now answer the precise question
'how?' From a severely practical angle there are so many aspects of an
efficient school administration that any searching review of them is
bound to become rather confusing and nitty-gritty in character. In
addition, since any administrative machine must be designed to satisfy
individual needs and circumstances — in this case those of a particular
school — our discussion is bound to be concerned more with general
principles than with specific details. Nevertheless, it is hoped that the
analysis which follows will prove to be of some interest to individual
readers, in considering those aspects and instruments of administration which particularly concern them and their schools. To make
this easier to accomplish, related devices and procedures have been

grouped together, under general headings, and these headings have been placed in alphabetical order, for ease of reference:

> Finance
> Forms
> Information
> Procedures
> Records and filing systems
> Technical services

1 *Finance*

The basic purposes of a school's financial administration should be to use its resources to the best advantage and to relieve the head and his colleagues of responsibility for all routine financial transactions; these would include the checking of invoices, the receipt, recording and auditing of school supplies and stock of all kinds, the maintenance of account books, ledgers and records, and the handling of cash, whether in the form of payments (e.g., petty cash) or collections (such as dinner money, or contributions to the school fund or towards the cost of visits, journeys and expeditions, etc.).

All decisions on questions of policy, and ultimate responsibility for financial administration would, of course, remain with the head, in consultation with his colleagues (e.g., the distribution of capitation and departmental allowances, or the authorisation of expenditure from the school fund); but the routine implementation of those decisions would then become the responsibility of the accounts section of the school's general office, under the bursar or registrar. Heads of department and other members of the staff would still be held responsible for indicating their needs and claims, in accordance with established regulations, for such supplies as books, materials, equipment or furniture; but, once these proposals have been approved by the head the teaching staff should then be relieved of all routine financial and administrative responsibility for them except that they would, of course, still be entirely accountable to the head, for the selection, custody, and use of the teaching materials and resources issued to them.

As with all administrative operations it is of great importance to standardise financial forms and procedures (see Sections 2 and 4). By this means each operation can be analysed by its separate stages, leading to the completion of a check list or action sheet. This will furnish guidance for those who are responsible for seeing each financial operation through to its conclusion. It will also provide a guarantee of information to all those who are interested in or affected by the school's use of its financial resources.

2 *Forms*

These are of three basic kinds:

 (i) Those imposed upon the school by the DES (such as Form 7, the annual return on which many of the national statistics relating to secondary education are based);

 (ii) Those required by the LEA, which can sometimes engender as much friction as the forms prescribed by the central government; and

(iii) Those which the school designs and uses for its own purposes.

Now, all forms tend to be:

Repetitive such as school reports, examination entries, forms used by children and parents in determining choice of course in the middle school or in the sixth form, and a school leaver's clearance form (designed to check the return of all school property in his possession).

Restrictive and selective (e.g., in the nature of the information demanded, the individuals who are expected to provide it, and the amount of space available for furnishing it).

Quickly out of date, so that they soon become only partially relevant or even wholly irrelevant to the purpose for which they are still being used.

For these reasons it is of the greatest importance that, with every form designed by the school for its own use:

The 'customer' — i.e., whoever will be expected to complete it — should be consulted about its design.

Great care should be taken over its layout, arrangement and format. The appearance of a form, and its immediate impact on the 'customer', are of profound significance. So much is this the case that the quality and reliability of the information which a form elicits will be in direct proportion to the extent to which the design and purpose of the form itself can win the 'customer's' confidence and willing cooperation. For this reason, once a new form has been designed, it should be used for a quick series of dummy-runs, with appropriate revision following each run, to eliminate doubt and confusion in the questions asked, to adjust the space provided for the answers, and to make quite sure that all the questions are absolutely relevant and necessary.

The stock of any particular form should be small enough to ensure that it will come under scrutiny at regular intervals, and be subject to frequent, critical review.

The number of school forms in use at any one time should be reduced to an absolute minimum. All those who are required to complete them must have a feeling of certainty that the information asked for is genuinely necessary, and that effective use will be made of it. Where this essential confidence between designer and user is weak, or lacking altogether, then there will be a rapid deterioration in the accuracy and goodwill with which the form is completed.

By the nature of the circumstances, schools can do much less about the design and effectiveness of forms imposed upon them. This would apply, for example, to forms used by the DES, local authorities, examining bodies, the Universities Central Council on Admissions (UCCA), or the Central Register and Clearing House. But, in these cases, too, it is of very real importance, in the interests of the education service as a whole, that there should be direct communication between those who design and impose the form, and those who are required to complete it. Constructive criticism and suggestions from 'customers', intended to increase the ease and accuracy with which the form can be completed, will seldom be summarily rejected, and will often be warmly welcomed.

3 *Information*

The processing and distribution of information has an important part to play in the daily life of a school. The initial task is to identify the different kinds of information which are required, at different times in the school year, by different groups of people. Once this task has been completed, then a process of standardisation can begin, and a distribution list for each separate item or series of information can be drawn up by the head, in consultation with the bursar. There can, of course, be no guarantee that information, however skilfully framed and timed, will always reach the individual concerned just at the moment when he needs it, or that he will invariably understand and absorb it, when it reaches him. School information services should be designed to minimise the number of occasions when things go wrong, by following these six principles:

(a) Repetitive information (such as that contained in Bulletins or Information Sheets) should be issued only as often as is realistically necessary.

(b) The information being made available should be carefully and persuasively worded. For this reason it must always be edited, preferably by someone on the staff who is interested and skilled in the art of communication. This also ensures that all information is directed and filtered through one channel.

(c) The form in which the information is conveyed should be attractive and eye-catching in appearance (e.g., by using different coloured paper for different purposes),be clearly arranged, and so far as is humanly possible in the hurried intercourse of daily life be free from ambiguity.

(d) The way in which information is conveyed should be appropriate to the nature of the information and of the occasion. This will dictate, for example, whether it should be announced in public (e.g., at morning assembly or at a staff meeting), whether copies of a notice should go only to some or to all members of staff, whether receipt should have to be acknowledged (e.g., by initialling a list of recipients), or whether it should merely be posted on a notice-board for the information of those whose attention it may happen to attract.

(e) General notice-boards and special display-boards (e.g., for posters), individual pigeon-holes and staff 'in-trays' used for the dissemination of information, should be regularly checked and cleared. The limited experience which is available suggests that the nomination of someone with taste and imagination to be responsible for all the school's visual displays and exhibitions (including notice-boards), and for all the points for the collection and distribution of information (including pigeon-holes and 'in-trays') would reap a rich reward, not only in terms of the school's general appearance, but also in the efficiency of its administration.

(f) Those who persistently fail to offer the degree of individual cooperation which the system demands, should be identified, and be persuaded to see the error of their ways!

LISTS AND REGULATIONS   Another broad aspect of administration, under the general head of information, concerns the issue of routine lists and regulations. There are many kinds of lists in a school — staff lists, form lists, house lists, fixture lists and distribution lists (maintained in the school office, for all routine information and documents, to ensure that copies are sent to everyone who ought to be informed). There are also regular practices and regulations, such as the preparation of agenda and minutes for all formal meetings, and the publication of standing instructions and regulations, such as fire precautions, school rules, a staff handbook and the routine information and instructions issued to parents at the time of a child's admission. These should all be regarded as part of the school's information services, and the responsibility for revising, collating and issuing them should be assigned to the administration although, of course, the head and members of the staff will always have to be consulted.

4 *Procedures*

The design and control of internal procedures and procedure systems (like the control of forms and information services) is much more wholly within the school's own competence and resources than some other aspects of administration. At the same time, the scope for skilful administration in this area is enormous, with all the complicated and interrelated communications and transactions of a large community. There are, indeed, a great many repetitive events and occasions in the life of a school. They include some obvious circumstances such as:

the daily assembly, moving about the school, and wet dinner hours or occasions when the weather is unsuitable for physical education lessons to be taken out of doors;

the drafting and placing of advertisements, the arrangements for the reception of applicants, and the steps to be taken for the preparation of an appointing committee or a meeting of the governors;

booking arrangements for transport or entertainment, the reservation of rooms within the school for specific purposes, and the planning of visits, journeys and expeditions;

lists of those to whom information should be sent and actions reported, the inclusion of fixtures and engagements in the school calendar, and the procedure to be followed in the event of fire, accident, sudden illness or staff absence.

This list could be extended almost indefinitely, to include all the main routine events in the school's life; but the purpose of specifying circumstances and situations which call for precise decisions and for particular courses of action, is to establish agreed procedures, in order:

to ensure economy of time and effort;

to achieve a degree of stability and continuity, so that similar circumstances will lead to similar action on different occasions;

to make sure that important considerations and details are not overlooked under pressure of events, or in the excitement of the moment, and to provide for emergency action to be taken, in the absence of the head or his senior colleagues, by any member of the staff, however junior or inexperienced, because the appropriate procedures have been worked out and promulgated.

Having identified the occasions and circumstances which justify a measure of standardisation, a good deal of careful planning and precise definition is still necessary, in order to prescribe the exact procedure to be followed in any particular situation. This will call for consultation and discussion, and it is essential that procedures, once defined, should be published in a readily accessible form (e.g., by inclusion in the staff handbook), and should then be subject to regular overhaul and revision. Nothing is more moribund and ineffective than a procedure or course of action prescribed for a particular circumstance which is still followed when that circumstance has changed or no longer obtains. At the same time it must be remembered that procedures which involve or concern children should be made equally well known to them as to the staff; ignorance, or panic or misunderstanding can cause chaos in an emergency as quickly as incompetence or deliberate sabotage.

5 *Records and filing systems*

The records which a school maintains are an essential part of its organisation and administration. The most important records are those
relating to the progress of individual children.

The record of each child begins with the information provided by
his previous school. Perhaps the best way of maintaining this record is
to open, for each child, a file or folder in which can be placed all the
relevant information about him, prior to his admission. The folder
should indicate clearly, on its outside cover, the address of the child's
parents or guardians, and their telephone number (if any).

Thereafter, the folder should be a repository of all the school's
cumulative information about a child, on the basis of continuous assessment and pastoral care. Inside the folder it is helpful to have separate
pockets, or large envelopes, so that, for example, academic and medical records can be separated from general information. In any event,
unless complete copies of each school report issued on the child are
retained in the folder, summaries of each report must be recorded, in
order to maintain a continuous narrative. For the purpose of the folder
is to ensure that all the information about a child, including such
knowledge as is available about his home environment, should be
readily accessible. Much of it will be based on impressions, incidents,
conversations and interviews, over the years, recorded on standard
school memo pads by those who are consecutively responsible both
for teaching him and for his pastoral care, and by others who come into
contact with him in one capacity or another. When these comments
and impressions find their way into the folder, they will add to the
cumulative and continuous record of his growth, progress and development.

There is considerable divergence of practice about where these
folders should be kept. Increasingly, the responsibility for their custody is being assigned to house or year masters, who then also carry
responsibility for all school reports which are issued, from time to
time, on individual children. In a large school this may well mean that
these folders are no longer kept in the head's room, or in his secretary's,
but in the room of an individual housemaster, or in a room used by
all housemasters, which is properly equipped for the maintenance of
records. Wherever they are kept, the folders must be 'tidied up' at
regular intervals, the information and comments on separate memo

pads being transferred to a continuous record; they must also be accessible to members of the staff who have need to consult them, either because they seek information, or because they wish to add a new piece of evidence.

This right of access, however, raises the difficult question of confidentiality. Is some information about a child of such an extremely personal and confidential nature (e.g., that he is illegitimate or adopted or that his father is serving a life sentence for murder) that it should be in the possession only of whoever is ultimately responsible for his overall welfare, to be used only at his discretion? There are good arguments in favour of such precautions and, in that case, the confidential information should, perhaps, be kept in a separate file, while the child's folder might be distinguished in some simple but clearly recognisable way, to show that additional but confidential information is available. This is an area where particularly sensitive procedure and judgement are required. The position should be regularly reviewed and, when the circumstances which caused the confidential file to be opened, in the first place, have either changed or lapsed, then the distinguishing mark should be removed from the folder. It is only too easy to give a lasting impression that a child is abnormal, in some way, long after the circumstances calling for particular notice have ceased to have any long-term significance.

The record of each individual member of the staff, teaching and ancillary, should begin with his original form of application, and with the notes made at the time of his appointment interview. His home address and telephone number should be clearly indicated on the outside of the folder, and it is a most useful practice to issue, every term, a complete staff list, with addresses and telephone numbers. Staff assessment will be examined, in some depth, in chapter 18, but it may be useful here briefly to indicate that the folder should include evidence of growing experience and maturity, in respect of tasks assigned, responsibilities assumed, additional training undertaken and qualifications acquired. Such evidence will come from many sources, personal and circumstantial, during the course of his career, and most of it will be provided by the master himself, by the head, by the head of his department or by other senior colleagues. The record should be as complete as possible, overcoming undue reliance on memory, so that its value is not diminished if, for example, the head is transferred to another school. When the time comes to answer a confidential enquiry, to draft a testimonial or to provide a reference, nine-tenths of the evidence and information available should be in the folder; the remaining one-tenth can then be derived from current subjective judgements and assessments. From time to time all the evidence which the folder affords should be up-dated, and translated into the form of a permanent record, partly in order to reduce the sheer bulk of accumulated paper, and partly as a step towards eventual disposal. When children and staff leave the school, their records must obviously be transferred to bulk storage, so that access can still be obtained, in case of need, for some appropriate time. How long this period should be, and whether such records should then be destroyed, is a contentious and difficult question. Since school records can be of tremendous historical and sociological interest, it is a pity that no generally accepted national practice has been developed; perhaps the most that can be said is to suggest that it would be wise for a school to consult the LEA and the local records and archives office, before embarking upon a policy of destruction.

FILING SYSTEMS   A simple filing system, easy to understand and to operate, is the very corner-stone of administrative efficiency. Such a system must be tailored to the precise demands of a particular school; the help and advice of commercial firms, who are expert in the operation of filing systems, will often be found invaluable, but it is a disastrous mistake to buy a commercial system, lock, stock and barrel, in the belief that it will meet the needs and circumstances of every school.

The basic purpose of an efficient filing system is to enable papers to be put away with accuracy and certainty, and to be recovered with speed and confidence. To make this possible, certain practices must be established:

(a) The categories and titles of files must be precisely defined, so that the file to which any particular paper relates can be readily identified.

(b) All files should be numbered, and a list of them, mounted on a piece of stout cardboard, should be in the possession of all who have access to the filing cabinets or shelves. The list should include the serial number of each file, and the exact category of information to which it relates. As an illustration of this principle, in operation, it may be helpful to consider the sub-division of files concerned with one of the school's major correspondents, such as its local education authority. Circumstances will differ widely from school to school, and from LEA to LEA, but some classification such as the following may be helpful and appropriate:

FILE NUMBER	MAIN HEADING	SUB-HEADING
500	LEA	*policy*
501	LEA	*finance*
		(with sub-files according to particular LEA regulations concerning capital expenditure, capitation allowances, furniture and equipment, etc.)
502	LEA	*premises* (i.e., buildings and grounds)
503	LEA	*teaching staff:* establishment
504	LEA	*teaching staff:* advertisements and appointments
505	LEA	*teaching staff:* salaries and salary scales

This pattern could then be followed with a series of files dealing with ancillary staff, and so on.

(c) Effective use can sometimes be made of files of different colours for different purposes, to increase the speed of identification, and this same principle can also be applied to memo pads, and to paper used for other documents in regular use. For example, green paper might always be reserved for staff notices, and yellow for the agendas and minutes of committees.

(d) When designing a new filing system it is important to begin, on a tentative basis, for the first few weeks or months, with serial numbers and titles in pencil, so that adjustments can be made, and obvious errors and omissions corrected. The numbering should also leave substantial gaps, after each category, so that additional files, subsequently found to be necessary, can be fitted into the sequence, without destroying the coherence of the system of numbering.

(e) The significance or relevance of each paper to be filed must be readily recognisable, so that one can decide, promptly and confidently, in which file it should be placed. A substantial degree of certainty can be attached to this process if the head and bursar, for example, will indicate to their secretaries, at the top right-hand corner of each paper to be filed, as they transfer it to their 'out-trays', the particular file in which it should be placed. This can be done quite quickly, by using a code or initials or by indicating simply the number of the file concerned. This may sound ponderous, time-consuming and complicated, in theory, but it works with surprising ease and smoothness, and establishes a most effective working confidence between, for example, the head and his secretary.

(f) All filing procedures for the maintenance of school records, whether in the custody of head, bursar, housemaster or other member of the staff, should use the same system. To this end, the practices on which the system is based should be set out in precise detail, and copies of these instructions should be made available for the use of all those who have responsibility for and access to school records.

(g) The system must allow for a degree of doubt, overlap and uncertainty. The most malignant bane in the experience of those responsible for operating a filing system is the letter which deals with several different subjects. When such a letter is from a parent it need cause no particular difficulty, so long as it concerns only one child, but this proviso is unlikely to hold good when there are two or more brothers or sisters in the same school. Some relief can be obtained by encouraging the school's major correspondents to confine each letter to a single subject, and to put the title or subject at the top of each letter; and these two practices should invariably be followed in the school's own correspondence. Effective cooperation can only be expected, however, from correspondents who have to understand and operate their own filing systems! So, whenever there is any doubt about where a paper should be filed, because its contents straddle the territory of two or more files, the best way out of the difficulty is to make one or more copies of the paper concerned, and to place a copy in different files, each concerned with one aspect of the paper being filed, with cross-references as appropriate. Modern photocopying machines make this a much easier procedure to adopt than it would have been a few years ago.

(h)   The efficiency of the filing system can be checked by the speed with which particular papers can be recovered and made available for reconsideration. If this process frequently takes longer than thirty seconds, then it is possible that there is some confusion either in the design of the system or in the way in which it is operated.

6   *Technical Services*

MACHINES   Educational machines of all kinds, especially mechanical teaching aids. are becoming more complex and more expensive every year. They demand technical knowledge for their effective use and maintenance. Sometimes this is provided by the suppliers (e.g., typewriters, internal telephone systems or language laboratories): but it will become increasingly important for schools to include among their staffing resources the skills of an expert in audio and visual aids, who can handle tapes, films and machines of all kinds, organise their availability for particular lessons, maintain a catalogue of available teaching material, and record radio and television programmes, when they are first broadcast, to be used for teaching purposes on subsequent occasions.

MAINTENANCE   Efficient school maintenance also depends upon adequate staffing. A capacity to deal, on the spot, with minor repairs (such as leaks, overflows and breakages) is an invaluable asset: it not only contributes to general morale, but also saves time and money. However much the caretaker is a handyman, and has been trained in the use of fuels, polishes, abrasives, cleaning materials and mechanical equipment, he cannot be expected to cope, unaided, with the full range of technical problems arising from school maintenance. There is, indeed, a growing and welcome shift away from the traditional situation (in which the head was expected to be concerned with suppliers, contractors, clerks of works, joiners, plumbers, decorators and electricians) towards an organisation in which these contacts and concerns are carried by the bursar and the school's administrative services.

SECRETARIAL   All secretaries and clerks in a school are bound to be in contact, in varying degrees, with staff, children, parents and visitors. They therefore carry an important public relations responsibility, in addition to their administrative duties, and they must be trained to exercise this responsibility tactfully and persuasively. It is found to be helpful if one member of the clerical staff can work in a separate room, where she can deal with telephone calls, receive visitors, and prevent continual interruption of the main school office.

The head's secretary holds a position of particular importance. She is bound to be in close and continuous touch with staff, children, parents, governors and visitors of all kinds, and to be in possession of highly confidential information. The position therefore calls for efficiency and diplomacy of no mean order. For the headmaster's perfect secretary will identify herself with him and with the school community, while maintaining an appearance of calm detachment. Since she eschews gossip, and is able to keep a secret under provocation, her integrity and discretion will be beyond reproach. Sifting telephone calls, she will know when to deal with them herself, and when to pass them on. She will never fail to deal tactfully and sympathetically with visitors, doing her best to ensure that, even when they are not fully persuaded or convinced, they go away impressed by the courtesy and efficiency extended to them. She will make sure that relevant files are always available for consultation (for example, between making a telephone appointment and the arrival of the visitor concerned); and she will guarantee that, whenever the head goes to a meeting or conference, all the papers which he may need are put before him. She will remind him of his engagements, and make sure that he fulfils the programme to which he has committed himself: yet she will be sensitive and alert to those occasions when he needs protection and freedom from interruption, no matter what pressures are building up outside his room. And — through it all — this paragon will remain calm and serene, radiating confidence and good humour, and demonstrating, to all who come into contact with her, many of those aspects and purposes of good administration with which this chapter has been particularly concerned.

III   THE USE OF RESOURCES

13   Manpower and time I

Among the most important questions which a head ever has to answer, are these: 'Who is to teach what subjects, to which children, in what size and composition of teaching groups, and for how many periods in the week?' For the answers to these questions affect the deployment of manpower in the curriculum and time-table. Their importance is emphasised by two significant truths: *all* members of staff are closely involved, as individuals, in the structure and operation of the curriculum, whereas not all of them will necessarily be equally concerned with interests and activities outside the classroom (although most of them will be involved in pastoral care). In the same way children spend a greater part of their school lives in the classroom, laboratory or workshop than in following any other school interests or pursuits. This means that the ways in which the resources of manpower and time are deployed in the curriculum and time-table, and in the provision of pastoral care, will affect both staff and children more dramatically than the decisions which are taken in any other sector of school life. It also means that the achievement of non-academic, as well as of academic, aims and objectives will have to be accomplished almost entirely through the attitudes, standards, qualities and relationships which are established in the teaching situation.

Confronted by these two factors, it is both comforting and salutary for a head to remind himself that, in seeking to find answers to these complex questions, he can create for himself more room for manoeuvre than is commonly supposed. To take an example, at the extreme limit of absurdity, it would be 'possible', in a school of one thousand children, with a staff of fifty, to make forty-nine of the staff 'free' for every period by requiring the fiftieth to supervise the whole school in the assembly hall, although this would obviously be both nonsensical and impracticable. At the other extreme limit, almost equally absurd in its assumptions, it would be 'possible' to allocate one teacher to every twenty pupils, for every period in the week, by giving the staff no 'free' periods at all. Yet, in between these two extremes there is room for a great variety of practice, dependent partly upon the determination of priorities, and partly upon the devising of solutions which are not only practicable but are generally acceptable, and which most nearly match the needs of a particular school.

A head may decide to begin the whole process with a general review of the curriculum and time-table, in order to decide what changes, if any, he wishes to introduce. Having done this, and having calculated the total number of teaching periods per week which will be required to carry out his intentions, he can then work out the number of non-teaching periods which he can afford. Immediately, however, he is likely to find that there is conflict between the number of non-teaching periods which he can offer to all the members of his staff, and the number of such periods which he and his colleagues conceive to be necessary. For provision must be made, not only for his own role as head, but for the execution of the responsibilities assigned to the deputy head, senior master (or mistress), heads of department, heads of house (or year), and all the other members of staff who hold posts carrying major degrees of responsibility. As schools become larger and more complex, making adequate provision for such non-teaching time becomes increasingly difficult, for most heads find themselves dependent upon a fixed teaching staff establishment, while having to meet all the needs of the children, as well as the demands of external examinations, employers, colleges and universities, from a strictly limited pool of resources. In addition, they often find themselves bound, in varying degrees, by established practices, hallowed by long usage, which it is very difficult to justify except on grounds of tradition.

Upon examination, however, many of these traditions turn out to be not matters of deliberate policy or design at all, but simply an amalgam of established custom on the one hand (with or without philosophical support), and of hard bargaining and compromise between subjects, which are all competing for the time available, on the other. Why, for example, do mathematics and French commonly have an allocation of five periods a week, history two and religious education one, while physical education has four? Is there some profound professional significance in these figures? Why is French commonly the first — and often the only — foreign language taught in English schools? Do experiment and research provide any evidence that the study of *any* subject in repeated small doses of thirty-five or forty-minute spoonfuls really offers the most effective teaching and learning pattern?

Most, if not all, secondary schools involve a choice of subjects at about the age of 14, which inevitably means that one or more subjects have then to be dropped. Latin, history, geography and one science (physics, chemistry or biology) are among the subjects most commonly found in this category. But, when a subject is dropped from the time-table of a particular pupil (after one, two or three years), what has been gained by its study up to that point, and what has been learned which has significance and relevance on its own account? Or, consider the allocation of exactly the same number of periods to all subjects at A-level compared with the sharp discrepancies in the allocation of periods to those same subjects at O-level: can both be equally valid and meaningful? Again, is it possible to justify the frequent and total omission of the creative and aesthetic subjects (such as art, crafts and music) from the time-tables of those who are following a predominantly 'academic' course? In some circumstances it can be argued that there are good and proper reasons for all these practices, but it is salutary to be reminded of these, and many other similar questions, if only to prevent expediency, compromise and usage from hardening into another generation of established traditions, however untenable they may be on educational or professional grounds.

What this all means is that, despite external pressures, and despite all the demands and constraints imposed upon schools, in designing a curriculum and time-table there is still substantial scope for innovation, initiative, enterprise and imagination. For example, the amount of time devoted to the 'direct' teaching of a subject (within the number of periods allotted to it) might be reexamined and reassessed, in comparison with the amount of time set aside for private study. In the sixth form, where some subject groups are often small, and sometimes very small indeed, could not the lower and upper sixth groups be taught together, at least for part of the week, or for part of the academic year? Elsewhere in the school, in a subject such as art, in which individual work and direct experience, subjected to informed criticism and assessment, is more important than the imparting of knowledge, might it be possible for one teacher to supervise more than one teaching group, or for two teachers to supervise three such groups at a time? On the other hand, in those subjects in which exposition by the teacher of a new topic or theme is an essential part of the learning process (such as history, geography, mathematics or music) it should often be possible to combine teaching groups, within a particular year, for individual lessons, and then to split up into smaller groups for discussion and development. Again in English, and perhaps in other subjects as well, such as history or geography, it might be sensible for children to do a good deal of the reading required on their own, and then for them to come together, with a teacher, for elucidation and discussion and for assessment of their written work. None of these possibilities is mentioned because it is novel or revolutionary, or because it has any particular merit or significance in itself, but only to indicate that the head's room for manoeuvre is still very considerable.

It is at this point in the consideration of a curriculum and time-table that the aims and objectives which were fully discussed in Chapters 5 and 6 became of paramount importance. For, in determining the answers to the many and complex questions which are raised by planning a curriculum and time-table, heads find themselves driven to the compilation of some order of priority among their immediate objectives. Calculations may show that it is not 'possible' to introduce a new subject into the curriculum, to multiply the number of combinations of optional subjects in the middle school, or to cater for the special needs of the most able and/or of the least able. But the conclusion that any such proposal is 'impossible' is valid only if a head is not prepared to accept any other change of practice which would *make* it 'possible'. Any number of constraints can be overcome if the consequences are found to be acceptable, and many of these constraints will be considered in the course of this chapter. In fact, the whole problem of manpower in relation to the curriculum resolves itself into an exercise in the determination of priorities. Three further examples may be considered at this stage, all illustrating the fact that every proposal has its price in curricular terms.

First, what relative weight should be attached to each year group, or ability group, in terms of teacher time and teacher skill? If it is decided, for example, to set mathematics, for five periods a week, across the second year, and to provide one more set than the number of forms in that year, then the 'extra' five periods which will be required, in order to effect this change, will not be available for any other purpose anywhere else in the school.

Secondly, if the senior and most experienced teachers are confined to the fourth, fifth and sixth years, then there is an inexorable compulsion to use junior and less experienced teachers in the middle and lower schools.

Thirdly, if it has been decided to offer a generous range of minority subjects in the sixth form, it is unlikely to be 'possible', at the same time, to achieve many other desirable goals, such as reducing the size of teaching groups in the lower school. Two boys doing A-level music, or one boy taking A-level Greek, will use up teacher time, which must inevitably mean either larger teaching groups or inadequate provision of time for those subjects elsewhere in the school unless, perhaps, the music and classics departments were over-generously staffed to begin with.

There are, of course, formidable difficulties in resolving these and other similar problems. Their solution must depend upon the clear determination of educational aims and objectives; but the clarity with which each proposal can be considered will be enormously increased if the exact cost of each alternative can be calculated. When it is known precisely what a particular provision or proposal will cost in terms of manpower, then this cost can be balanced against the advantages to be gained from making that provision. Only then will it be feasible to determine which year or group will be paying the price of each alternative; *for, in the last resort, the 'price' of any curriculum or time-table proposal will be paid by a group or by several groups of children.* So it is to this problem of costing curriculum and time-table changes that attention must now be directed.

Suppose that a new head has been appointed to an existing 4-form entry, mixed, grammar school, with 600 boys and girls (post-RSLA) in the first five years (the main school) and 160 in the sixth form. Before giving consideration to any possible changes in the curriculum and time-table, the head will wish to achieve a thorough grasp of the existing situation. He knows that the staffing ratio has been calculated to allow one teacher for every twenty pupils in the main school, and one for ten in the sixth form: this gives him a total of 46 teaching staff. Thirty of these 46 are employed because there are 600 children in the main school, and the other 16 by virtue of the fact that there are 160 pupils in the sixth form. The school operates a 40-period week, and the average number of non-teaching periods is 8. Therefore, in the main school:

30 teachers each teach, on average, 32 periods per week, thus providing a total of 960 teacher-periods.

In the first five years there are 20 forms, each taught for 40 periods a week. This means that simply to teach these forms as teaching groups each of thirty children, will require a minimum of 800 teacher-periods.

The difference between these two figures, which establishes the head's room for manoeuvre in the main school is, therefore, 160 teacher-periods.

In deploying these 160 periods at his disposal the previous head must have had in mind a number of fairly obvious competing demands. These may well have included, for example:

More non-teaching time for those members of the staff carrying the heaviest administrative load; or

Smaller classes than the norm in certain subjects, or smaller teaching groups in certain parts of the school, such as the first or fifth year. (In a comprehensive school, of course, this particular priority would offer a very much wider range of problems.)

Whether or not the previous head considered and abandoned these particular proposals, he actually decided to devote his 160 available teacher-periods to the following purposes:

An options scheme in the fourth and fifth years, offering a variety of courses for 20 of the 40 periods in the week, leading to GCE O-level and to CSE. During these 20 periods, on average 6 sets are taught from the 4 forms. This means that 2 more teachers are occu-

teacher-
periods

pied for 20 periods a week, in each of
the 2 years, thus using from the avail-
able surplus: 80
Half-classes for craft subjects for 3
periods a week in years one, two and
three, and in each of 4 forms per year,
thus involving a total of: 36
An additional set in French and in
mathematics in years two, three, four
and five, for 5 periods a week in each
subject, thus absorbing a total of: 40

Total	156

Therefore, of the 160 periods surplus to his basic needs, the previous
head had deployed 156 periods in the main school.

The position then seems to be that the previous regime had
allocated a 'fair' share of the available teaching resources to the main
school, since only 4 of the 160 periods available were used to subsidise
the sixth form. This is confirmed, by an analysis of the sixth form
itself, in which the two years (lower and upper sixth) are taught
separately throughout the week. The sixth form curriculum shows
that:

teacher-
periods

Games and Physical Education occupy
3 teachers for 3 periods a week each,
in each year, involving a total of: 18
General Studies takes 4 teachers for
4 periods a week each, in each year,
amounting to: 32
Religious Education is taken in
groups of 34 pupils, and uses
5 teacher-periods in each year: 10

Total	60

The following courses are offered at A-level:

> *For 7 periods per week:* English (2 sets), History, Geography (2 sets), Economics, French, Latin, German, Russian, Art, Music, Mathematics (2 sets), Further Mathematics (double subject), Statistics, and Engineering drawing.
>
> *For 8 periods per week:* Physics (3 sets), Chemistry (2 sets), Biology (2 sets), Woodwork, Metalwork, Needlework and Home Economics.

	teacher-periods
A-level subjects, therefore, take up 214 teacher-periods in each year, or a total of $214 \times 2 =$	428
In addition, three O-level courses in English, Mathematics and French (all basic to subsequent career patterns) are offered in the sixth form. English and Mathematics have five periods per week each, and French has four, in each year, making a total of :	28
In the sixth form, therefore, the total number of teacher-periods is :	516
This total of 516 is made up of 16 teachers each teaching for an average of 32 periods per week, thus contributing a total of :	512
plus 4 periods 'borrowed' from the main school :	4
	516

An analysis such as this can be carried out on any existing school curriculum. The actual number of teacher-periods which are surplus to basic needs will, of course, vary with the size of the school and the generosity of its staffing ratio: but, once the number of teacher-

periods has been calculated, it is possible to consider alternative proposals, the implications of which can be measured and costed, before
any changes are introduced. In the example analysed above it is very
probable that the new head will be disturbed by the fact that, below
the fourth form, a great deal of the teaching is being carried out in
form groups, and he may well wish to consider a number of other
proposals. He may, for instance, wish to offer 'open access' to his
sixth form, without insisting on minimum academic qualifications
for entry. This proposal would bring with it a demand for more
O-level, CSE or general courses in the sixth form. (He would have to
remember, however, that while there is a great deal to be said for
widening the intellectual horizon of individual pupils, some combinations of O-level or CSE with *one* A-level may well offer no greater
opportunities in the employment market than the original O-level
or CSE qualifications. Indeed, they might prove a positive disadvantage, because the candidate is now one or two years older, but is no
better qualified in terms of career opportunities, and has missed the
chance of apprenticeships which are available at 16.)

Alternatively, the new head may be anxious to introduce a new
subject, such as sociology, into the sixth form. Any addition to the
curriculum, or any expansion of optional courses will, in general,
have to be staffed within existing manpower resources. To add to the
number of teacher-periods deployed in one part of the curriculum
must necessarily involve a corresponding reduction elsewhere. Again,
the head may wish to improve the existing provision for half-classes
(which is only 3 periods per week, at present, in each of the first
three years) by extending this provision to cover an additional
2 periods per week (making 5 in all) in those three years. This would
cost a further 24 teacher-periods and, on top of the existing provision for half-classes of 36 teacher-periods, would make a total of 60,
thus demonstrating the fact that the provision of half-classes is very
expensive in terms of manpower. To extend the range of options in
the middle school (years four and five) on the other hand, by providing seven teaching groups instead of six, for 20 periods a week, would
cost 40 teacher-periods. Two questions then arise: first, how can
these extra teacher-periods be found and, secondly, if they are found,
what price will have been paid, and by whom, and can the cost of
the change in curriculum pattern be regarded as acceptable?

Many other possibilities might be examined and, in each case, the exact 'saving' can be calculated. For instance:

1　Some colleagues could be asked to accept a heavier teaching load.

2　Without completely abandoning music, art, German or Latin in the sixth form, if the subject teachers concerned were able to overcome the difficulty of teaching the two years in these subjects together, as one group, then 28 teacher-periods would be saved. A smaller saving would result from putting the two year-groups together for only part of the week.

3　Alternatively, such minority subjects might be catered for, at sixth form level, by making arrangements with a neighbouring school or college of further education, to collect together a viable group of students in a single institution (although, of course, this is liable to produce severe time-tabling problems).

4　By contrast, in those subjects which attract large numbers of pupils at A-level, it might be possible to combine teaching groups for part of the week. For example, if the two chemistry sets were taught together for five periods in the week, but were separated for 3 periods of their practicals, then there would be a 'saving' of 5 teacher-periods in each year, making a total of 10.

5　A reexamination of inherited practices might reveal possible 'savings'. If circumstances allowed for a reassessment, in contemporary terms, of some of the many traditional features of the curriculum and time-table which were questioned in the earlier part of this chapter, then the head's room for manoeuvre might well be substantially increased beyond 160 teacher-periods.

All the calculations which have so far been made have ignored the fact that the majority of teachers are specialists. This causes serious problems in the process of translation from the broad planning of a curriculum to the detailed construction of a time-table. Indeed, an increasingly significant limitation upon the head's freedom of action is the growing specialisation imposed by the rapid advance of knowledge, and by the development of new techniques appropriate to the teaching of particular subjects. That now all-too-rare treasure, the general subjects teacher, who could teach in more than one sector of the curriculum, provided a valuable element of flexibility in the deployment of staff, as well as making it rather easier to develop a degree of integration and of cross-fertilisation between subjects. He also made it rather less difficult to introduce changes into the curriculum, and to consider time-table innovations, without having to wait for corresponding changes in the composition of the teaching staff. There is, in fact, a curious paradox in the current secondary school scene. At the very moment when there is a strong movement towards integrated studies, designed to blur the boundaries between subjects, there is so great an advance in the pace and content of knowledge, and in the development of specialist teaching techniques, that to teach any one subject, with competence, demands both specialist knowledge and specialist training. Association or integration even between subjects which are closely related, may present difficulty: in 1975, for instance, a teacher who understands and has mastered the methods of the Nuffield Science project is unlikely, at the same time, to be equally competent in 'new' or 'modern' mathematics, despite the close links between mathematics and physics. Moreover, the dilemma is reinforced by the undoubted fact that promotion goes, most often, to the full-blooded specialist! There is, in fact, a desperate need for those who are responsible for the education and training of teachers to consider how two factors (the demand for competent specialists, and the need for teachers who can cross subject boundaries) can be reconciled. For there can be no doubt that, in the next ten or twenty years, there will be major developments, both in curriculum practice and in teaching techniques, which will have profound implications for the generations of teachers who will be expected to put them into practice.

After all the decisions have been taken about the competing demands upon the curriculum, and the determination of priorities has produced a firm pattern of principles and objectives, there still comes the stage at which 'a' teacher has to become 'the' teacher, 'a' housemaster to become 'the' housemaster. Before a time-table can be prepared there are delicate human decisions to be taken about who should teach a particular group of children. To expect each member of a subject department, for example, to teach a complete cross-section of the school, both by age and by ability, may appear fair and sensible, but it may ignore the needs and interests of particular groups of children, and it may fail to make full use of the knowledge, enthusiasm and expertise of particular members of staff. An historian may be better versed in Roman rather than in economic history, a scientist more at home in organic than in physical chemistry, or a teacher of English have a strong passion for Elizabethan literature, rather than for contemporary poets or dramatists. To ignore these needs and preferences would be to make less than maximum use of staff potential. Again, is it wiser to concentrate, or to spread as widely as possible, the influence and impact of a particularly effective or of a particularly weak teacher? Are the interests of probationers fully recognised and protected by the provisions of the time-table? Does it lie within the power of the head to match a particular teacher with those teaching groups with whom he is most likely to communicate successfully, and thus to convert the process of learning into an exciting adventure?

These are all crucial, human problems, affecting both staff and children, to which answers must be found. Yet, here again, conflict will occur between competing priorities, all of them desirable, perhaps, but not all of them immediately practicable within current resources. The head may make the time-table himself, or he may delegate its composition to others: but, however he does it, he must keep in very close touch with its development so that here, too, as with the reaching of all decisions affecting the curriculum, the solutions adopted may be based upon firm principles, rather than upon expediency or upon mere convenience.

14 Manpower and time II

'The governors of a school never have to take a more crucial decision than when they appoint the head of their school.' This assertion, even if faintly exaggerated, is certainly grounded in truth: for the quality of school life —its vigour, ethos, effectiveness, sensitivity and motivation —has been shown by long experience to depend, to a very substantial degree, upon the quality of that appointment. In the same way, it can be safely asserted that the most important single factor which determines the head's success in pursuing his aims and objectives is his skill in selecting his staff, in developing initiative and a sense of corporate endeavour among them, and in fostering their several interests and capacities. On his talents in these operations will largely depend the quality of the school's relationships, the effectiveness of its teaching, the concern and resourcefulness of its pastoral care, the texture and vitality of staff morale, and the whole quality and temper of the school's community life and spirit. If the head is successful here, then his colleagues will be aware of, and in sympathy with, his policy; they will appreciate his enthusiasm and his encouragement of their work, and his success in recognising and developing their full potential; they will grasp the opportunities which he affords to them, through his patterns of communication, consultation and delegation, and they will value the support which he secures for them in the shape of competent administrative services. On the other hand, if he falls short of their role expectations for him in these areas, then they are likely to experience disappointment and frustration, and to feel that they are marking time, instead of growing in expertise and maturity.

Inevitably, the selection of staff, at any one moment, will be largely determined by the curricular and time-table demands of the posts which happen to be vacant. There is some danger in this fact, however: if an exact correspondence is always sought between a master who is leaving and his replacement, the result may be to confer an element of rigidity and conformity both upon the curriculum itself, and upon the composition of the staff. In an era of continuous innovation, this is a factor which has to be watched very carefully. Nevertheless, even if the head is determined to introduce changes into his curriculum, the first step towards filling any vacancy should always be an examination of the exact nature of the job as it is being carried out at present and this analysis should be checked with the teacher who is doing the job at the moment. For it is of the greatest importance to arrive at an accurate picture of the job, with a precise knowledge of its present total content and implications, without overlooking any of the responsibilities which have become attached to it. This is necessary, first, so that these responsibilities can be redistributed and, secondly, in order that the qualities, qualifications and experience necessary for the successful performance of the job, in future, can be identified, taking full account of the changes which it is intended to effect. Only then can an appropriate advertisement be drafted, and a suitable application form (or a special supplement to a standard form of application) be designed. At the same time it will be necessary to prepare a cogent and convincing account of the school, its circumstances, purposes and *modus operandi*, which can be sent to all who ask for application forms. By all these means applicants should be left in no doubt about the exact nature of the job, about the qualities required for its performance, or about the general flavour and character of the school. For the fundamental purpose of advertising is to attract applications *only* from those who are genuinely interested in this particular job, who are competent to perform it, who share the general philosophy and outlook of the school, and who would be sympathetic and welcome members of the school community. There is no advantage whatever (except to the post office) in attracting a large number of applications, a substantial proportion of which have to be discarded as soon as shortlisting begins. The process of selection, in fact, poses two fundamental questions:

1　Can the requirements of the post which is to be filled, and the qualities and qualifications of the applicant who would exactly match those requirements, be specified with precision, before the post is advertised?

2　Are there any particular procedures which would enable the members of a selection committee to be more confident in recognising such an applicant when he appeared before them?

It is obviously essential to make each applicant feel at ease, by means of a short introductory conversation, but the selection committee should not give the impression to the applicant that this part of the interview has any significance, apart from breaking the ice. Thereafter, it is of vital importance that much the greater part of the interview should be devoted to listening to the applicant; otherwise, precious time may be wasted by members of the committee making contributions to the discussion instead of asking leading questions solely designed to give the applicant an opportunity of justifying his application. Attention should be concentrated upon those aspects of the applicant's career and experience which are particularly relevant to the post for which he has applied, especially those which have not been revealed in his form of application. Again, the interviews of all the applicants should be so planned and structured that comparison between them is made as easy and effective as possible. If a head of a department of mathematics is being appointed, for example, then part of each interview, for each applicant, should explore the same areas.

For instance, what evidence can be deduced from his record and experience to suggest that:

(a) He has a clear philosophy and motivation for the teaching of mathematics, and would be able to differentiate, in teaching content and method, between groups of varying academic ability?

(b) He would be able to set about syllabus design and revision? (Would he depend entirely on his own department, or would he welcome consultation with other departments, and with external sources of advice?)

(c) He would be anxious, within the department, to involve his colleagues in responsible and independent tasks concerned with the teaching of mathematics?

(d) He would consider it to be his responsibility to supervise and control the work of his colleagues in the department? (How would he set about it?)

(e) He would know what action to take if he found that a member of his department was an ineffective teacher?

(f) He can establish warm and constructive personal relationships with other people, and win their cooperation? (Are his
personal interests and out-of-school activities such as to
involve and encourage such relationships?)

To assist in the process of comparison between applicants, members should be given adequate time, after each interview, for making
careful notes, before the next applicant is ushered in. For it is important that the final recommendation should be based, not only
upon memory (however reliable) or upon impression (however experienced) but also upon first-hand recorded evidence. First impressions can be particularly dangerous, and a sound judgement can be
reached only after all the evidence has been sifted and assessed. For
the purpose of the exercise is, by eliminating hunch and chance (so
far as is humanly possible) to select the applicant whose qualifications
and experience most nearly match the specifications of the job. When
this match is less than perfect, however, it will be necessary to decide
whether the gap between this applicant's qualifications and the specifications of the job is, nevertheless, small enough to justify his
appointment.

The education service has much to learn about improving its advertising and selection techniques, which demand a great deal more
systematic hard work, detailed preparation, professional skill and careful follow-up than is often devoted to them. In all this there is no
doubt whatever, in our own minds, that the central part should be
delegated to the head; but he would, of course, be wise to seek all the
advice and support to which he has access, more especially that
available from his own senior colleagues, from his governors, and his
authority, and from his professional advisers, including administrators
and consultants. Nevertheless, it is our conviction that, in the last
resort, the head must be given a major voice in the selection of members of his own staff (including a right of veto), and that he, in turn,
must be prepared to accept accountability for the way in which he
exercises this responsibility.

It would be idle to pretend, however, that in making appointments
to his staff a head is ever an entirely free agent. He is subject to constraints in this area of his responsibilities, as in all others. To begin
with, he can only select from among those who apply, and who are
willing to accept appointment. Quite often, too, the exigencies of the

employment situation will mean that he is unable to make an appointment which exactly matches his immediate requirements and objectives. Furthermore, he is normally restricted to a staffing ratio determined by his employers according to a formula (even though that formula may be subject to adjustment in the light of particularly urgent and special considerations), and it is not in the nature of formulae to be sensitive to circumstances, or to all the factors affecting individual schools. A straight staff-pupil ratio, for example, which would be appropriate for a school consisting of homogeneous groups of selected children, is unlikely to be sufficiently flexible or generous for a large comprehensive school. Yet even for comparable schools, these ratios still vary, from one local education authority to another, to a surprising extent! Moreover, with so many subjects in which the supply of competent teachers falls short of the demand, however adaptable the staffing ratio may prove to be, the total resources of manpower available in the country, at any one moment, are bound to place restrictions upon the head's freedom of choice. There are additional constraints, too, upon the curriculum itself, which cannot be ignored: they arise from the extent and nature of the available accommodation, from external examination regulations, and from the entrance requirements laid down by higher and further education, by professional bodies and associations, and by industry and commerce. A head who decided not to include mathematics in his curriculum, for instance, or to make Chinese or Esperanto his first foreign language, would certainly have some explaining to do to his children and their parents, to his governors and his local authority, as well as to local industry and the general public!

From a consideration of particular constraints, it is now appropriate to turn to the general question of how to make the best use of staff resources, and of the extent to which time should be regarded as an ally or as an enemy. For even when the new time-table goes into operation on the first day of the autumn term, representing (as at that moment) the best use of the school's teaching resources which it has been possible to devise, the school's manpower resources still cannot be taken for granted, or be left to their own devices. Responsibility for the guidance, appraisal and planned career development of every single member of the staff must remain the head's constant and abiding concern. This will apply particularly, of course, to those who are at

the outset of their teaching career, or have been recently appointed
to the staff after experience elsewhere. The rate of staff turnover in
secondary schools has added an urgent significance to the provision of
appropriate staff programmes of induction and initiation. Not only the
head but heads of department and heads of house must be involved in a
positive schedule of induction, with the object of ensuring that new-
comers are initially welcomed, are made aware of the school's outlook
and philosophy, are introduced smoothly to its patterns of organisation and working practice, and are encouraged to feel that they have a
contribution to make to its welfare, which will be recognised and
appreciated. For probationers (the real beginners), however, this would
not be enough. They need (and all too seldom receive) a sustained
degree of pastoral and professional care, extending over at least their
first two or three years. Their initial teaching programme must be
tailored with imagination and compassion, they must be encouraged
to continue their own reading and study, and they must be enabled
by visits, and by attendance at courses and conferences, continuously
to broaden their knowledge and experience. The James Report on
'Teacher Education and Training' has given a powerful fillip to the
suggestion that schools should appoint professional tutors, who would
not only exercise particular responsibility for the welfare and performance of probationers (or 'licensed teachers'), but would also
maintain a close liaison with teachers' centres, colleges of education,
polytechnics and universities. However it is accomplished, and techniques will happily vary from school to school, probationers must be
given sustained encouragement and guidance in the classroom, including the provision of opportunities for observing experienced
teachers at work, of teaching alongside them, and of having a chance
to discuss their own ideas, achievements and difficulties with sympathetic and experienced colleagues. Only by such means can it be
reasonably expected that the practice of professional assessment, with
which they have been familiar during their training, will become
firmly established in their experience as a natural process; only so
will they be encouraged to reject the prevailing attitude towards
teaching as a private and personal relationship, and towards the classroom as a bastion of independence to be defended against invasion.
And, only when these objectives have been achieved, will the profession be entitled to an easier conscience about the way in which, at

present, it so often fails to nurture and foster the teaching skills and enthusiasms of its most recent recruits.

For the staff, as a whole, the provision of a staff library is important to stretch minds, and to introduce new ideas, developments and techniques. Visits to other schools, as well as to colleges and universities, should be encouraged, and full advantage should be taken of courses of in-service training. These are only some of the ways of making sure that staff resources, both of the individual and of the school, are used to the best advantage. A reconsideration of the established pattern of staff meetings, which has already been suggested in Chapter 10, would be a move in the same direction, in order to increase the opportunities for sustained discussion of philosophical questions and attitudes, and of professional problems. There are some who suggest a 4½-day week for the children and a 5-day week for the staff, the half-day being devoted, by the staff, to their own further education in one way or another. Another way of achieving the same purpose would be to close the school on one day a month, or on one day in each term, in order that the staff may spend a whole day in continuous consideration of questions of 'great pith and moment'. Much more justifiable in principle, and probably more attractive in practice, would be to extend the school year for teachers beyond the minimum laid down for pupils, using the time thus gained for staff meetings, and for different forms of in-service training, both within the school and, externally, at teachers' centres and elsewhere. Such a practice might succeed in devising an acceptable form of productivity agreement within the special circumstances of education.

Often, of course, the school's concern for the professional development of individual members of the staff may involve the provision of additional training, or the attainment of additional qualifications. This, in turn, may well involve, for an individual, the delegation of additional responsibilities within the school, or transfer to another post, elsewhere, whether on immediate promotion or not. But this is not a process to be feared or restricted; however much the loss of a particular colleague may be regretted, there is abundant evidence that a school which secures a regular number of promotions for members of its staff will, in turn, achieve an enviable reputation, and attract a steady flow of applicants of good quality. This aspect of the head's responsibilities is of such importance that it will be further examined in Chapter 18.

Turning now to other general considerations relating to the most effective deployment of teaching staff resources, for some tasks traditionally performed by teachers it is perfectly legitimate to ask: 'Do we, in fact, need a teacher for that particular job?' Should the library, for example, in a large school, be in the care of a trained librarian, rather than added to the responsibilities of a master (very commonly the head of the English department)? Current practice in different parts of the country is certainly pointing in the direction of professional librarians for large schools, and this can be readily justified as school libraries expand from their original function, as book stores, to their new, exciting task of furnishing not only books but teaching and learning resources of all kinds for both staff and children. Could the same arguments apply to the provision of careers advice? Are there some schools which would benefit from, and be able to make good use of, the services of a professional trained in industrial psychology and careers guidance, rather than expect a teacher to perform this most responsible and onerous task on top of all his other duties?

These are only two of the ways in which a school's manpower resources might be materially strengthened by the appointment of those possessing qualifications and experience in fields other than teaching; but, perhaps the most interesting and most promising of all such comparatively recent developments is the reinforcement of the teaching staff by the recruitment of trained professionals to act as counsellors. It is, clearly, of the greatest importance, from the outset, that the appointment of a counsellor should be regarded as a buttress for the teaching staff and not as a substitute. So important is this general principle that we ourselves should hope no counsellor would ever be appointed until such time as careful consideration and consultation had guaranteed the willing collaboration of at least the majority of the staff with whom he would be working. Much of the significance of the counsellor's contribution would lie in the field of diagnosis and identification, which can present problems far beyond the normal training and experience of a schoolmaster. In addition, he would offer a point of referral outside the school's authority structure and, by talking their language as one professional in their own field to another, the counsellor could enlist the ready understanding and collaboration of psychologists and psychiatrists, probation officers, police liaison officers, child-care officers and many other skilled professional workers in the field of social service and welfare. Such contacts would often lead to the calling of case-study conferences about particular children or families, representing all the interests involved, in a way which it would be very difficult for a schoolmaster to achieve on his own. It would be sheer humbug to pretend, however, that there are not a number of fundamental issues, arising from the appointment of counsellors, upon which no substantial measure of agreement has yet been achieved. There is, for instance, considerable variety of practice between the appointment of teacher-counsellors (who continue their teaching on a part-time basis) and of teachers, who have added counselling to their teaching skills, but whose contribution, within the school, is felt to be most effective if they are no longer involved in the daily classroom situation. There is also much anxiety over the contentious issue of confidentiality. Should all the information obtained as a result of counselling remain strictly confidential between counsellor and client, or should it be fed (without the client's consent, if necessary) into the school's pastoral care machinery and records? There is also some perfectly natural concern about whether the recruitment of a counsellor might not weaken the resolve of some members of the teaching staff to remain actively involved in the practice of pastoral care, now that a colleague, specially trained and equipped for this purpose, has been appointed. Some heads, moreover, are concerned lest the appointment of a counsellor should stimulate the development of fantasy in children, and so lead to the creation of imaginary problems, to the fostering of unhealthy relationships, and to the fertile coinage of difficulties to which adolescence is particularly prone. There is also genuine anxiety lest the appointment of a counsellor, by the operation of Parkinson's Law, should lead to the sustained propping up of children whose difficulties are such that they ought to be encouraged to face their own situations, and to work out their own solutions.

These are all rational and legitimate concerns, which must be resolved in the context of each individual school, and it would do the skill of counselling no service to pretend that they do not exist. For our own part, however, we are firmly convinced that these are anxieties which will prove to be unfounded so long as, from the beginning, the right personal relationship can be established between head and counsellor, and between counsellor and his colleagues in the staff-room. Once scrupulous planning and consultation have established confidence in the minds of the staff, then a counsellor can make a significant contribution towards strengthening and widening the scope of their own concern for the pastoral care of individuals. Given that these, and other similar questions, have been squarely faced and honestly answered, and given that the necessary fund of good will and confidence has been established, then we ourselves are deeply convinced that the manpower resources of large schools can be significantly enriched by the appointment of counsellors.

So far, this chapter and the previous one have been mainly concerned with teaching staff, but enough has already been said, earlier in the book, to indicate the importance of supporting services of an administrative, secretarial or technical nature. Whenever a teacher's time is misused in any of the ways described in Chapter 7 there is a waste of trained manpower, and it must be the head's constant concern to maintain an appropriate balance between teaching and ancillary staff. Moreover, the deployment and efficient use of ancillary staff is no mere sinecure, but makes significant additional demands upon the head's skill in the establishment and maintenance of good human relationships, and his capacity to tap the resources of skill and service upon which the smooth running of the school so greatly depends. It must also be remembered that there are available still further resources of manpower, which are at the head's disposal. HM Inspectors, educational administrators, consultants of all kinds, governors and parents offer him, between them, a wide range of experience, expertise and concern, which can often be drawn upon and harnessed to the school's manifest advantage. Some of them, indeed, have a dual role as assessors and as consultants, but their experience will invariably be put at the school's disposal, if they are rightly approached; and they can contribute a great deal when questions of policy or principle are under consideration, or when particular situations and problems call for the exercise of all the wisdom and expertise upon which the school can depend. By making use of all the available resources, both internal and external, it becomes possible to satisfy every member of the staff that he is making his maximum contribution to the life of the community.

The use of time, as a resource, has so far been considered only in the context of its association with manpower; but time is a resource in its own right. Besides being the scarcest and the most inflexible of all the resources at the head's command, it calls for the exercise of clear principles and priorities in its use. Heads will also recognise the importance of submitting themselves to rigorous cross-examination in order to discover whether they are using their time effectively. Indeed, a scrupulous and detailed analysis of the way in which their time is used, as a matter of established practice and habit, will often reveal a sharp discrepancy between the rosy conception of a head's own intentions, and the sober truth revealed by exacting scrutiny of the ways in which he is actually using his time in practice. For our own part, we have found it salutary to ask ourselves some pertinent questions. For instance, in our use of time, are we giving priority to those aspects of our work which are manifestly of most importance? Do our priorities in the distribution of our time stand up to rigorous examination? Are we doing those things which, if we ourselves do not do them, will not be done (such as reading widely and thinking deeply about our work) or are we only too easily satisfied by performing comparatively routine tasks, because we enjoy doing them and do them well, although many of them could be readily performed by someone else? If the head teaches, for example, is this the most effective and most rewarding use of his time, or is it, perhaps, in the context of the seventies, no more than a pleasant professional indulgence, designed 'to keep his hand in', to encourage his colleagues to believe that he still understands the classroom situation, to set an example, and to bring him into regular contact with particular groups of children? On this question theory and practice differ very widely from school to school, and it is no part of our intention to come down firmly on one side of the fence. But we cannot dodge the uncomfortable conviction that, in a large school, when a head is teaching there must be many other things, of even greater importance, which he might well be doing instead. Similarly, when he delegates responsibility to a head of department or a head of house, for example, can the head ensure that an appropriate allowance of time can be set aside for the performance of these additional responsibilities? If not, is there, in fact, an element of in-built unreality in the structure of delegated responsibilities as planned and practised in many secondary schools today?

The searchlight should not fall only upon the head's use of his time, however. Nowhere is there room for more rigorous examination and research than in the way in which time is used in the class-room. Of how many lessons can it be truthfully asserted that they have used forty unforgiving minutes to maximum advantage? To strike an accurate balance between the preparation of material, exposition, discussion, recording, correction and revision is a delicate process, which achieves complete success only in the hands of master craftsmen. For a teacher to examine and analyse his use of time in the classroom, for a head of department or head of house to scrutinise the way in which he uses the limited amount of non-teaching time made available to him — these are projects deserving of every encouragement. To take the process one stage further, nothing but good can come from a searching enquiry into the reasons for so many established secondary school practices concerned with the use of time, such as the length of teaching periods, the duration of the school day, the number of weeks in each term, and the number of terms in a year. But, if these practices are to be objectively reassessed (as we believe they should be) there must exist, as a prerequisite, first a willingness to recognise the facts as they are, however uncomfortable they may be, and then, secondly, a determination to subject them to a process of rationalisation. Those which can be justified only on the grounds of custom or expediency, but not on the basis of philosophy or priority, must then be subjected to particularly careful re-examination. For if there is one phrase which crops up more regularly than another in the professional discussion of school-masters, it is the familiar, despairing cry of '. . . but, alas, there is no time!' If only the profession were just one degree more critical and more courageous, it might become convinced that it is not lack of time which is always the worst enemy, but lack of a clearly defined table of priorities, designed to *make* time, and to guarantee that every minute of the time available shall be spent to the best advantage.

15   Money and materials

Many of the principles discussed in the two previous chapters, which concerned the effective use of manpower and time, also have implications for every head as he grapples with the important question of how to make the best use of his financial resources. For example, it was suggested, in the previous chapter, that it might be sensible to start a small staff library, but money for this purpose would have to come from somewhere, and the provision of a staff library is likely to mean that some other desirable school objective has to be postponed or pared down. The systematic encouragement of staff to attend conferences, and to take part in courses of in-service training, is a further example of the financial implications of manpower planning. Such courses and conferences are normally financed outside the school, from an LEA budget, but the link with the school's financial resources is a very real one. What decisions have to be taken when a master returns to school after attending such a course? If he has been seconded for a term or a year, for example, to study the use of film and television in the teaching of English in secondary schools, not only has a considerable sum of money been invested in him, but also in mounting the course itself and in providing a temporary replacement on the staff of his school. This investment will not be fully productive and profitable if, on his return, he is unable to put his new ideas, methods and techniques into practice, because he cannot be provided with the necessary films, projectors, cameras and television equipment. The wise head, of course, will have foreseen this need, and will have made budget provision for it, so that the tide of the master's enthusiasm can be 'taken at the flood', and his new-found expertise can be put into practice. Without such provision his ideas will remain academic and sterile, his enthusiasm will rapidly wane, and the original investment of resources will have been unproductive, except for his own intellectual and professional development. So it becomes clear that the head carries a heavy responsibility for the establishment of priorities between competing claims. When there is not enough to go round, there is bound to be such competition for resources, and many heads prefer to share the necessary decisions with their colleagues, or at least to engage in full discussion and consultation, as a preliminary to the taking of these decisions.

In these respects we believe that the head has more power, more responsibility and more patronage than is generally recognised. Patronage is a word which causes hackles to rise and carries unfortunate and unacceptable overtones; but a moment's consideration will carry conviction that a head's responsibilities in the realm of finance are fully comparable with those of a manager of a fairly large enterprise in industry or commerce. Although he himself does not handle so much hard cash, the capital cost of his buildings, expenditure from both capital and revenue accounts on their maintenance, together with the cost of staff salaries and wages, books, equipment, apparatus and furniture are more than enough, in total, to put his financial responsibilities in the big league. Promotions represent patronage, and they also represent a solid investment in promising work; but there are, of course, many other spheres in which the head has financial discretion and responsibility. For some years it has been the common practice for heads of schools to have an allocation of money, on a *per capita* basis, for the purchase of books, apparatus and other materials (the 'capitation allowance'). The allotment of these funds between subject departments, the school library and other school activities has long been at the head's discretion, but it is becoming common for such discretion to be extended to allow the head (acting through his governors) to transfer expenditure from one budget heading to another. Given this discretion, a head can decide to buy a major piece of equipment, instead of a number of small consumable items; in some local authorities such transference of expenditure can even be extended to include manpower. For example, if the head were to appoint a secretary to the staff common room who was equipped with appropriate technical aids, he might well be putting his staff in a position to teach more effectively by providing them with secretarial support and by facilitating the production of teaching materials.

In all such decisions it goes without saying that the staff should be consulted, and that their confidence in the school's financial policies should be secured and maintained. Indeed, the more a head is given, and chooses to exercise, discretion the more important it is that his colleagues should be involved in, and should clearly understand, not only the purposes and principles behind his decisions, but the processes involved in reaching them. In some schools it has been the practice for the head to play his financial cards very close to his chest, by holding the purse strings tightly, and by not disclosing the total sums which he has at his disposal. His colleagues are then invited to ask for what they want, at any point in the school year, and the head tells them whether they can have it or not. Such a method of allocating financial resources is in danger of breeding distrust and frustration, and it deprives the staff of the opportunity of widening their own experience and responsibility by a full consideration of all the competing claims involved. Any teacher or head of department worth his salt will constantly have in mind the next development which he would like to see in the teaching of his subject, and be anxious to add to the school's stock of relevant literature and other material; he will know of the existence of apparatus and equipment which he would like to see available in his department. Yet it is extremely unlikely that everyone can be fully satisfied, at one and the same time, from a pool of resources which is bound to be limited. Indeed, a staff which is ever satisfied with its resources is probably a staff which is intellectually and professionally moribund! Even at the best, then, members of staff are likely to want more than they can have; at the worst, when information both about the resources, and about the way in which they are allocated, is a closely-guarded secret, the common room is likely to be shot through with curiosity and suspicion. Every master knows that some of his colleagues are more powerful than others; everyone suspects that some are more adept than he is at capturing the ear, the attention and the support of the head. Such a head, suspected, however unfairly and unreasonably, of listening more attentively to some of his staff than he does to others, or of bending to the latest or strongest wind to blow through his room, has not only lost the confidence of his staff but, by his very methods, he has already set about destroying it.

But if any noticeable lack of openness and fairness in the allocation of school funds is to be deplored, it must not be assumed that strict fairness, by itself, is necessarily and always acceptable. There is danger in resorting to formulae of some kind, in order to achieve 'fair' distribution, and to resolve a difficult dilemma. It is possible, for example, to calculate the proportion of the common funds which should be allocated to each department and activity, according to factors such as the number of children studying a subject, the number of advanced level candidates or the inherent cost of teaching certain subjects, such as science. Clearly these are factors which must be taken into account; but such formulae, if rigidly applied, can easily serve to frustrate legitimate enterprise and desirable experiment. A pattern of financial distribution which is repeated from year to year, however sound the basis on which it was orginally devised, is in danger of leading to a situation in which no department ever has enough money in any one year to undertake a major revision of teaching content or method. It would not be feasible, for example, to consider the introduction of a Nuffield Science programme, or of an audio-visual language scheme, or to abandon an obsolete series of text-books and to restock completely with one which is contemporary. It would probably be much fairer, in the long run, to ask heads of departments to submit fully documented budget proposals, well in advance of the beginning of each financial year, and then arrange for their proposals to be carefully scrutinised, uncluttered by formulae, and unprejudiced by adherence to a customary pattern.

But who should undertake this formidable review? The head must carry ultimate responsibility, of course, for the use of his monetary resources, as he does for all other aspects of the school's activities; but a strong case can be made out for asking heads of departments (or heads of faculties) to meet together, under his chairmanship, and in the presence of each other to present and argue their case. Some decisions will be reached readily enough, and will be accepted by the body as a whole, but there will always be conflicting claims which the head alone can resolve. He will be aware, of course, that even in an open meeting of this kind powerful, informal influences are at work. There will always be some who are not prepared to risk offending their colleagues when they are sitting together round a table, but who would be prepared to be more frank and forceful in a private discussion; for this reason the head will have studied the written departmental submissions, in advance, and may well have had consultations with individuals to elucidate their real needs and to clarify their arguments. There will often come a point, however, at which he must shed his role as chairman, and resume the role of head, charged with the responsibility of arbitration. In approaching this task he must remember his duty to invest in enterprises which are likely to be most profitable to his school and to his children. He will know, on the one hand, which of his colleagues have both ideas and imagination, and the energy, expertise and tenacity to follow them through in practice and, on the other hand, which of them appears to be brimming over with enthusiasm but is, in fact, relying on sudden inspiration and has not thought through his proposals with sufficient care, understanding or thoroughness. He will also recognise that there are some, unhappily, who are content to tread the same path as in years past and who cannot, in good conscience, be rewarded with additional resources until they can be stimulated into new thinking and fresh activity. Quite often two or more claims will appear to be of more or less equal merit and, here, the advantage of making (or, at least, promulgating) decisions in an open meeting of heads of departments is at its most telling. A head of department who has to wait for the implementation of his proposals until the next financial year will understand (even if he does not wholly accept) the reasons for the decision, which will have been made apparent to him during the discussion. It will also be obvious to his colleagues that, although he has been kept waiting on this occasion, as a matter of deliberate policy, he will become entitled to some measure of priority in subsequent allocations of financial resources.

At the same time, all those concerned with the annual review of a school budget must remember that many, if not all, decisions about expenditure have long-term implications. The two examples quoted earlier, of Nuffield Science and audio-visual language teaching, are obvious cases of a continuing commitment, because they will involve not only a considerable capital investment to set them up, but, for a number of years, they must have substantial injections of materials, equipment and apparatus (in addition to normal replacement and maintenance) if they are to operate effectively. They become, therefore, a charge upon the school's budget in a planned and phased programme, if the initial investment is to be fully productive. Moreover, throughout their discussions, and most particularly at the point of final decision, the head and his colleagues must always have, in the very centre of their thinking, the school's agreed aims and objectives. For the dilemma of competing claims involves the identification of the next most urgent and essential step in the progress towards the attainment of those objectives. Only when the objectives, themselves, have been placed in order of priority, both in respect of their long-term educational importance, and of their relative urgency in the immediate time-scale, can the dilemma be resolved.

At this point it may be helpful to have a brief look at the financial relationship between schools and local education authorities. Mention has already been made of the welcome increase in the financial discretion extended to schools. Such discretion is, of course, always operable only within the budgets of the school and of the LEA. Immediately, it can be seen, however, that there is, within LEA policy, exactly the same inherent difficulty as has been discussed in relation to a fair distribution of resources within a particular school. The most obvious and, superficially, the most obviously 'fair' way for an LEA to allocate money to a school would be to base its budget on the size of the school, and the age range of the children within it. Such a decision would seem to be perfectly acceptable, at first sight, for these are factors which are bound to affect the expenditure which a school must necessarily incur. Nevertheless, some books, materials and equipment are required by all schools, whatever their size, and there are undoubted circumstances in which it would be 'fairer' to operate on a 'to him that hath not' principle. For example, additional resources are certain to be required by schools in deprived areas; and when an old school is scheduled for ultimate closure, it is entirely unreasonable that it should be put at the wrong end of the queue for resources, until the day comes for it to be replaced. Indeed, there would be strong justification for attaching priority to such circumstances, and for putting new books, equipment and furniture into old schools, prior to their closure and resurrection. Moreover, smaller schools would always suffer if an authority based its calculations *solely* on the principle of 'fairness'; and such a practice would encourage a degree of rigidity which might well mean that no school, in any one year, could spare enough resources for a major professional development. Thus, initiative would be cramped and experiment stifled. Perhaps the best way out of this dilemma would be to take account of size and type of school but, in addition, to expect heads to submit budget proposals to the chief education officer, very much in the same way as it has been suggested that heads should invite proposals from their heads of departments. Allowance could then be made for local and individual considerations, including the age and condition of the buildings, the range of amenities available in the area, the particular skills, knowledge and expertise of the staff and the special and particular needs of the children concerned. In this way, urgent needs and encouraging growth-points would be identified, and could be met and nurtured to fruition; and it may then become clear that it would be sounder for the authority to support experiment in a few enterprising schools (for example, by the provision of video-tape equipment) rather than to standardise provision for all its secondary schools on exactly the same basis. An approach, such as this, to the distribution of resources may well depend upon close liaison between the chief education officer and the advisory services of all kinds available to him; the better he really knows exactly what is going on in the schools under his control, the better can he assess the needs and demands of individual heads, against a background knowledge of current developments in his own area and in the country as a whole. Specialist advice is clearly most valuable in carrying out such a formidable task and, in some areas, specialist advisers are themselves given an allocation of money which they can use for pump-priming operations in their own subjects or for the support of promising developments in the schools which they serve. Here again, however, a word of warning is necessary. Without good cross-communication between advisers it would be only too easy for one particular school to receive more than its fair share of such additional resources; and the same danger could arise in the degree of priority extended to a particular class or year within a school, by several heads of departments all operating independently.

Once decisions have been taken within a school about the financial resources which are to be made available for a subject department or any other major aspect of the school's organisation, then the head of department or house (or holder of a similar post of major responsibility) must assume full charge. This would include the final decision on which books, materials, apparatus and equipment to order as well (of course) as responsibility for the care, maintenance and stock-control involved in using his resources to the maximum advantage.

But the responsibility which he is exercising is a delegated responsibility.

The head himself and, ultimately, the chief education officer, must be prepared to render account to the community as a whole for the decisions of the head of department; and herein lies a dilemma. At each level, any one member of the education service is accountable to his immediate superior for husbanding his resources. His superior in turn, is responsible for seeing that everyone who reports to him is obliged to render an account. But exactly how much discretion a chief education officer, a head or a head of department can allow to those working under him is (as we saw in Chapter 11) a matter of delicate and subtle judgement. On the one hand experience suggests that people work to maximum effect only when they are doing those things which they want to do, by methods in which they have confidence and by employing techniques which they can use effectively because they themselves have chosen them. On the other hand, we have argued in the same chapter, that discretion may well involve diversity, and this may present real problems in an increasingly mobile society.

A master 'doing his own thing' may be extremely successful but, if his methods are too strikingly individual, and are too far out of the main stream of current educational practice, very real difficulties may be created for pupils who move to other schools, as well as for his successor when he moves to another post. School stock rooms and cupboards are crammed with books and equipment which are no longer in use. In seeking an acceptable course to follow between the conflicting alternatives of uniformity and diversity, account must always be taken of local and individual considerations: it is simply not possible to suggest a universal touchstone. Nevertheless, uniformity can easily seem to encourage dull mediocrity, and the risk involved in backing colleagues and schools with ideas, initiative and boundless energy is often justified by results. It is comparatively easy to avoid major mistakes by sticking to established practice, but adventurous experiment and exploration are often excitingly fruitful.

Perhaps it would be possible to devise schemes for the pooling and redistribution between schools (or even between LEAs) of books, materials and equipment which are no longer in use. It would obviously be complicated and difficult to arrange, and the cost of administration might exceed the advantages to be derived. But, if appropriate financial and administrative procedures could be devised, perhaps it might become possible, by agreement between all the parties concerned, for a master to take with him, when he moves to another school, those materials and teaching aids which he has developed, and which he uses expertly but which his successor does not intend to use. This would leave the field clear for his successor to develop his own teaching methods, while employing his own choice of teaching materials. The difficulties are obvious and there might well be dangers, too, in that frequent changes of staff might mean that particular groups of children were subjected to constant changes of methods and materials. Moderation and wisdom would clearly have to be exercised by all concerned; but teachers are often found to be working with textbooks and materials which they have 'inherited' and in which they have no confidence, but which they cannot afford to replace. Any practicable alleviation of this difficulty would not only save substantial sums of money, but would encourage teaching initiative and enterprise, and so bring positive advantage to generations of children.

It is an obvious truism that money is wasted when books and equipment are no longer in use; but distressingly often, it is a truth which is ignored or overlooked. When expensive apparatus spends most of the school year locked in a cupboard, only to be brought out to show to visitors, or on 'open days', the situation has usually arisen for one or more of four main reasons.

First, the equipment may have been bought by a master who was taken in by clever advertising, or who knew of its effective use by another school or heard about it on a course, but had not, himself, fully understood its use or application.

Secondly, the purchase may have been made by a head of department who has since moved to another post, and whose successor either does not wish, or does not know how, to use it effectively.

Thirdly, there may be a problem of availability. If apparatus has to be shared among a number of teachers, there must be some 'advance booking' arrangements; if this means that lessons have to be planned in detail too far ahead, or that room changes or porterage are involved, then there is a strong probability that teachers will simply not make the extra effort involved to use the equipment. A slide projector or an overhead projector, for example, is often needed only for a few minutes at some particular stage in the course of a lesson. If it is immediately available it will be used; if it is not, then the relevant visual material may not be shown to the children. It is important, therefore, to give careful consideration to the extent of the provision which is to be made, and to its availability. Over-provision, which ensures that every teacher has immediate access, in his own room, to every piece of equipment he is likely to use, will obviously mean that much of it will lie idle for a great deal of its useful life. Under-provision, on the other hand, though less obviously wasteful, can be a false economy. If a department which really needs three overhead projectors in fact has only two, then it is not only under-equipped, but experience suggests that the two projectors which it possesses are unlikely to be fully used.

Fourthly, some heads of department may be over-protective and cautious. It is certainly their clear duty to cherish and maintain the equipment and materials which they control; but, in some cases, this duty may be interpreted to mean that the stock must be used as little as possible (and certainly not by anyone else!) in order to preserve and extend its working life. In turn, this emphasises that money spent on the maintenance, repair and replacement of apparatus which is in constant use is likely to be a sound financial investment; and all of this draws renewed attention to the fact that, if heads are going to enjoy a greater measure of financial discretion and independence, then they must also be prepared to accept an equivalent measure of accountability.

16   Space

Has any head ever been completely satisfied with the accommodation of his school? Certainly, most heads are concerned about their buildings, to a greater or a lesser extent. This is not because they are cantankerous or over-critical, but because space confronts them with problems which are less easily resolved than those which arise from any of the other resources at their disposal. Schools are living, developing communities, subject to constant change and growth; school buildings, on the other hand, are comparatively static and rigid, subject only to long-term modification or improvement, and then only at considerable expense. There is, of course, a direct link between the philosophy and practice of secondary education, and the buildings designed for the achievement of its aims and objectives. But a number of major factors impose substantial constraints upon architects and planners, so that exact congruence between intention and practice, in terms of buildings, is extraordinarily difficult to accomplish.

To begin with, the time lag between the definition of purposes and principles to be embodied in the design of a new school and its actual occupation is in the order of five years, give or take a few months and, during any period of five years, advances in educational thought and practice are considerable. In consequence, most new schools are, to some extent, out of date by the time they open. Then, it is most unusual for the head who will actually organise and run the new school to have been identified soon enough for him to be able to play a significant part in its design; by the time he has been appointed, major modifications, which he may wish to suggest, will either be wholly impracticable or unreasonably expensive to attain. Again, the design of schools is subject to statutory building regulations and cost-limits. Under the guidance of the Department of Education and Science these constraints have undoubtedly encouraged a great deal of research and ingenuity, and have brought about a vast improvement in the

design, equipment and furnishing of schools. They impose considerable restrictions upon an individual architect, however, especially
when (as so often happens) the lowest estimate, on tender, is appreci-
ably higher than the cost-limit allows, with the result that substantial
economies have to be effected in the final stages, on financial rather
than on educational grounds. Moreover, when a new school opens, it
seldom accommodates even approximately the number of pupils for
whom it was intended. Either it is partially empty (only very occasionally, as when the development of a new housing estate has taken
longer than expected), or (most frequently) it is overcrowded, and is
compelled to wrestle with inadequacies and shortcomings from the
very first day of its life.

There are, however, other deeper and far more significant reasons
why there may be a gap between theory and practice in the design of
schools. To begin by asking, for instance, in what the teaching process
consists, is quickly to discover that it is not possible to frame a defini-
tive answer. At one end of the spectrum, teaching may consist of
talking to a class, with or without a blackboard or other audio-visual
aids, and with the teacher remaining in front of his class for the whole
lesson. At the other end, a group of pupils may be working on its own,
under direction and supervision, either answering questions in writing,
collecting information, reading, or preparing material as a basis for
subsequent use and development. During this time the teacher may
be working at his own desk, calling particular children up to discuss
their work with him or moving round the room, from desk to desk,
talking to individual children. In between these two extremes there
may be an infinite variety of practice, including working from assignment cards, visiting the library, or undertaking projects outside the
classroom and even outside the school. The class may remain seated,
with periods of oral discussion, or its members may be free to move
from their desks and their room as their work demands. The class
may work as a coherent unit, or it may break up into groups, or be expected to work as individuals. Only one teacher may be involved in
any particular lesson, or there may be close cooperation between a
number of teachers working together, with two or more of them
present in a classroom at the same time. These, and many other per-
mutations and combinations, are all recognisable and acceptable
aspects of the practice of teaching and learning adopted by individual

teachers, and it would be wholly invalid to assert that any one technique is 'right' and another 'wrong'. Indeed, a skilful and experienced teacher may, in the course of a week or a month, use many if not all of these methods, varying his techniques according.to the content of his material, the capacities, interests and needs of his pupils, his own particular skills, and the extent and nature of the facilities available to him.

Perhaps, then, greater certainty can be achieved by considering something which is, surely, much more straightforward, namely the precise composition of classes. After all, there are many thousands of such classes, and there must be some identifiable pattern among them. Pattern — yes; but unanimity of practice — no. Most teaching groups are, by long tradition, established on a basis of age. But there is still great variety of practice within an age group. Children, for example, may be segregated strictly according to assessed ability, either in a 'streamed' situation or in subject 'sets', or they may be integrated, for teaching purposes, on a social, rather than on an intellectual basis, and so may be split up into house or year groups, with the natural consequence that such groups will cover a wide span of ability and attainment. Sometimes there may be combinations of these methods, so that children may work in forms, in sets, or in house groups, for different subjects. Sometimes separation by ability may be achieved by rather coarser, less refined, grading than would be acceptable in streams or sets; when this practice is adopted then two or more roughly parallel forms are 'banded' together to form an identifiable teaching sector (although each form within a 'band' will still be taught, for most purposes, as a separate entity). So it becomes clear that it is practice and usage, in addition to philosophy or proven methods, which determine these decisions. Yet it must never be forgotten that each different method of organisation into teaching units implies a difference of teaching content and technique: *if it doesn't mean that, then there is clearly no point in making the distinction at all.* For all systems of classifying children in teaching groups are intended to offer maximum advantage and opportunity to each individual child, on the one hand, and the most favourable teaching circumstances and conditions for the staff, on the other. It is seldom, however, that these two factors exactly coincide: nor is there often unanimity about their merits even within a particular school. There is a growing body of hard evidence that co-education has positive advantages over single sex, and that streaming is much less disadvantageous than its opponents maintain. But there is simply no practical or theoretical agreement about all these issues.

Perhaps then, greater certainty and precision can be found in the size of a class; and, at first glance, the position here certainly seems to be much more favourable. For all teachers are agreed, without any controversy, that a class of 40 or more children is too large. Temporarily, as a target which is politically and economically practicable, the figure of 30 has come to be accepted, but there is still considerable dispute over whether this target should be the same for both primary and secondary schools. Ask the question: 'Why 30 is particular?', however, and there is no clear answer, except that 30 is fewer than 40 and, therefore, clearly more acceptable. There is no hard evidence whatever to suggest that 30 is 'right', whether professionally, administratively, financially or constructionally. After all, 25 is fewer than 30 and 15 or 20 fewer than 25. Ought the size of classes to be continually adjusted, as economic prosperity is established, then, or is there a known size of class, proven by experience and experiment to offer the most favourable opportunities and circumstances for both pupil and teacher? The answer, yet again, must be an unhappy and emphatic negative. There is, indeed, some disconcerting evidence that size of class may be a much less significant factor in individual progress than most teachers would maintain; but there is no evidence whatever to substantiate any argument that a particular size of class, whatever it be, is the most favourable, to be followed as a guiding professional star, through all adversity, until its universal attainment.

Perhaps, then, the size of classrooms and teaching spaces will offer some authoritative evidence? But the size of teaching spaces varies from subject to subject, by reason of the different teaching processes and operations which they require. It is no surprise to find, therefore, that, in current practice, certain sizes have come to be accepted as norms, not only for the size of 'standard' or general purpose classrooms, but for laboratories, workshops and other practical rooms, and for the largest teaching spaces such as halls and gymnasia. Even so, it is difficult to justify the planning of science laboratories for a maximum of 36 pupils, while workshops and other practical rooms are designed for 20: is a science laboratory only half as dangerous as a cookery room? Moreover, 20 is more than half a normal class of 30 so that, when classes are split into two groups for these practical subjects, some of the teaching space is unused; and the acceptance of norms still leaves unanswered a great many questions of philosophy and practice which directly affect the design and organisation of schools. Ought there to be, for example, variety in the size of teaching spaces not only between subjects but within any one subject? Is it an advantage if all the rooms in which a particular subject is taught are grouped together; if so, would liaison between related subjects be fostered if all their teaching spaces were planned as a coherent unit? Again, should each classroom be an isolated and independent unit, or should teaching spaces be separated from each other by sound-proofed and movable partitions, rather than by party walls, so that they could be expanded or contracted to meet particular circumstances? This would mean. of course, that in order to provide for maximum freedom of adaptation and use of rooms, internal walls could not be load-bearing. This is a practice which has already become commonly established in designing new blocks of offices, and is beginning to make itself felt in the shape of 'open plan' schools, which offer teachers flexibility for experiment and for the development of new teaching practices.

Again, should as many teachers as possible have their own subject teaching rooms, with all their teaching resources and materials around them, or would it be in the greater general interest to reduce the surge of children's movement about the school, between periods, by expecting members of the staff, who are not dependent upon specialist teaching provision, to move from lesson to lesson, instead of the children? Does a school need a large all-purpose hall and, if so, how can it be used to maximum advantage throughout the day? How can a school's needs for social and dining areas be best satisfied: are house or year blocks, each with its own recreational and dining facilities, necessarily the best answer, and can rooms which are designed primarily for social, dining and recreational purposes be equally effective when they are used as teaching spaces? These are all questions upon which it is important that the teaching profession should develop a positive outlook, since the answers to them materially affect the different ways in which a school can be organised and run.

So far, in all that has been said about the internal planning of a school, very little reference has been made to the size of the school itself. This size will have been determined by local and practical considerations of 'roofs over heads', rather than upon proven theoretical concepts of minimum and optimum size. Indeed, as in so many other aspects of school design, it would be quite unrealistic to adopt a dogmatic or authoritative attitude. By convention and tradition, grammar and modern schools were generally much of a muchness in size, and seldom exceeded four- or five-form entry. But when comprehensive schools began to appear, the initial tendency was to make them very much larger than anything previously known in this country. This was partly because an increase in the size of secondary schools was becoming a world-wide phenomenon, as they became comprehensive; but it was also felt that such schools needed to be really large if they were not only to produce and sustain a viable sixth form, but were also to secure effective teaching groups, in minority subjects and in optional courses in the middle school, as well. Subsequent experience has somewhat punctured this belief, however, and there are now unmistakable signs that size, itself, can present a school with intricate problems of organisation, communication and control.

There are other aspects of school design which are of great interest and concern to teachers, but they are of a more technical nature, and are mainly outside the scope of teachers' expertise. They include the questions of lighting, ventilating and heating classrooms, the problem of acoustics, and the design of school furniture and equipment. Two major features of school organisations, however, in relation to the use of space, must be considered. The first concerns the problems which arise from divided or 'linked' premises. This commonly occurs when two or more schools are combined in a scheme of reorganisation. When this happens, what were originally operated as separate schools are now regarded as forming part of a new school. They may be 'linked' by paths across a single school campus, involving only two or three minutes' walk, or they may be situated a mile or more apart, and be separated by a complex of busy public roads involving a journey between them, on foot, of five, ten, fifteen or even twenty minutes. Such a situation clearly gives rise to major problems of internal organisation. It emphasises the complexities of control, and creates new and significant problems of communication and consultation. Movement of staff and children between buildings will have to be restricted and time-tables develop greater complexity. It may be difficult to accomplish a real sense of cohesion and purpose, both for staff and children, however skilfully the organisation is planned. If there is uneven distribution of teaching accommodation between the different sets of buildings, then heads of department will find it harder to achieve effective contact with the school as a whole, when the school's total teaching programme takes place in two or three sets of buildings which are widely separated from each other. All these problems call for imagination, initiative and sustained enthusiasm on the part of all concerned if they are to be successfully overcome.

A second, and most particular, problem in the use of space, concerns the school library, which is now becoming much more widely recognised and deployed as a resource-centre than simply as a repository for books and magazines. Films, film-strips, records and tapes (both audio and video) all now find a place in many libraries, together with a wide range of teaching materials and resources. By established tradition a school library has often been regarded as providing access for staff and children to the book shelves, at certain stipulated times; in addition, it has offered a suitable environment for sixth-form teaching and, when not in use for that purpose, for sixth-form private study. Some schools also adopt the practice of allowing whole classes to have access to the library, during what are known as 'library periods', within the time-table, in order to encourage training in the finding and use of books. These practices are unlikely to be tenable, however, if the library is to become the intellectual dynamo of the school, providing not only free access for staff and children at all times (which presupposes the appointment of a professional librarian) but acting as a clearing-house and information centre for ideas, references, illustrative and source material, bibliographies and suggestions. There is, of course, no reason why neighbouring rooms, associated with the library, should not be used for teaching or private study; and there is every reason to provide nooks, corners and alcoves within the library itself, together with individual desks, designed for private study and equipped with storage space, technical aids and services, where books of reference, tapes, records, newspapers and journals can be studied on the spot. At the moment, the provision for private study, in most schools, is either wholly non-existent or totally inadequate. But it is unlikely that a library can maintain its new enlarged role if it is still to be put virtually out of action by reason of being set aside for teaching, the instruction of classes in library practice, or for continuous private study. Moreover, the opportunities which the library affords will not be fully exploited unless the staff so plan and orientate their teaching that children are continually directed to the resources which the library commands, not as an occasional point of reference, but as a consistent and enthusiastic policy.

This rapid (and, necessarily, superficial) survey has touched upon only some of the problems which arise when trying to design the most effective teaching spaces for the most enlightened teaching practices. It has indicated the multitude of decisions and compromises which are involved in the design of a school. There are so many competing priorities between which a choice has often to be made. An architect may have to choose, for example, between more teaching accommodation or better quality facing materials and finishes; between venetian blinds and carpets or wider corridors and staircases. The survey has also revealed that there are many professional issues upon which there is not even a measure of general agreement. It is hardly surprising, therefore, that there is so much variety of practice in the provision of teaching accommodation. There are, it is true, many schools in which a positive attitude is adopted to the physical circumstances and environment in which they operate. But, as a body, teachers have not given consistent or profound thought to the design and planning of schools, although they are often irritated by the deficiencies of the buildings in which they work, and frequently indicate a powerful wish to be involved in their planning, especially of alterations and extensions. This being so, it is not surprising that changing educational ideas impose ever new demands upon school buildings, and there is unlikely to come a day when educational ideas and architectural skills achieve a state of perfect harmony and accord. Nevertheless, nothing but good would accrue from a determined professional assault upon many traditional practices and usages in the secondary school, in order that they may become rooted in proven experimental theory and may be sustained by enlightened planning and design.

It would be out of step with the general theme of this book, however, not to recognise that, once a school is in operation, a particular burden rests upon the head. Space is, indeed, apart from time, the least flexible and the most intractable of all the resources at his disposal; but his freedom of manoeuvre is still very much greater than is often supposed or realised. Basically, the questions confronting him fall into two categories. On the one hand, there are those which are fundamental. which do not respond to expediency or compromise, and which are only susceptible of modification by the exercise of patience and persistence over a long period; on the other hand, there are those questions which are capable of partial if not complete solution in the short term. Fundamental questions presuppose a basic conflict of purpose and intention between the design of the school's teaching accommodation and the fulfilment of the school's current objectives. For example, a school might be seriously short of accommodation for science or music, so that it would be wholly impracticable to adopt a curriculum in which science or music played a prominent part; or the wide physical separation of teaching accommodation for related subjects (such as art, crafts and engineering science) would make integration between them particularly difficult. Again, the design and distribution of classrooms might be such as to prejudice, if not to preclude, any policy of team-teaching, or of any teaching technique involving flexibility in the use of space. The absence of house or year blocks might seriously diminish the opportunities for social education, and the development of a full community life. An inadequate gymnasium, poorly drained playing fields, and swimming-bath facilities at a considerable distance from the school, would hamper and might even prevent the growth of a fully integrated programme of physical education. Such shortcomings and deficiencies impose constraints which can only be overcome on a long-term basis, and can probably only be eliminated altogether either by additional building, or by extensive adaptation and remodelling. There are, however, many examples of what can be accomplished when architect, administrator and head are all of one mind, and are determined to meet the challenge by which they are confronted.

The second category of problem may be described as one which is capable of solution, either by modifying the pattern of the school's organisation, curriculum, time-table and teaching methods, or by experimenting with other ways of interpreting the school's philosophy and objectives. By such means the school will be able to take full advantage of the facilities which the buildings afford, and will not be wholly restricted or frustrated by their shortcomings and deficiencies. Ideally, of course, no school building should entirely determine the nature of the school's organisation and objectives. Inevitably, however, most school buildings last a very long time (often far too long!) and so, in succeeding generations, they are bound to impose restrictions upon the way in which the school can be run, and upon the changing nature of its objectives. The task of the head, then, in this as in so many other situations which we have already considered, is first to identify the exact nature of the accommodation problems with which he is confronted, and then to devise solutions which are most nearly in accord with his long-term philosophy and purpose. If the teaching accommodation is restrictive or wholly inadequate for example, it may be possible to modify and vary the size of teaching groups. To accomplish this it would be necessary to make an exact analysis of the number and size of all teaching groups, in every period of the week, and then to compare this analysis with the maximum accommodation which the building affords. Many a school is overcrowded and under-used, at one and the same time, just because the size of its teaching groups does not match the capacity of its teaching spaces.

If there is a shortage of teaching accommodation in a particular subject, then some relief may be gained by staggering the dinner-hour, or extending the length of the school day: this would make it possible, for instance, to use the available science laboratories or workshops for a longer time each day. Neither of these solutions is free from disadvantages, of course; they make it very difficult to organise clubs, societies and activities when part of the school is working and part is dining or free; they restrict the opportunities for getting the whole staff together, as a body, during working hours, even for a short meeting; they give rise to problems of noise and distraction when some children are working and others are playing outside the classroom windows; while an extended day, with different parts of the school beginning and ending at different times, may well cause acute problems for the public transport service. But these difficulties are not insuperable, even if no ideal solution is possible. Further education encounters and overcomes all of them. Some colleges of further education, indeed, have shown how to make greater use of scarce teaching resources by lengthening the college year, so that expensive plant and equipment are in use for, say, 48 instead of for only 36 weeks a year. Moreover, secondary education is moving in this same direction, as the concept of community schools catches on. It is no longer fanciful to picture a secondary school open from 8.30 a.m. to 10.30 p.m., whose library is also the public library, whose teaching and recreational facilities are used as much by adults as by children (having been designed with this purpose in mind) and whose operations include a youth club, a health clinic, a centre for the careers advisory service, and a social club. In comparison with such imaginative ideas as this much contemporary bickering over the 'dual use' of school buildings pales into insignificance.

Problems of circulation, on the other hand, which can be acute in congested corridors and on narrow staircases, can be met by modifying the length of periods, in order to reduce the extent of movement by staff and children. The present practice of adopting periods of 30, 35, 40 or 45 minutes, throughout the day, imposes a rigidity which has become almost a tradition. It is hard to see why a length of period deemed suitable for eleven-year-olds, or for religious instruction, should also be expected to be equally relevant and appropriate for eighteen-year-olds, or for mathematics or languages. For this reason, some schools now adopt a more flexible time-table, based upon unit modules of 20 or 30 minutes, which can be used as single or multiple blocks of time for different classes, age-groups or subjects.

In choosing between all these possible organisational changes, in response to the constraints and restrictions imposed by the nature and extent of the available accommodation, some degree of compromise will often prove to be necessary; but it is generally possible to strike a rough balance between advantage and disadvantage, and this is exactly where we began this final section of the chapter. The head's task, in this section of his responsibilities, is to be realistically aware of the limitations which his school buildings impose, and of the opportunities which they afford. He is equally under an obligation to adapt his organisation and methods, and to devise ways and means of making the maximum and most flexible use of *all* his resources — not only of manpower and time, of money and materials, but of space as well.

IV ASSESSMENT

17　Pupils

We have now reached the last of our four questions: *How will you know when you have got there?* In Chapter 4 we suggested that assessment was fundamental to the whole process of running a school, and we emphasised that it was a basic operation of good management. Education, however, cannot employ all the quantitative criteria of good management which are relevant in industry and commerce. If sales or profits fall dramatically short of expectation, or if actual costs grossly exceed initial estimates, then the position can be analysed in precise terms. If a television set or an aeroplane is badly designed or carelessly assembled, its weaknesses will be quickly and alarmingly revealed. The educational process, by contrast, can rely on no such 'criteria of manifest disaster', and while this may be a source of comfort, it is, at the same time, a disadvantage. Because schools are concerned with boys and girls, on their way to becoming men and women, and with the assessment of the infinite resources and capacities of the human spirit, they would reject out of hand — even if they could be shown to be relevant — crude mathematical methods of measurement. For schools, there can be no precise auditors' certificate, no conclusive statement of operating profits and losses, no exact balance sheet of assets and liabilities. They have to be satisfied with much less precision, to accept qualitative rather than quantitative judgements, and to depend upon subjective assessment of objective evidence. Nevertheless, despite these handicaps, the process of assessment is central to the whole practice of education, and cannot be shirked or neglected with impunity. Schools dare not disregard such indicators of success or failure as are available to them; for, without some careful and continuous system of evaluation, there is grave danger that their aims and objectives would falter or be taken for granted, and their standards be in danger of atrophy or decay. Indeed, it is probable that they will even have to become accustomed to the use, in an adapted form, of some of the instruments of measurement which operate in the harsh world of business and economics, such as cost-efficiency, cost-benefit analysis and measurements of productivity, however sharply they recoil from them in perfectly genuine horror.

For there can be no doubt that, with the enormously increased resources of money, plant and manpower which the education service now commands, society will seek to apply some standards of measurement, in order to be satisfied that educational facilities are being put to good use, and that the nation is receiving good value for its money. No one would be happy to pour his own resources into any organisation, however philanthropic, which bluntly rejected all idea of external assessment, but ruefully admitted that it possessed only the most rudimentary and imperfect tools of internal evaluation. Even in the operation of charitable organisations, subscribers look critically at the cost of administration in relation to total income, and seek for evidence that their subscriptions have been well spent, and that there is an identifiable end-product to show for the expenditure of their support and good will. Why, then, should society adopt a different attitude towards the assessment of education, however deeply entrenched the vested interests of education may be? No; the uncomfortable truth is, we believe, that the education service must learn courageously to accept the need for such assessment, and to apply itself vigorously and systematically to the development and refinement of such tools and measures of evaluation as may be found to be genuinely relevant in the educational context. Otherwise, the service should not be surprised if the task is undertaken by those whose skills lie rather in the rigid application of quantitative data and procedures, than in the substantiation of subjective judgements.

Now, at this stage, it is important to remember that, in education, assessment is not to be thought of simply as a postmortem or as an attempt to reach a verdict of guilty or not guilty. Educational assessment is a continuous process, a journey which never ends, for there is always another stage ahead. Those who love the mountains and fells will know how their eyes become fixed on some attainable ridge or spur, hoping that it will presently bring them within reach of the summit; but, as they struggle upwards, new vistas and prospects are continually revealed. So it is with educational assessment. There is never a stage at which it is sensible to stop, except momentarily to rest, to regather energies and to confirm purpose and direction for the next stage of the climb. The fact that the principle of assessment is enshrined both in our first and in our fourth questions — *Where are you?* and *How will you know when you have got there?* — emphasises that it is not a linear but a continuous or circular process. Experience continually leads back to the reexamination of aims and objectives and to the refinement of methods and techniques, not only in the light of organisation and performance but in accordance with the continuously shifting expectations and demands of society. It may be found, for example, that objectives have been set too low and that far more can be achieved than was at first assumed to be possible. Alternatively, it may become apparent that targets have been set beyond immediate reach and that they must be redefined. In either case, not only ultimate destinations but the routes and tactics necessary to get there, may have to be revised.

It would be idle to pretend, however, that thorough-going assessment is as easy to accomplish in practice as it is arguable or desirable in theory. Assessment, in fact, is one major aspect of the art of judgement, that rarest and most delicate of human skills; and just because it is difficult, evaluation which is routine, incomplete and second-hand may come, too easily, to be accepted. Heads are often the prisoners of their own experience. They become so familiar with people, circumstances and things that they may cease to be aware of their significance; they are in danger of spending so much time in the engineroom of the school that they are far too infrequently on the bridge, scanning the horizon, checking their position, confirming their direction and speed, and estimating the conflicting influences of current, wind and tide. Indeed, they may become so heavily engaged in the operation of their own school that they have a vested interest in their own organisation and its performance, and develop a predisposition to believe in the rightness of their own decisions, particularly when they have been reached as a result of prolonged consultation and discussion. In consequence, unless they are very careful indeed, they may develop a tendency to recognise as evidence only those indicators which support their own expectations, and fail to discern testimony which should cause them furiously to think. If the results of a public examination are poor in a particular year, how often does a staff-room console itself with the thought that 'the fifth form this year were a particularly poor lot, anyway'? Lack of enthusiasm among children, or even downright antagonism, are blamed upon an apathetic or rebellious generation, without consideration of the effectiveness of the stimuli provided by the school or the relevance of its curriculum. So schools become frighteningly selective in their search for evidence, and tend to make judgements which are self-fulfilling; they are much less ready to accept evidence which suggests that their very assumptions and practices call for radical reexamination. Moreover, since the definition of their aims and objectives is often rather woolly and imprecise to begin with, their assessment is inevitably in danger of being equally vague and indeterminate. This is particularly so when evaluation is concerned with the relation between intention and individual performance and with the assessment of such qualities as initiative, independence, tolerance and integrity, none of which is easily measurable in quantitative terms.

Nevertheless, schoolmasters, however much they may take shelter behind the theoretical difficulties and dangers, do not hesitate to pronounce judgement in daily practice. They comment regularly upon colleagues, governors, local authorities, parents, examining bodies, and even occasionally upon themselves, as well as upon children's performance in the classroom, on the playing field or stage, or in the orchestra. If a head is consulted about a boy who is to be transferred, or a master who is applying for a post elsewhere, he will respond with an immediate and spontaneous assessment in qualitative terms, reinforced by such supporting evidence as is available. Not once in a thousand times will the enquiring head be told that the evaluation of children or staff is either impossible or inappropriate. Yet there are many heads who shrink from taking the one further step which would develop their own expertise in assessment into a systematic, continuous process, defending their resistance with the argument that as soon as it became systematic it would become 'inhuman', 'mechanistic', 'bureaucratic' or (in the case of staff) 'unprofessional' — according to whichever pejorative term they prefer. If, then, schools are to avoid the charge of shutting their eyes to the spotlight's blinding truth, and of preferring the comfortable twilight of their own inbred and indigenous methods of assessment, how are they to set about developing a more open and objective system? There are three major areas with which any school machinery of assessment must be concerned — children, staff and external relations. The rest of this chapter will be particularly concerned with the assessment of children: staff and external relations will be covered in subsequent chapters.

Having first established their objectives, in relation to the children, schools then have to ask themselves whether these objectives have been achieved. The difficulties and pitfalls are obvious. One such difficulty, for example, is that a single internal examination paper may be inadequate, in that it will only test some among the many objectives of teaching a particular subject (such as speed, accuracy, manipulative skill, reasoning power and the ability to collate and use data). In these circumstances, to set additional papers will not improve the value of the assessment, if they merely measure the same limited number of skills over again. If they are to be productive, further tests must measure the extent to which other teaching objectives have been attained. A comparable pitfall confronts schools which seek to recognise and to reward individual talent, in whatever sphere it reveals itself, but which then adopt the very common practice of labelling groups of children, while failing to realise that their assessment is self-fulfilling. There is now abundant research evidence to emphasise the appalling dangers of the labels which are attached to groups of children, since they catch on very quickly to the significance of these labels, and are content to accept them or to live down to them. Sometimes the consequences of rigid streaming, for example, have been shown to involve damaging assumptions by many children which may be wholly unjustified, and which have a motivating or a demotivating effect, far from the original intention of the school in deciding to adopt this pattern of organisation. Children who have been judged to be unsuccessful in one sphere of activity are often assumed to be (and therefore become) unsuccessful in other spheres as well. In the same way, undue emphasis on examination results quickly communicates itself to children, generating an inevitable distortion of values and a sense of failure in those for whom external examinations are irrelevant and inappropriate. Again, because external examinations inevitably tend to concentrate upon those aspects of a subject which can be readily examined and measured, teaching in the classroom often concentrates on those very same aspects, ignoring the critical survey of available evidence, the coordination of complex information and the capacity to improvise a spontaneous argument or to exercise judgement between alternative hypotheses. A head who frequently emphasises the importance of neatness, tidiness and punctuality, and concentrates exclusively upon the assessment of these qualities, can expect to develop a neat, tidy and punctual school but, in so doing, he will be in danger of obscuring qualities and characteristics which are of equal or greater importance. The danger, in fact, is that the methods of assessment which are employed may actually determine the objectives, so that the very instruments of assessment become masters instead of servants!

To safeguard against this danger the assessment of children must be both continuous and systematic; it must cover the full range of objectives and must consider all the evidence available. It must be concerned not only with every aspect of the life of the school, but with every individual child, identifying, understanding and supporting the quiet conformist, who causes no trouble and is never outstandingly successful but, equally, never in conflict with authority, with as much patient perseverance as is exercised in concern for the brilliant or the deviant. By far the most difficult objectives against which children are assessed are those concerned with social adjustment, temperament, personality and initiative. Here, assessments are inevitably subjective, but they are not to be decried or ignored as long as they are based upon sound professional experience. It is always necessary, however, to look carefully and objectively for evidence which supports, and also for evidence which tends to destroy, an impression. Hunches which remain totally unsupported by evidence should be regarded with great suspicion. The aim is to produce a balanced picture which will stand up to penetrating scrutiny. Schools must continually ask themselves not only what they think about each individual child, but why they think it: what aspects of his conduct or behaviour have been directly observed and have led to a conclusion. It is dangerous, for example, to make statements about a child's initiative, capacity for leadership, integrity, poise or powers of judgement without being able to quote instances and incidents in which those qualities have been tested or exercised; such circumstances should be observed and recorded, in order to build up a total assessment of qualities which by their very nature are difficult to quantify but which are, nevertheless, of supreme importance.

There is one sphere in which schools do not shrink even from quantitative assessment, for progress in the classroom is generally measured in familiar, rough and ready, quantitative terms. Five marks out of ten, 63 per cent, B+, pass, fail or distinction are all acceptable assessments, so long as there remains a healthy suspicion of all marks and grades and they are never thought of as having any absolute validity; but familiarity with such symbols and the confidence with which they are used, should, in themselves, provide a warning signal. A great deal of work has been done on the reliability and validity of examinations and on techniques of marking, and new kinds of tests and examination questions are being devised with the object of minimising the subjective element in the assessment of the answers. But it is probable that marks, grades, percentages and classification of degrees will remain in use in education for many years yet, and it is essential that the profession should arm itself against accepting them, or allowing others to accept them, as being related to any absolute standard. The award of a first-class degree, or of a grade in an examination, means no more and no less than that an examiner or a group of examiners, considering the work of a particular candidate in relation to a group of candidates in a particular subject at a particular time and in particular circumstances, considered that the quality of the candidate's work entitled him to a particular place in the order of merit in which all the candidates in that examination were placed on that occasion. There are dangers, too, in performing mathematical operations upon marks. Adding 'raw' marks together to produce a total, with a hard and fast line between success and failure, is extremely misleading because it ignores the varying contribution made to the total by sets of marks with different patterns of distribution between the maximum and the minimum. Doubling marks in certain subjects in an attempt to increase the significance of those subjects in the final total (which has sometimes been the practice) is also largely ineffective. Conversion of raw marks into 'standardised marks' (which relate all marks to the same mean and 'standard deviation') does enable them properly to be added together; but, even then, what needs to be remembered is that, however accurately these calculations are performed, they do not add one jot to the value or validity of the initial subjective judgements on which the original marks were based. Numbers can produce a dangerous illusion of precision!

For this reason many schools have now abandoned marks in favour of grades, often on a three- or five-point scale, which appear to offer greater security just because they do not pretend to achieve any precise mathematical accuracy. But it is easy to be deceived into assuming that grades have any greater objective validity. When a grade is awarded to a child, is he being rated in relation to his own performance or potential, or in relation to his contemporaries in his form or set, or in relation to his complete year group in the school, or in relation to his age group in the population as a whole, or in relation to some hypothetical absolute standard of attainment? Which of these criteria is adopted will make a world of difference to the particular grade awarded, and experience shows that those who award grades in schools are often as vague and uncertain about their significance as they are about the validity of marks. Subject teachers vary widely in the extent to which they are prepared to use the full range of marks or grades: it is possible, for example, to gain a mark of 95 per cent in mathematics or handicraft, while a top mark in English seldom exceeds 75 per cent or less: it is possible to be 12th in a form for mathematics with a mark of 65 per cent but 3rd in history with a mark of 49 per cent. With grades, too, those who award them are often diverted by the perfectly right and proper wish to encourage, to reward or to warn individuals; but in any of these circumstances the validity of the grade has been distorted, and when communicated to other people, it is highly likely to be misunderstood. For example, grades which are related to the standards of the group in which a child works, or which are deliberately designed to be encouraging, may well mislead parents when the time comes for their children to be measured against external criteria, such as those demanded by entrance for an external examination. Another difficulty, and one of particular significance, arises from the assessment of children who are working in groups of mixed ability. If their teaching is subject-based, then some subject specialists, with only two or three periods per week with each teaching group, may be involved in trying to assess as many as 300 individual children, without any norms of expectation such as apply when teaching groups are streamed. Moreover, in the assessment of children (and equally in the assessment of adults) they themselves should be closely involved in their own assessment. The more a pupil can take part in discussion with his teachers about the merits, weaknesses and potential of his work, the more likely he is to accept the judgements which he has been invited to share, and to be prepared to act upon the encouragement and criticism which are directed to his advantage. This is clearly in line with good teaching philosophy since, as a result of this process, the pupil is closely involved in his own learning.

There are, then, three natural steps which must follow every major stage in the assessment of an individual pupil. First, the teacher should review the teaching methods which he has adopted, in order to discover whether they can usefully be revised and reorientated, and so be made more effective. The pupil, for his part, should recognise errors and tendencies to be avoided in future, and changes in attitude or practice which would bring about an improvement in the quality of his work. Secondly, some record of the assessment must be made, on each occasion, in order that a cumulative inventory may become available. This record must take its place in the pupil's individual folder, which was discussed in Chapter 12. Thirdly, steps must be taken to communicate the assessment to those who are directly concerned, particularly the pupil's parents, the authorities of universities and colleges to which he may be seeking admission, or employers to whom he has applied for a post.

When a school is in a constructive relationship with parents, in an enterprise aimed at furthering the welfare and progress of individual children. then the periodic communication of the results of that continuous assessment will present far fewer difficulties than when they are enshrined in an occasional and portentous report. It is always necessary to decide just what parents are anxious to know and exactly what they ought to be told. Many parents are conditioned by their own school experience, and will believe that they understand the significance of marks and grades and of individual assessments, even though the terminology has changed. They are unlikely to know just what 'form', 'class', 'set' or 'group' mean in respect of their own children, and they will have little understanding of external examination procedures and grades, of the complexities of further and higher education or of the employment market. When the reports submitted to them are in a traditional form, with some details of marks, grades and positions, supported by verbal interpretation, they are likely to assume an understanding of the meaning of these symbols and comments which, in fact, they do not command. Sometimes, they will be puzzled or frustrated by language or jargon with which they are not familiar. There is still a temptation, in writing school reports, to substitute a witty or well-turned phrase for a down-to-earth explanation and such phrases often reveal themselves to the initiated as more of a report on the teacher concerned than on the pupil's progress. What is clearly necessary, and extremely difficult, is to put oneself in the position of each individual parent, and to devise a school report which will achieve its purpose very much in the same way as a personal letter. Indeed, some schools have begun to cast their reports in exactly this mould. For school record purposes full details are collated in standard form, but a housemaster (or whoever has final responsibility for an individual's report) interprets all the relevant information, and summarises it in the form of a simple letter, in terms appropriate to the parent concerned, varying from cogent academic prose to the simple directness of language employed by the popular press. This is clearly an exacting process; but if the object of reporting to parents is to tell them what they need to know (whether they are aware of the need or not), then such a letter is far more likely to be effective, and to be more productive of genuine collaboration, than a formal and traditional report which has to be interpreted, and leaves so much unsaid.

When traditional practice is to be followed, however, the standard form of school report, which has become something of a ritual, calls for drastic reconsideration. The little boxes, with narrow columns for the tabulation of marks or grades on each subject, leave room for an interpretative comment of not more than ten or a dozen words, thus putting a premium upon brevity rather than upon a helpful explanation. The significance of the marks or grades themselves is seldom explained in a way that is wholly intelligible to laymen, and there is often not the faintest suggestion that the school recognises or accepts any degree of responsibility. The school's only concern, it seems, is to report its assessment, and then blandly to assume that the pupil is wholly responsible. Often there is no invitation to parents to comment or to indicate how they think that they themselves, their son or daughter, or the school can do anything constructively and collectively to meet the situation, although it is becoming quite common for parents to be asked to acknowledge and, sometimes, to initial a report, before returning it to the school. Yet the purpose of a school report, apart from its contribution to the cumulative school records, is presumably to develop a conversation or dialogue between parents and school, so that all concerned may recognise the problems and be prepared to take such steps towards their solution as are available to each of them — school, pupil and parent. What the parent needs to know and the pupil to understand is whether, in the judgement of the school, Johnny is (or is not) developing according to his capacity and potential, how he is performing in relation to his peers and contemporaries, what forecasts can be made about his final school attainments, what steps the school is proposing to take to improve current performance, and how it is suggested that parents can help both Johnny and the school to achieve the objectives which they all have in mind.

A similar, although not precisely congruent, situation arises in the relationship between schools and prospective employers. Although the purpose of the communication is different, the principle still obtains: the employers should be told what they need to know as clearly and accurately as possible, in terms free from professional jargon, which they can readily understand. Because they share the bewilderment of parents over the significance of marks, grades and the detail of examination performance, or because they find it convenient to use the results of external examinations (designed for a quite different purpose) to produce a short-list from among their applicants, employers will sometimes demand qualifications or attainments which bear little relation to the demands of the vacancy which they are seeking to fill. At best this kind of misunderstanding can only be overcome by the establishment of trust and confidence on both sides. This confidence will be built upon a realisation, over the years, that the school's judgement can be relied upon. Experience will then have proved that the school's recommendation is concerned with a total assessment of the school leaver, and not merely with piecemeal evaluation of some isolated aspects of his school career.

18   Staff

Exactly the same principles apply to the assessment of staff as to the assessment of pupils: but, in practice, there is a major difference between these two processes. There are few, even among the most egalitarian, who would question the necessity for assessing the progress and development of individual pupils. Indeed, this responsibility is accepted as an inescapable and essential aspect of a school's responsibilities however much variation there may be in the ways in which it is accomplished. But when it comes to staff assessment there is a great deal of hesitation and suspicion. In fact, there are probably few such strictly professional issues on which there is a wider range of views, each of which is sustained by varying degrees of passionate conviction. Initially, such suspicions stem from the semi-autonomy of each individual school and the semi-independence of each individual teacher. The traditional philosophy which regards the head as *primus inter pares* (a philosophy which is much more relevant in the circumstances of today and tomorrow than it has ever been in the past) has developed an eccentric offshoot which suggests that any attempt at staff assessment is, at its best, strictly unprofessional, and, at its worst, is almost indecent and improper. Accusations of prying or snooping are frequently heard, and there is a fairly widely-held opinion that the teaching profession could get on perfectly well without any process or system of staff assessment at all. Let each teacher be his own judge and jury, and estimate his capacity, potential and performance entirely from within his own professional resources!

Such an attitude is wholly untenable. To begin with, however unpopular and difficult it is, staff assessment happens, and it happens continuously. Indeed, it is of the greatest possible concern to a great many teachers that it *should* happen, for it represents an essential stage in the process of career development or promotion. Every enquiry, testimonial or reference is dependent upon the fruits of

assessment, even if that assessment be of the sketchiest kind — off-the-cuff, spontaneous and occasional. Teachers would be monstrously aggrieved if heads were to refuse to answer an enquiry on their behalf or to provide a reference, on the grounds that they had no means of assessment. If, then, members of staff depend upon accurate and willing assessment, whenever it is to their advantage, however much they may dislike it in principle, surely it would be better for such assessment to be systematic, reliable and comprehensive, based upon direct evidence as well as upon subjective judgement, and giving full credit for strengths and assets, as well as acknowledging weaknesses or shortcomings?

Without doubt, the writing and interpretation of confidential staff references is an occupational hazard to which all heads are exposed. Moreover, common experience suggests that they are equally difficult to draft and to interpret. So let us begin our discussion of staff assessment, by looking at a typical confidential reference about Mr Buchanan, who is applying for promotion. Here is a letter from Mr Buchanan's headmaster, to the head of Woolley Comprehensive School. The latter has sought for further information about Mr Buchanan, who has applied for the post of second deputy head at Woolley.

Confidential   Copthall County Grammar School for Boys
Hayling Road
Copthall, Midborough

The Headmaster
Woolley County Comprehensive School
Overchester

Dear Headmaster,

Mr Alistair Buchanan

I am pleased to have the opportunity of supporting the application of Mr Alistair Buchanan for the post of second deputy head at your school.

Buchanan came here as head of the English department after eight years' service in two other grammar schools. He has given this school five years of devoted service. He teaches English throughout the school up to A- and S-level, and prepares candidates for university scholarships. Each year he has, of necessity, to omit one year-group from his own teaching programme but he rotates this omission so that he keeps in touch with all age groups as far as possible. He also assumes responsibility for the school library.

Buchanan is himself a sound scholar with a special interest in twentieth-century literature, and he communicates very effectively with all his classes, although he is most successful with the brightest boys. He keeps a firm control in the classroom, but has to work hard to interest those boys with less than an enthusiastic interest in literature.

Outside the classroom, Buchanan runs a well-supported debating society and, encouraged by him, one of his colleagues produces a lively school magazine. He is successful in welding together a closely-knit team in his department. In the common room he is well liked and forms easy personal relationships, although (apart from his skill as an opening bat in the staff cricket team) his interests are largely confined to his own subject. This comparative narrowness is my one reservation.

Buchanan is, in my view, ready for promotion and I think you will find him a strong candidate.

> Yours sincerely,
> *J. J. Jones*
> Headmaster

Now what does this letter tell us? Well, at first sight, very little. From initial impressions, it seems to be a rather inadequate and disappointing document (although it would be rash to dismiss it as either unrealistic or untypical). It certainly tells us far more about the writer than about the person on whose behalf it was written (and this is still commonly true of many school reports!). What it does tell us about Mr Buchanan has remarkably little relevance to the post for which Mr Buchanan has applied; and it never explains why Mr Buchanan's headmaster believes that Mr Buchanan is 'a strong candidate' for promotion to deputy head. On the face of it, it seems somehow unlikely that Mr Buchanan has seen the letter about him, or even knows of its content and general tenor. Indeed, we have a vague feeling that Mr Jones has fumbled through his headmasterly memories and impressions of Mr Buchanan, searching (in vain) for any relevant evidence. And so we become uneasy about the head's judgements, and we have an uncomfortable suspicion that an element of sheer chance has entered into the development of Mr Buchanan's career, just at the very moment when (so we feel in our bones) his application for promotion ought to have been supported by incontrovertible evidence. On the other hand, what light does the letter throw upon the admitted fact that heads find the drafting and interpretation of confidential references so difficult? Perhaps it may be illuminating to probe a little deeper.

First, there is undoubtedly an air of secrecy or semi-secrecy about such references which is professionally unhealthy. What, for example, does 'confidential' mean? Does it mean that these references are to be used in confidence, only at the point of final decision, and only then in the hands of heads or administrators using their professional discretion? If so, the proviso doesn't operate effectively, for copies of such references are often laid on the table for the selection committee, or even circulated in advance to all members of that committee. Alternatively, perhaps 'confidential' simply means that the subject of the reference has been kept in blissful ignorance of what is said about him, either in advance or in retrospect. In that case, perhaps, 'confidential' is really implying in effect: 'It's quite safe. I can speak frankly, because this chap doesn't know, and will never know, what I have said about him'. In our experience, in far too many cases, 'confidential' seems to mean just that, and we find this extremely disturbing. Or, from another angle, is 'confidential' simply intended to lull the recipient into a frame of mind in which he will amiably believe that the reference tells the truth about the applicant, the whole truth, and nothing but the truth? Again, if that is the real purpose of 'confidential', it fails miserably, for even the most gullible head immediately begins to ask awkward questions, to probe for the meaning hidden between the lines, and to search for the real message of the reference, behind its bland, and almost meaningless, façade.

Secondly, are staff references difficult to write just because they are inevitably based on subjective judgements, which are qualitative and intuitive in character, and have only a modicum of hard evidence to support them? In other words, does our anxiety arise from the fact that (as so often with our pupils) we only act in a stress or crisis situation, collecting and collating the information, upon which a staff reference depends, only at moments of critical importance, when success or failure, promotion or disappointment, are at stake? If so, it is hardly surprising that heads find themselves dependent upon scattered impressions, and hurried judgements, rather than upon sustained and valid evidence.

Thirdly (and it would be wholly unrealistic to obscure this aspect of confidential references), we have to recognise that if such a reference were to be completely objective and truthful, then one of two things would tend to happen. Perhaps a most valuable member of the staff would be 'lost', at a particularly awkward moment in the school year, thereby creating a vacancy which it would be very difficult to fill in the time available. Alternatively, a master, who had long outstayed his welcome in the common room, might fail to obtain another post elsewhere, at the very moment when his colleagues were preparing to celebrate his departure. In either event, would this knowledge make the writer pause, and persuade him to add a touch either of fantasy or ambiguity to his reference, or even a vivid splash of whitewash, so as to insure himself against both risks? There can be few practising heads who would dare to claim that they have never been confronted by such a temptation, and who would dismiss the very idea as a cynical attack upon their professional probity, deserving only of righteous scorn and full-blooded condemnation.

Fourthly, anyone who has had much experience of drafting references would freely admit that they are often extraordinarily difficult to compose. In these circumstances, it is only too easy to rely upon pleasant but innocuous and high-sounding phrases, which do not mean very much. Or we fall back upon concocting a piece of impressive and balanced prose, which sounds weighty and authoritative, but which does not even attempt a cogent assessment of the candidate for the particular post for which he has applied (and that is almost always exactly what the enquiry has asked us to do).

Finally, whatever the precise reasons for the difficulty which each individual writer of references experiences, there can be no doubt at all about the fact that these references are very seldom accepted at their face value. Those who receive and interpret them seldom regard them with the respect and reverence which their authors intended. Not so long ago the distinguished head of a well-known comprehensive school said, at a conference of secondary heads: 'Many of the references which I receive do not seem to relate to *real* people at all'. At the receiving end, then, despite all the concern and care lavished upon them at the production end, they are seldom regarded as wholly objective, and are often lightly dismissed as valiant attempts to dress up nondescript geese as elegant swans. And then what happens? Well, there can be no argument about that, for the recipient generally rings up the writer, to find out what he left *un*said, and to secure an accurate interpretation of the message which he intended to convey. So, in a few brief sentences over the telephone, the original reference is down-graded to a document of little importance. What now matters, in these circumstances, is a telephone conversation, unprepared, unscripted and unrecorded at either end. In this way, whatever the intention, a strong element of mystery and secrecy has been introduced into the process, so that an appointment may well be made on the basis of an impromptu, off-the-cuff telephone chat, rather than upon a carefully-prepared assessment and considered judgement. Is it surprising, then, that within the profession there is so much misgiving and cynicism about the way in which confidential references operate, and so little trust in the whole business of staff assessment, upon which such references depend? Has the time come when all the professional associations should get together, in order to hammer out (and it would take some hammering!) a realistic and acceptable code of practice?

Before we go any further, let us assume for the moment that we are just setting out on our professional careers, and try to identify the hopes and aspirations which would then be uppermost in our minds. To begin with, it is probable that we should stress the importance of a sense of security, and a feeling of belonging. This would involve having a clear picture of what we were expected to do, for whom and by when, and a knowledge of all the resources and aids which were at our disposal. Then we should want to be sure that we could rely, all the time, on the professional sympathy, understanding and support of our colleagues on the staff. We should want to be able to chat to other beginners about our difficulties, and even to share those difficulties with more experienced members of the common-room, without shame or embarrassment. We should welcome supervision and guidance from whoever was directly responsible for our work (whether head of department, head of house or year, or other senior member of the staff). We should confidently depend upon his advice just because it was based on a sustained and continuous interest in our progress, including the overcoming of our weaknesses, and the development of our teaching techniques. Beyond that, we should look for a general feeling in the staff room of professional responsibility, in which all shared, and to which all contributed. We should hope that arrangements would be made for us to visit other schools, as part of our professional training, we should expect to be encouraged to read and to discuss significant books and articles, and we should rely on being given facilities for attending in-service courses and conferences. On our return to school, we should then like to think that our colleagues would be eager to discover what we had learned, and to share with us the elucidation, testing and development of any new ideas or methods which we had picked up. Finally, we should expect all members of staff to be embarrassed by, and to accept a measure of responsibility for, any individual contribution to the school's total teaching expertise which fell below an acceptable standard, just as they would expect to rejoice and share in every individual teaching success.

Further, in addition to security, we should assuredly look for appreciation and encouragement. This would, of course, include not only congratulations when we had done well, but constructive help and criticism designed to identify our shortcomings and so enable us to do better. We all need encouragement, both for its emotional satisfaction and for its professional fulfilment. We need it in order to acquire a sense of achievement, and to develop a confidence in our own powers of self-assessment. This would enable us to monitor not only our general progress and development, but also the particular degree of mastery which we had attained in the craft of teaching. We need it, too, most emphatically, to stimulate and motivate us, to keep the pump of our enthusiasm working at full pressure and to generate, deep down inside us, a sense of professional commitment, and the prospect of appropriate reward.

Yes, we shall certainly and most reasonably look for reward. But, beyond a modest competence to enable us to maintain professional, personal and family standards, purely financial reward, as such, is likely to come fairly low in our order of priorities and motivating factors. For most of us, our reward means the assumption of greater responsibility, the opportunity to exercise greater initiative and independence, to assume greater authority and to stretch our professional wings. We need to justify ourselves to ourselves, and to develop a sense of service which, however derided, is still deeply rooted in British character and professional tradition. In other words, we should look for the fulfilment of our aspirations through promotion.

But how can that promotion be achieved? A tiny minority seem to manage it unaided, and to fall on their feet almost spontaneously. Most of us, however, need to find ourselves with the right qualifications and experience, in the right place and at the right time. For this we need continuous expert guidance and advice. We need a determination, on our own part, to fulfil ourselves and, on the part of others, especially our head, a willingness to evaluate our achievements and progress, to broaden our experience, to indicate possible avenues of career development, and to ensure that we are encouraged to apply for the right post at the right time, with the promise of a confidential reference which will do us full justice, without equivocation or ambiguity.

So we find ourselves confronted, once more, by the importance of references, and we wonder why our early hopes and expectations are later so often constrained by deep-seated professional doubts and fears. Over the years, for some reason, it has become part of the mythology in staff common-rooms that assessment is always assumed to be fundamentally critical and destructive in character; perhaps this is yet another result of attempting to maintain a status of individual professional independence, suggesting that once assessment is accepted, faults are much more likely to be apparent than achievements to be recognised. Yet if there is one aspect of assessment more than any other of which all teachers stand in dire need it is the factor of encouragement. The price of professional isolation is often professional loneliness and one of us knows, from long experience as an external assessor, how disconcertingly frequent it was for a word of encouragement and appreciation to be followed by surprise and amazement expressed in some such terms as these: 'Thank you very much. That is the first time in five (or ten or twenty) years that anyone has ever expressed approval of my work!'. Such reactions are every bit as common from heads as from teachers of all ages and experience, emphasising the fact that appreciation, encouragement and approval are among the scarcest but most powerful motivating factors, while their absence can easily induce a sense of uncertainty, frustration or neglect. There is no more effective way to build a career than to build from strength, and a recognition of strengths and positive qualities is a fundamental characteristic of successful assessment. Praise and encouragement are, in fact, every bit as important for teachers as they are for pupils.

Another reason why assessment is important is that, at the other end of the spectrum, the revelation of weaknesses or the sharing of problems can lead to positive and creative action. In other words, effective assessment must take place in an atmosphere which predisposes a willingness to accept constructive criticism and to entertain advice, and it must always be followed by appropriate action. As we saw with the assessment of pupils, the cooperation of the assessed is essential to the process of assessment: but in order that it may become a cooperative enterprise, assessors (whether they be internal or external to the school) must approach their task in such a way as to secure for themselves an atmosphere of welcome and receptivity. For only in such a mood of mutual trust and confidence can discussion be genuinely free from antagonism and be directed to maximum advantage. Here is another instance in which education may have something to learn from industrial and commercial practice. The concept of 'management by objectives' implies that the job to be done and the targets to be aimed at are agreed between employer and employee. Subsequent performance can then be examined and discussed, so that targets or methods, or both, may be reviewed and new objectives set. Now, it is not suggested, for one moment, that a teacher's objectives can be set in anything like the same mould as those for a worker on a production line, a sales representative or a shop assistant. But positive advantage must surely follow in any teaching situation, or any post which combines teaching with administration, from joint examination of what is being attempted and how far it is being achieved. By this means every member of the staff can be encouraged to define and seek to attain his full potential, with benefit both to himself and to the school in which he serves.

Yet another reason for developing a deliberate policy of assessment is that it provides a means of checking and validating selection and appointment techniques. Without some such systematic check it is impossible to discover whether qualities and capacities presumed to be detected at interview have been subsequently revealed in practice, or to identify weaknesses in selection procedures. In an earlier chapter the importance of retaining interview notes was stressed and it can now be seen how significant a part notes can play in the validation of appointment procedures. It is a curious characteristic of the education service that it expends so much money and time upon advertising and selection procedures, but seldom invests anything like the same degree of concern in investigations which would reveal whether these procedures have justified themselves in practice, or need to be revised and improved.

So far, in this chapter, the case has been argued for a positive staff assessment programme, which would embrace all members of the teaching staff (and would apply, with equal validity, to secretarial, administrative and ancillary staff as well). The next step must be to discuss how such a programme can be instituted and sustained. But before embarking upon a consideration of the practical issues involved, there is an interesting paradox which deserves some consideration. This suggests that it is the duty of a successful head to encourage maximum turnover of his staff. This proposition will seem, at first sight, to be in violent conflict with the attainment of stability and security in staff common-rooms, and will fill with dismay and unbelief those heads who are already wrestling with an unprecedented annual turnover of staff. Nevertheless, there is a truth in the paradox which should not be overlooked. If the potential capacity of every member of the staff is regularly reviewed, it will often happen that additional opportunity, training or experience is required, in order that the next stage in fulfilling that potential can be achieved. Very often, of course, those opportunities can be found by providing extended responsibilities within the same school. Although movement from one school to another, for minor promotions, may not be as common in future as it has been in the past, nevertheless it is sometimes bound to happen that an appropriate enlargement of experience can be attained only by transfer or promotion elsewhere. This has always been recognised by most heads, even if they would hesitate to frame their belief in terms quite as disturbingly realistic as those which are now being considered. But it may be salutary to remember that the interests of the education service as a whole, as much as those of individual members may best be served by strategic movement from one school to another. We ourselves deplore the tendency which has grown within recent years for number two in the hierarchy to succeed number one (whether in schools, colleges or administration): despite many successful illustrations to the contrary, we believe that the appointment of heads, principals, and senior administrators should be made from outside rather than by internal promotion.

Having considered staff assessment from the angle of 'whether?' and 'why?', it is now appropriate to turn to the question 'how?', and its corollaries. From the outset it must be apparent that, if assessment of staff is to be acceptable, it must be systematic, continuous and carefully planned. Occasional, haphazard or spasmodic assessment is bound to arouse uncertainty and antagonism, and to give rise to emotions of doubt and insecurity. If there are frequent exceptions to the general rule, or if assessment is confined to the few or to a minority, then it will assume an unhealthy character, and be presumed to be for purely personal and prejudicial reasons. Any process of assessment which gives rise to the question 'Why me?' or 'Why now?' is to be condemned as a failure. A casual, or occasional, visit to a classroom, laboratory or workshop by the head or a head of department is bound to assume a portentous significance, and will appear to be designed for a specific and particular purpose; but regular visits will come to be accepted by the staff as normal procedures as they will by the children, whose curiosity will not be aroused and whose sense of loyalty will not be strained. At this stage, however, it must be recognised that the very idea of classroom visits by the head, or by anyone else, would be regarded as anathema in many schools, both by heads and by their colleagues, and would be labelled as unwarranted interference in the professional relationship between teacher and pupils. Many heads and heads of departments, regard the ideas here put forward, as the philosophy of the devil, undermining professional integrity, and developing feelings of insecurity and resentment far outweighing any possible advantages to which such a system might give rise. Only a few years ago, at a conference of secondary heads, the head of a large school, with a common-room of about a hundred members, declared with conviction that he could write a testimonial or reference for any one of them, off-the-cuff, as occasion arose, without hearing them teach, but solely on the evidence which he collected on his frequent journeys about the school; and, since he was a very experienced and devoted head, his confidence cannot be dismissed with contumely.

Is there, in fact, any alternative way of achieving the same result without using methods which are, to many, unacceptable? Without assuming for a moment that a colleague's contribution to the school is confined to the classroom, it cannot be denied that a teacher's prime duty is to teach. Are there, then, any ways of satisfactorily assessing teaching capacity which do not involve direct observation in the classroom? Pupils' work can be seen regularly, for example, and this will reveal a good deal about the way in which they have been taught. Internal tests and examinations will furnish some additional evidence, reinforced by the teacher's own comments and assessments on school reports. The pattern of pupil choice in the middle school, and in the sixth form, will tell something about the comparative popularity of particular subjects, although it will always be tempered by pupil realism in recognising that even a subject currently unpopular may be necessary for their own course pattern. External examination results, which are assessed in the light of all the circumstances, will add to the stock of first-hand evidence, particularly over an extended period; in addition, pupils will chatter naturally about their subject likes and dislikes and will hint obliquely at teacher strengths and weaknesses, while parents will sometimes discuss the work of a particular teacher in its impact upon their own son or daughter. Even an occasional visit to a classroom, ostensibly with a message or an enquiry, will furnish some evidence about discipline and class control, and passing impressions from a walk along a corridor will at least establish whether there is silence or noise. But silence itself is a measure of nothing except the degree of silence. It may indicate an atmosphere of concentration, in which all are working methodically and enthusiastically; but it may equally mean only that nothing whatever is happening except that teacher and class have come to a mutual understanding that they will not disturb each other! Noise, too, can be disruptive and uncontrolled, or it may indicate a purposeful and busy activity which is wholly acceptable. None of these factors, whether taken in isolation or in concert, would furnish sufficient first-hand, reliable evidence on which to form a judgement about a teacher's competence and skill. Far too many of the intangible, qualitative characteristics of a skilled, resourceful and imaginative teacher would remain unrevealed, even if all these methods were systematically employed.

Moreover, the pastoral care of staff (which is just as much an integral part of the philosophy of pastoral care as that which is so much more generally recognised, the care of individual children) involves a concern for a teacher's total contribution to the life of the school. A significant addition to his skill as a teacher is his membership of the school community: the impact of his personal enthusiasms and interests on the playing field, in the choral society or orchestra, or in one or more of the many school activities which take place outside the classroom; his membership of the common-room and his part in committee and in debate and discussion; the quality of attitudes and relationships which he engenders among his colleagues as well as with pupils and parents; his intellectual and professional awareness and sensitivity, together with the range and depth of his vocation as a schoolmaster — these are all crucial factors to be included in any total reckoning. But, since these are largely intangible and immeasurable, does it mean that full-blooded assessment of a colleague must be abandoned as unattainable, and that schools must rely on the bits and pieces which emerge from casual contact and haphazard impression? Heads and their colleagues would find this a very negative and unsatisfying philosophy: teachers would develop a deep sense of grievance and frustration if it were admitted that testimonials and references could only be based upon half-truths and upon partial evidence. For this reason, there is no escape from assessment in depth, wherever such assessment is possible, and this must clearly include classroom performance; indeed in discussing delegated responsibility in chapter 11 it was emphasised that such responsibilities must include assessment of all those included in the area of delegation, whether it be house, year or subject department.

The basic question, therefore, is one not of strategy but of tactics. Clearly, if a school has been unused to such procedures, it would be the utmost folly to launch it upon the common-room by assault. Probationary teachers, who are familiar with tutorial assessment of classroom performance, will happily accept its continuance in the school situation, if approached in the right way. If the head himself teaches, he should invite the head of the subject department concerned to visit and to share his lessons; in the same way the head and his most senior colleagues should establish the practice of visiting each other's lessons; one or more heads of department willing to experiment, by visiting the lessons of their colleagues, should be encouraged to do so; the impact of team teaching will encourage a sense of cooperation and support, and break down the loneliness and isolation which is at the root of all suspicion and fear; and the whole problem of staff assessment should be the subject of discussion and ventilation in the common-room. The purpose of such moves should be to secure general acceptance of the philosophy, and willing participation in the practice; but a very great deal will depend upon the extent to which classroom visits, by whomever they are undertaken, are friendly in intent, easy in relationship, purposeful and constructive in subsequent discussion. Once adverse criticism is seen not to be their primary objective, but they have been accepted as a mutual sharing of knowledge, experience and techniques, to the advantage of individuals and to the enrichment of the staff's stock of professional expertise, then the battle is more than half won. All that is then necessary is to ensure their frequency and regularity so that they are seen as perfectly normal and routine occasions, applicable to all, and in the interests of all (both as individuals and as members of a professional community). They should, of course, invariably be arranged in advance, and the more a visit can be seen as a cooperative venture the better, with visitor and teacher sharing in the lesson together; moreover they must invariably be followed by some discussion, however brief, about the content, methodology and success of the lesson, such discussion always being based on constructive use of the first-hand evidence which the lesson afforded.

There are still three further problems to be faced. The first concerns records. Even among heads who recognise the need for a process of systematic assessment there is often an intense dislike of recording impressions and conclusions in writing. The suggestion is made that this introduces an element of secrecy, and implies an organisation of confidential 'police' files. But human memory is so fallible and so selective in its operation that, particularly in large schools, it would be sheer folly to rely upon hit-or-miss recall when evidence is required for a specific purpose. Nor can the theory be sustained that no head should keep an individual record on each member of his staff; indeed he would be wholly failing in his duty to his colleagues, himself and his Authority if he did not do so. The only unresolved question, therefore, is what should go into that record and how it should be maintained. Our own belief is that it should be continuous, detailed and cumulative. If the practice of using a school memo pad for recording a brief summary of conversations with parents or individual children, or of incidents, developments and circumstances affecting them, were also to be applied to staff, then this would be seen to be a perfectly normal part of the school's record system. Such notes would often be of the briefest kind, perhaps only a sentence or two in many cases, but they would make sure that relevant evidence or judgement was not overlooked when the time came for a sustained assessment of an individual's career development. Moreover, it should be a fundamental principle of operation that such records should not be furtive and should contain no surprises; in other words no note or comment should be placed on record, the significance of which is not already known to the individual concerned, and has not already been discussed with him, whether the note refers to a particular lesson or to a specific incident or stage in his career.

To take this principle a stage further, it should also apply to testimonials and references. Such documents should contain nothing which is not already known to the colleague about whom they are written. The practice of revealing in confidential references either a qualitative judgement or a personal opinion of which the applicant is unaware is wholly to be deplored. This leads to the conclusion, of course, that if a colleague wishes to apply for a post for which his head considers that he is either unsuitable or unready, then, before drafting his reference, the head must make his standpoint clear to the applicant, and must indicate that, while he will do his best to be as fair and positive as possible, he will not quibble or haver on the basic issue. For, unless the integrity of references can be preserved, the profession as a whole will suffer. The truth, the whole truth and nothing but the truth is as important in a professional reference as it is in a court of law: the successful head in this respect is he whose judgement is respected by those who rely upon it and who, at the same time, carries with him the confidence of all his colleagues, because they know that he will not be deterred either by embarrassment or fear from stating the whole truth as he sees it, without expecting others to fill in the gaps or to interpret hints and suggestions which he has deliberately left vague and imprecise. Heads are as fallible as other mortals and are as liable as anyone else to errors of judgement. It is important, therefore, that they should be sure of their evidence, and should not pretend to certainty which they cannot sustain. There will be occasions, of course, when clashes will occur with individuals; but if the head has constantly discussed their progress with his colleagues over the years — their strengths, responsibilities, enthusiasms and achievements, as well as their shortcomings — then there should be no room for disagreement on facts, although there may still be opportunity for differences of interpretation. This may seem a harsh and unbending doctrine, almost impossible of fulfilment, but the health of the education service depends upon implicit confidence in the integrity of such professional documents.

The second problem relates to the factor of external assessment. It is to be hoped that the recent reorganisation of local government will bring about a dramatic improvement in the size and quality of LEA inspectorial and advisory staffs, so that the best current practice will be accepted as a standard by all. It is unlikely, however, that a situation will ever again arise in which every individual school can expect to receive an external inspection at regular intervals. Such a task is now certainly beyond the numerical strength of HM Inspectorate, although there are some signs of a renewal of faith in the value of external and independent assessment of schools. Henceforward, visits by HMI or by LEA inspectors and consultants are likely to be irregular in their frequency, often to be concerned with particular subjects or aspects of a school, rather than with the school as a whole, and to affect individual members of staff or groups of members, rather than the staff as a body. If this forecast is correct, this new pattern will impose considerable strain both upon those who visit, and upon those who are visited. It will be difficult to achieve a sense of normality or habitual practice in such circumstances, and the more infrequent the visitation the more likely it is to give rise to feelings of tension, anxiety, and disquiet. The days of regular inspection of every school, as practised until the early 1960s, are certainly over; it is now, therefore, of crucial importance that the teaching profession should make up its mind about the advisory services which it needs, so that schools can guarantee to provide that atmosphere of trust and confidence in which, alone, external assessment and advice can operate successfully, without causing friction or arousing opposition.

The third and final aspect of the assessment of staff concerns the heads themselves. In the context of the writing of references it has been suggested that heads are fallible, and so they are in other ways, too. They are charged with the task of securing the attainment of certain agreed objectives, and they carry the burden of decision-making and of offering guidance over a wide field of knowledge and expertise. Quite clearly, they too will have their particular strengths and weaknesses and they are unlikely to be equally strong, equally sound or equally successful over the whole range of their activities. It is therefore, necessary for the head to carry out a close and systematic scrutiny of his performance. Internally, he must be prepared deliberately to look for and to welcome comments and criticisms from his colleagues and his pupils. Although straight questions may not produce frank answers, it is possible to talk to colleagues about their jobs, and to children about their progress, in such a way as to discover what they believe to be their frustrations and their advantages. The head must then decide to what extent he is responsible for creating the conditions in which the frustrations are being felt and in what ways he can change the circumstances in order to improve the situation. He must also look at himself, not in a morbidly introspective or neurotic way, but coolly, honestly and as objectively as possible. Reference has been made in Chapter 14 to the necessity for the head to look closely at how he is using his own time, and there is no doubt that a carefully-kept diary, or a pause for five minutes at the end of a day to look back on what has been done, can produce some disquieting reflections. He is concerned not only with the distribution of his activities over the time available, but also with the question of how effectively those activities are being carried out. A frequent review of targets and an assessment of the extent to which they have been attained is essential at school or at home, in quiet and calm retrospect. Moreover, external assessment is available for the head if he chooses to invite it, shows that he welcomes it, and that he genuinely regards it as a natural and acceptable process. Governors, parents, former pupils, administrators, advisers, inspectors, local employers and members of the local community all have a viewpoint which the head should ascertain.

This whole question of a school's external relationships is so important that it will be considered in the next chapter. So let us close this discussion of staff development and assessment with a brief summary of the principles upon which it must operate, if it is to be established as a normal part of the routine life of a school.

Ten principles upon which successful staff development and assessment must be based:

1 It must be universal and apply to all: there can be no exceptions, no favouritism, no victimisation, and it must involve no secrets, surprises or comparisons. The crucial factors are integrity and intent.

2 It must be systematic, normal and continuous. It must take place openly, 'on the job', on the basis of agreed procedures, and must be diagnostic as well as corroborative.

3 It must be a cooperative enterprise, involving trust and confidence. It must always include consultation between assessor and assessed before any final conclusions are reached.

4 It must embrace all aspects of a teacher's career and performance, including his teaching capacity, and take account of his full potential. *All* the evidence must be collected, sifted, assessed *and agreed between assessor and assessed.*

5 When conclusions have been agreed, then appropriate action must always follow (such as the acquisition of additional knowledge, qualifications or experience, the elimination of weaknesses or shortcomings, the assumption of new responsibilities, and the acceptance of new career targets and objectives).

6 These principles must be followed by middle managers in the exercise of their delegated responsibilities for the assessment of the colleagues under their control.

7 Staff development and assessment must start from strength, develop naturally, and take advantage of every opportunity for securing unspectacular success.

8 It must be cumulative, and must maintain continuous

records. For example, 90 per cent of the information, evidence and qualitative judgements, which are required for drafting a reference, should be available in a teacher's file at any one time, leaving only 10 per cent to be collected, collated and assessed when a detailed and comprehensive assessment is required for the purposes of career development.

9 Advantage must be taken of every source of assessment, whether internal or external. Heads, and their most senior colleagues, must be seen to be taking particular trouble over their assessment of themselves.

10 Any effective system of staff development and assessment must furnish answers to the following seven questions, and the answers must be acceptable in the common room.

Whether?
Why?
How often?
By whom?
On whom?
For whom?
Then what?

19   External relations

The part played by a school in a child's life and development is not
capable of exact definition, and is subject to infinite individual variation. The impact of the school, compared with the influences of
home, environment, social pressures and peer groups, is a matter of
some uncertainty and controversy. This is not surprising, considering that these factors are complex and are closely interwoven; the precise balance of influence is bound to vary from child to child, from
family to family and from school to school, while the total situation
undoubtedly varies from generation to generation. Not so very long
ago it was the accepted philosophy and practice, both of parents and
of schools, that children should be virtually handed over to the school,
where they would be educated by schoolmasters, who were almost in
a position of unchallenged authority, and were free to prescribe not
only academic patterns and courses, but dress and conduct and even
social attitudes, standards and values. Nowadays, however, research
has clearly demonstrated that the earliest years in a child's development are of paramount importance (which ought to involve secondary schools in a process of fundamental reassessment!), that the
influences of home and environment play a crucial and often a pre-
dominant part in a child's education, and that the impact of the school
will be effective only to the extent that the child is seen by the school,
not only as a pupil, but as a member of a family, of a peer group, and
of a community, including the community of the school. It follows
that no single factor in this process of interaction can make its full
contribution in isolation; all must be aware of and responsive to what
the others are doing and are planning to achieve. For the threads
which make up the fabric of a child's experience of learning and growing are very closely interlinked, and cannot easily be disentangled. So
it is important that, for the sake of its children (and for many other

cogent reasons) a school should be sensitively aware of, and involved with, the world outside its walls.

There are two main aspects of this awareness and concern which must be considered but they, too, are difficult to separate from each other, so clearly do they dovetail and intertwine. First, a school should make the maximum use of all its external relationships in order to furnish additional evidence for an assessment of its own progress, achievements and shortcomings. Secondly, it is important that careful consideration should always be given to the presentation and explanation of the school's own philosophy and practice to those individuals, bodies and institutions who are, as of right, interested in and concerned for the school and its children. These include parents, governors, the local authority, other schools, colleges, universities, employers, the welfare agencies and examining bodies, together with press, radio and television. In what follows, these groups and institutions will be discussed in the context of their relationship with the school; it must be remembered, however, that there are other external relationships, and that any local community also includes the police, and the courts, in addition to a very large number of churches and clubs, societies and organisations, both religious and secular, which are too numerous to be mentioned here, but with all of which the school is concerned, directly or indirectly.

Looking, first, at the children themselves, in relation to their world outside, every school will be anxious to obtain some information about its pupils after they have left. This information will cover not only their progress at college or university, or in employment but, most particularly, it will indicate the kind of men and women they have become: it will be concerned with the quality of relationships which they have established, their maturity and stability, their range of interests and leisure pursuits, their beliefs and values and convictions. Such information, however, cannot be assembled regularly or systematically. It will arise, rather by accident than by design, from informal conversations and casual contacts; but schools will cherish any such evidence which they are able to collect about the welfare of former pupils, as a means of measuring the extent of their own success or failure. Happily, in other directions, such as choice of career, important evidence about the degree of success which the school is achieving can be gained from a systematic review of the information available in the records of the school's careers advisory service. How many children leave school as soon as they are entitled by law to do so, and how many of them were, in the school's judgement, mistaken in that decision because it was taken contrary to advice and persuasion? Such data, seen against the school's background of geography, community attitudes and job opportunities, will throw some light upon the effectiveness of the school's curriculum, syllabuses and teaching methods, upon the extent to which the children's interest has been aroused and upon the degree to which they have become willingly involved in their own intellectual, educational and social development. For many children it will be appropriate that they should go on to some form of full-time higher or further education, and the numbers who do so will provide a measure of the school's success in meeting external requirements, and in fulfilling its obligation to develop the full potential of its pupils. For many others, of course, immediate employment, combined with apprenticeships and part-time further education, will constitute a proper choice. The extent of the demand for such careers will be a measure of the school's success in arousing intellectual interest and excitement, combined with vocational purpose, and in generating faith in the development of individual capacities, even at the cost of postponing social and financial independence. The nature of the first appointments obtained by school leavers, the school's standing with employers and the ease with which children are placed in jobs, will all reveal a good deal about the school's success in achieving its objectives and, incidentally, about the effectiveness of the careers service which it offers from its own resources and in collaboration with the local authority's careers advisory service. The extent to which former pupils are happy in their jobs, whether there is a reasonable match between the chosen career and their capacity, and how rapid is the turnover between one job and another, will also offer corroborative evidence.

It is certainly well worth while making an effort to collect such evidence, though it may be difficult to devise a regular system for keeping in touch with former pupils. A good deal of random feed-back is generally available to schools, but it is inclined to be haphazard and incidental. Employers who are pleased with former pupils will often telephone to ask if another suitable candidate can be found for a similar vacancy; but this, too, is fortuitous, because it is far less com-

mon for schools to receive from employers positive indications of
failure when things have gone wrong. Nevertheless, whenever former
pupils visit their school, a wise head will take the opportunity to probe
their reactions to their job, or to their college or university life, particularly in relation to the preparation and training which they
received at school. Did they know what to expect; was the advice
they were offered relevant and useful; were they given adequate
training in learning to work independently, to stand on their own
feet, and to meet the demands imposed upon them in these new situations? All of these questions, and many others of a similar nature, will
elicit home truths from young men and women who will have shed
many of their inhibitions about talking to their head. But it must
still be recognised that those who come back to school and talk
freely about themselves, in this way, are likely to be a biased sample,
in statistical terms.

It might be possible to put such a casual and continuous review
on a more reliable basis by asking the school's careers service to undertake an occasional systematic enquiry, through a questionnaire sent
to a sample of former pupils, the sample being based upon sound statistical techniques; but such a procedure would encounter many difficulties, not the least among them being that it would be expensive,
and would require a good deal of clerical support. Perhaps the most
that can be said, with any confidence, is that schools should make
the maximum use of every shred of evidence which can be obtained,
whether from former pupils themselves, or from employers, colleges
and universities.

In the relationship between schools and parents the basic aim must
be to achieve genuine two-way communication. There is, first, an
obligation upon the school to explain to them its aims, philosophy
and methods, and to seek their advice when major changes of policy
or practice are under discussion. But secondly, the school must use
its best endeavours to stimulate and encourage parental response and
initiative, in order to establish a genuine working partnership; this
will involve the deliberate encouragement of parental assessment,
particularly of their own children's work and progress but also, more
widely, of the school's successes and failures. By such means as these
the school, which is at the centre of an intricate web of family and community relationships, can become the main agent in the synthesis of

all the influences which bear upon the children; but such a process depends upon genuine involvement, and will not be achieved by superficial lip service to the idea of collaboration. This process of involvement should begin with consultation about the establishment of aims and objectives, as was discussed in Chapters 5 and 6, in order to attain effective parental identification with the school's philosophy and policies. Such an identification will not be easy to achieve, however, because parents generally fall into a number of fairly clearly-defined categories. The first group consists of those parents who are deeply concerned for their children's welfare and progress, and who are also sufficiently poised and articulate to join in a dialogue with the school, and to take part in its corporate activities. With this group the two-way process of communication, consultation and assessment is likely to be pretty straightforward. In the second, much smaller, group will be those parents who are less actively concerned for their children's development, and are content to leave major decisions to the school and to the children themselves. The third group is likely to contain parents who, despite their deep and genuine concern, are prepared to leave decisions to the school, either through intellectual and professional discipline, or because they are traditionally moulded into believing that the school knows best, or because they are acutely aware of their own lack of knowledge and understanding of educational jargon, and are not only inarticulate but are genuinely scared of headmasters. There may sometimes be a small, fourth, group of parents who are themselves anti-establishment, and who visit the school only to ventilate and support their children's complaints. The second, third and fourth of these categories will demand a deliberate and energetic effort from the school, if genuine communication is to be established. Invitations to these parents to visit the school will have to be carefully, often individually, worded and they may have to be personally delivered. When all else fails the school must be prepared to visit them, so that discussion can take place on their home ground, and on more equal terms. The problem of getting from many parents any assessment containing even a hint of adverse criticism of the school is enormously difficult, but it is worth a great deal of effort to obtain; it will often have to be achieved orally, rather than in writing because the formality of written communications and questionnaires will be least effective with many such parents. There is, unfortunately, no magic measuring stick by which the school's success in achieving collaborative communication can be assessed. Nor will it normally be possible ever to know the full story of parental assessment of the school. Recognition of the need for such assessment, on the part of the head and all his colleagues, is a major step towards achieving it, however; thereafter, it is a matter of looking constantly and patiently for pointers and indicators, whenever and however they occur. School reports offer an excellent illustration of the difficulties. Even when parents are invited to comment upon their children's reports, only a minority (consisting, mainly, of the satisfied and the dissatisfied), will take advantage of the opportunity, and of those few only a handful will offer objective and meaningful observations. If parents are critical, how much notice should the school take of their criticisms? If parental response in such circumstances is poor, and attendance at parents' meetings is disappointing, are the parents wholly to blame or must the school accept a substantial measure of responsibility for the failure to communicate? These are uncomfortable questions which cannot be shirked if genuine partnership is to be achieved.

In Chapter 6, and again in Chapters 14 and 18, the relationship between schools, governors, local authorities and their professional advisers was discussed. The head who has the confidence of these 'external allies' is in a strong and fortunate position, but such confidence will not flourish if it is based on a one-way process. Many governing bodies, for example, leave the head to do his job with the barest minimum of comment or criticism, and many heads regard this as an entirely satisfactory situation, counting themselves lucky to be trusted and supported in this way, as indeed they are. In our view, however, not only is this situation one which is likely to encourage the head into a misleading sense of security and complacency, but it indicates a quality of relationship which ought to be unacceptable to both parties. Often enough, school governors are regarded by heads as no more than rather tiresome rubber-stamping cogs in the administrative machine, to be endured with good grace, to be expected to initiate action only when the head asks for their support, and never to be invited to make their own positive contribution to the school's philosophy and policy. In such a situation not only is the status of the governing body diminished, so that the position of school governor is unlikely to be attractive to men and women of ability and experience, but the school's resources are impoverished. On the other hand, when governors are expected to play a central and active part in the life of the school, and are invited to appreciate and to discuss professional and academic as well as administrative and procedural matters, then a partnership can be established which is a source of comfort and strength both to the head and to the school. Explaining complex educational issues to a body of laymen can, of course, be a frustrating and exasperating experience for a head, but it can also be a salutary one; for it has been said that, if a head cannot explain his philosophy to a body of laymen, then there may be something wrong with his philosophy. A head who buttresses his relationship with his governors, by having regular meetings with his chairman, for example, can establish a partnership in which he can report progress, launch ideas or pose problems, confident that he will be offered a sympathetic ear, together with completely frank and candid advice. Such discussions will ventilate and clarify the issues which are to be put before the governors for their decision, and will furnish a source of refreshment and encouragement to the head, in what is only too often a rather isolated and lonely job.

Much the same attitude can be applied to lay members of the Authority (most of whom, of course, also serve as school governors). Many teachers tend to deride the part which laymen can play in the administration of education, particularly in relation to appointments; but our own direct experience is supported by the overwhelming majority of those who have been closely associated, in one capacity or another, with lay members of education committees, who pay tribute to their realism and common sense, their perspicacity and their devotion to the cause of education. In a service which makes such heavy demands upon the community's good will and support, and which relies so confidently upon a substantial share of the nation's resources, it is clearly to the general advantage that laymen should be directly associated with its administration, able to speak 'for the people', to represent their views and to protect their interests. It would be a poverty-stricken attitude which would argue that such an association should be concerned only with finance and with administrative procedures, and that considerations of educational principle and policy, and the definition of basic educational objectives, should be excluded from their provenance. Moreover, their right to embrace the full range of educational problems in their deliberations, and to express their own views, suggestions and criticisms, is powerfully reinforced by the fact that they are sustained, in their discussions, by the professional counsel both of their own officers, and of consultants, internal and external, such as inspectors, advisers, organisers and HM Inspectors. These two categories are also in direct relationship with the schools, and the wise head will regard them as invaluable reinforcements for his assessment armoury.

The administrative officers of an LEA are in a particularly strong position *vis-à-vis* the schools. Not only are they themselves professionals within the service, with direct teaching experience of their own, but they are in daily contact with local and national opinion, through the Authority's committees and sub-committees, and their own professional associations and societies. In addition, most of them find time to visit schools and colleges, to sit on external committees, such as those of universities and examining bodies, and to meet teachers on courses and conferences. They are able, therefore, to exert a powerful influence, by keeping schools and colleges in touch with each other and with contemporary trends and developments both within their own area and elsewhere, and by providing opportunities for practising teachers to continue their own professional development through courses of in-service training at teachers' centres and elsewhere. They are also in a position to command the good will and respect of teachers, and to play a part in educational policy which is as significant as it is informal. In consequence, some chief education officers and directors of education are among the most creative and fertile influences in the development of educational policy and practice. Their advice and experience is particularly valuable to heads, because they can talk the same language, and illuminate a head's problems by drawing upon such a wide range of information and experience. Their assessment of a school, therefore, however partial it may be, represents an external judgement working on inside knowledge and awareness, and bringing independent standards of comparison which add an extra dimension to the school's own attempts to assess itself, however determined and consistent those attempts may be. The wise head, therefore, will offer a warm welcome to all such visitors, will take them into his confidence, and pay the most serious attention to what they have to tell him, and to the advice and criticism which they may offer.

Turning now to the relationship between schools and other educational institutions in the neighbourhood, probably the most important question to ask is to what extent a particular school fits into the total educational provision in its immediate area. For a secondary school to establish such liaison can be a formidable task, especially when the number of primary schools contributing to a particular secondary school is very large; it may sometimes even exceed fifty, in a major city which offers a good deal of parental choice in its arrangements for transfer to secondary education. In situations such as this, the variety of approach between primary schools is likely to be extremely wide: for example, some children will be reading avidly and with intense enjoyment at 11, some with difficulty and hesitation, and others not at all; some will have learned a good deal of French, while others will have done little or none; some will have studied modern mathematics, while others will have followed a traditional mathematical course; some will have done a good deal of experimental science, while the scientific education of others will have been confined to a simple course of nature study; some will have approached the mastery of their own language through a restricted programme of reading, together with formal grammar and comprehension exercises, while others will have been given the opportunity to read widely, to express themselves freely, and to explore their knowledge and interests over a considerable range of topics; some will have enjoyed a broad musical experience, including the playing of instruments and simple composition, while others will not have ventured beyond singing lessons with a narrow choice of songs. Such contrasts could be multiplied over and over again, but enough has been said to indicate that secondary schools can be presented with situations of the greatest intricacy and complexity. It is no wonder that some secondary schools, despairing of finding any clear or identifiable pattern among the children whom they admit at 11, decide that it is safer to make no preliminary assumptions and that they must virtually start from scratch, muttering imprecations upon the primary schools for invading territory which rightly belongs to *them*, and yet failing to teach the basic skills upon which secondary education depends. It would be improper and impertinent in this context to suggest any solution of this problem, of which all primary and secondary heads are aware. What can be said with confidence, however, is that, for the sake of the children, the basic obligation upon all concerned must be to effect a smooth transfer from the primary to the secondary stage, with the greatest possible continuity of method and approach, and with the minimum of overlap and repetition. In this context, a major responsibility rests, surely, upon the secondary school, a responsibility which embraces liaison, the pooling of information, and an examination of its own contribution towards achieving the quality of transfer which we have outlined. There can clearly be no justification, for example, for reading over again, in the first year of the secondary school, popular favourites (such as *Treasure Island*, or *The Wind in the Willows*) which have been enjoyed in earlier years, or to cover again in history or geography ground which has already been explored before 11. Substantial progress towards harmonisation and integration will be dependent upon good will on all sides, a desire to achieve a measure of agreement upon basic principles, if not upon detailed practices, a recognition that the children's needs will be best served by continuous collaboration between their teachers, including a sensitive, constructive and circumspect use of school records, and a determination that major changes of content, approach or method should not be put into effect until all their implications and repercussions have been fully explored. At the same time, in all their contacts with primary and with middle schools, secondary schools should strive to increase their own knowledge of how young children learn and develop, and should be willing to reassess the extent to which a partial sacrifice of their autonomy and a modification of their methods would best serve the interests of the children and of their parents. There are a number of agencies which, either deliberately or incidentally, have improved the awareness of teachers of what is taking place in other schools. Participation in CSE and other examination and subject committees, discussions within professional associations, and the recent growth of teachers' centres, are all welcome catalysts in the process of cross-communication.

Similar difficulties arise in attempting to achieve liaison with other secondary schools and with colleges of further education which also cater for the 16-19 age range. At present it is not uncommon to find unregulated duplication, and even competition, between the schools and the colleges. On the face of it, it is very difficult to justify several schools and colleges, all within travelling distance of each other, organising (without even prior consultation between them) small teaching groups, or examination classes, in minority subjects. This problem certainly cannot be overcome by rigid regulations, for there are undoubtedly some pupils of 16 + for whom an adult college offers a more appropriate background than the secondary school. Moreover, the difficulties of interlocking time-tables are not to be lightly dismissed, while the transfer or exchange of pupils arouses fierce feelings of loyalty, independence and security, which stand in the way of even a modicum of rationalisation. Nevertheless, it has already been suggested, in the chapters on the use of resources, that the cold finger of economic realism is likely to be pointed, with increasing frequency and vehemence, at examples of wasteful provision and duplication, so that the schools and colleges will be under mounting pressure to achieve a sensible degree of cooperation and working partnership. The first step towards that goal must certainly be an increase in mutual knowledge and awareness, based upon regular consultation and exchange of information. In some areas joint secondary and further education committees have been set up, designed to foster this process. For as things stand at the moment, many secondary schools and colleges of further education are so woefully ignorant of each other that it is difficult to guarantee students, who seek advice, an adequate measure of choice and continuity.

Nor is the position very different, although in a somewhat divergent context, if we consider the relationship between secondary schools on the one hand, and colleges of education, universities, and external examining bodies on the other. Colleges of education and university departments of education are in a particularly privileged (and therefore, in a particularly vulnerable) position in their relationship with schools. Because they are engaged in the further education and initial training of the next generation of teachers, effective cooperation between them is of obvious and paramount importance. Where this cooperation is only marginal or ineffective the consequences are disastrous; then, the schools allege that the colleges know little or nothing about the art and craft of teaching, and are concerned only with theory and academic performance, while the colleges retort that they are burdened not only with all the problems of primary and secondary education, but with all the ills and shortcomings of society, and that they carry the whole temple of education upon their over-burdened but unappreciated shoulders. The tragedy of this failure of communication (for so it often appears) is that colleges of education and university education departments, in general, and college and university tutors and supervisors, in particular, enjoy a prerogative of unique significance. For, while they may appear to be acting only as internal assessors of their own students, they necessarily have their feet in both camps. Experienced teachers themselves, they are in continuous contact with schools; their awareness of the opportunities and difficulties which confront students in training is counterbalanced by their first-hand knowledge of the problems and labyrinthine perplexities with which the schools are faced. In this situation their counsel, comments and suggestions should be of enormous value both to the schools in which they are privileged visitors, and to the colleges and universities to whom they owe first allegiance; certainly the schools are missing a most propitious opportunity if they do not first glean, and then meticulously assess, the impressions and perceptions which are garnered by these go-betweens, as they move from school to school about their daily business.

In their relationship with universities and examining bodies, schools are particularly sensitive to the restrictions which these bodies impose upon them. In responding to their demands, they grumble over the loss of freedom and independence involved, and quiver with indignation over the dead hand of university and examination regulations. Yet, universities are genuinely aware of these difficulties, while examining bodies welcome teachers into consultation and partnership, and offer them a major voice in policy and practice; indeed, the whole machinery of public examinations is becoming more and more dependent upon teacher cooperation. While they complain bitterly about the constraints imposed upon them, however, teachers are often slow to take advantage of the freedoms and opportunities which are now offered to them, for devising special syllabuses to meet their own particular needs (witness the slow growth of CSE mode iii); and there is clearly room for much better liaison and a more effective dialogue between schools and universities, not only between heads and vice-chancellors but, locally, at head of department level.

The recent establishment, in many areas, of Local Authority Social Services Departments, will ease the manifest difficulty experienced by schools of achieving effective liaison with a whole host of social and welfare agencies. Even so, schools find themselves involved, not only with this new coordinating department, but also with courts, police liaison officers, probation officers, child-guidance clinics, medical officers, the careers advisory service, the churches, the youth service, hospital services, national voluntary agencies, such as children's societies, family service units and local organisations of a charitable nature. It is a fearsome and formidable task to keep in touch with them all, and yet the school is at the focus of a child's educational and social development, and must often be prepared to take the initiative in referring cases to the appropriate service agency, or in calling for a case-conference to tackle a particularly complex family problem. Most schools, unfortunately, find themselves without the resources or specialised knowledge to act in this focal role (although, as we have seen the appointment of counsellors may substantially ease them over the initial difficulties). This may well be an area in which widespread delegation to individual members of the staff, combined with skilful coordination of all the knowledge and information thus made available, will offer schools the best way of ensuring that the services of all these departments and agencies are harnessed in the interests of children's welfare.

The public communications media — press, radio and television — also confront schools with a major difficulty, which may sometimes appear in the guise of a fire-eating dragon. Day-to-day involvement with the media is rare, but a spicy titbit of news, however trivial, a threatened scandal, or the prospect of a conflict with authority, are enough to cause hordes of reporters, photographers and camera-men to descend upon a school, until the nature and significance of the incident which called them together is lost in a welter of competitive publicity. Such circumstances are apt to destroy the school's confidence and good will, and to stretch courtesy and patience beyond their breaking point. Nevertheless, these media can be good friends as well as dangerous enemies, and the wise head will establish contact with their local agents, and offer to guarantee that they are regularly offered items of news and information whenever any is available. Having thus made a positive contribution to their insatiable hunger for 'news', the head is then in a much stronger position to ask them to exercise restraint and moderation when the need arises. Success can, perhaps, be measured by the balanced treatment afforded to the school's affairs, over a period of years, although there are bound to be peaks and troughs of activity. Although it may at first sight appear distasteful, some schools have found it effective to appoint a member of the staff as press liaison officer. His prior function is to spot the occasions and circumstances which are likely to be of interest to the press and public, to make sure that appropriate information is promptly and freely made available, and to be always available for enquiry and consultation. The establishment of cooperation and good working relations which such an arrangement ensures, will go a long way towards alleviating the impact of those few occasions when the welfare of the school appears to be in conflict with the sacred inviolability of a news story.

Schools are often hampered by the prevalence of the 'us' and 'them' image. To destroy this image effectively the school must involve itself in the life of the community, and the community in the life of the school. It is of the highest importance to care about the quality of a school's external relationships, to nurture them, and to keep them healthy and robust. This will involve looking positively and systematically for any evidence of success or failure, whether invited or incidental, and however subjective; only so can the school assess the extent to which it is both contributing to and drawing sustenance from the enriched life of the community.

V CODA

20   Innovation

All through the book, and explicitly in the Introduction, we have stressed the changing and changeable nature of the contemporary secondary
school scene; we have indicated some of the problems to which this
continuous change gives rise, and the nature of the skills and techniques necessary to overcome them. Now it so happens that, like any
school time-table, the processes of change inside a school involve
nearly all the managerial principles and practices which we have been
discussing. For this reason alone, innovation provides an appropriate
peg on which to hang the message which we wish to convey, in our
closing pages. The planning, achievement and evaluation of change
afford an object lesson in the basic skills of running a school, all seen
in action in a single operation (as it were), so that they can be assessed,
not only in relation to each other but to their ultimate outcome. On
this account, we believe that the successful management of innovation affords a convincing illustration of what headship is all about.

But there is a much stronger reason even than that for selecting
it as the subject of our concluding chapter. Our predecessors could
count upon living and working in a world of agreed objectives and
stable values, of established traditions and accepted practices. We
ourselves find all these landmarks fast disappearing, so that we have
the gravest difficulty, on the one hand, in holding fast to those
values to which we adhere most deeply while, on the other, first identifying and then adapting ourselves to new ideas, new concepts and
new beliefs, as they emerge from the welter of continuous social
and educational change. Yet it may be realistic to suggest that the third
quarter of the twentieth century may well see some slowing down
of the pace of change in our schools. Externally, some leaders of
political thought, and some sections of our increasingly mobile
society, are clearly becoming anxious about current educational
trends, and about the enormous variation in curriculum, organisation

and method between one area and another. It is now possible, for example, in different parts of the country, for a child to transfer from primary to middle or secondary school at almost any age between 7 and 14. At the same time, internally, there is a heartfelt longing for a period of stability and security, during which loyalty to old values can be renewed, and new values can be tested and assimilated. Moreover, the nation's deliberate investment in educational innovation may well have to be curtailed, in the years immediately ahead, under the financial pressures to which central and local government are now exposed.

Nevertheless, we believe that it will be profitable to consider the factors which determine change, and the principles and practices which affect its achievement. How does the need or the desire for change arise, in the first instance? It may be that a disconcertingly small proportion of those in the fifth form are found to be opting for mathematics and science in the sixth; or the pattern of options and choices available within the curriculum may be exposed to the criticism that they are no longer satisfying the purposes for which they were designed. Alternatively, the appointment of a new member of staff may provide an opportunity for development: the fortunate recruitment of a physicist, for example, with a strong personal interest in astronomy, might provide a chance to strengthen the course of general studies in the sixth form. Again, it may be that the ways in which staff resources are deployed in the curriculum and time-table, are no longer felt to be acceptable; or, perhaps, there may be strong pressure in the common room to replace streaming, setting or broad-banding by a system of mixed-ability grouping. Equally, concepts and practices being tried out elsewhere may trigger off a desire for change, or members of the staff may come back from an in-service course or conference, bubbling with exuberance, and anxious to put new ideas into practice. At the same time, anxiety or enthusiasm within the school may well be reinforced by the fruits of research and experiment outside it, as with the curriculum projects launched and fostered, for example, by the Schools Council or the Nuffield Foundation. Moreover, there are many aspects of contemporary change that are not connected with curriculum practice at all, such as beliefs, purposes and convictions which are grounded in a desire for social justice, or which aim at a positive discrimination of resources towards the needs of the deprived and the handicapped.

Yet, whatever their origin and nature, such pressures to achieve change immediately resurrect our original questions: *Where are you?* and *Where do you want to go?* What advantage is expected to accrue from any change which it is proposed to make, and to whom? What weakness will be eradicated, what strength will be exploited or reinforced, what injustice will be eliminated or at least diminished? Above all, is the cost of the change likely to be justified by the results, whether the cost be measured in purely financial or in total human and social terms? For, at the outset, it is highly desirable to establish the objectives which are to be attained and the criteria by which the proposed change can eventually be evaluated. Indeed, it would be wise continually to guard against changes which are brought about by pressures imperfectly understood, by ideas which have been only partially grasped, or methods which are based only upon theoretical justification. Nothing is more dangerous or more misleading than the 'bandwagon syndrome', which leads to the adoption, lock, stock and barrel, of ideas and practices at second- or third-hand, without adequate examination, digestion, preparation or training.

Having decided, however, that a particular change has, on balance, sufficient merit to deserve thorough investigation, we have then to consider the resources at our disposal, and the constraints to which we are subject, in answer to the question: *How are you going to get there?* And here it is essential to take account of those factors which are likely to be adverse, as well as those which are favourable, so that we can eventually strike a careful balance between them. Perhaps some of those which are, at present, against us can be changed by judicious lobbying, while those which support us, today, may well be less favourable in the future. If, on balance, the omens are propitious, then we must decide whether the adverse factors are within tolerable limits, or whether their influence must be diminished, before it would be wise to make up our minds to go ahead. All this involves, of course, continuous communication and consultation, not only with those who advocate or resist the change, but with all those who are likely to be affected by it, whether directly or indirectly. And the latter are likely to include not only children, staff and parents, but governors, the local education authority, and even examining bodies, employers, colleges or universities, according to the nature and impact of the particular change which we are considering.

At this stage, therefore, it may well be expedient to set up a working party, to explore the proposed change in all its ramifications, and to identify all the probable consequences and repercussions of the change; for the latter are often likely to be far more extensive than is at first apparent. Everyone likely to be concerned must be made fully aware of the exact nature of the proposal under consideration, and of the part which they will be expected to play in its operation. Some or all of them may well require a period of preparation and re-training, for the acquisition of new skills and attitudes or of additional experience. At the same time, too, particular care must be taken to protect those who may feel threatened by the change, either in status or prestige, or by the rejection of their own familiar methods and the adoption of new ones; or the change may seem to cast professional doubt upon hitherto accepted practices, which have become established by tradition, and in which they have long believed. Patient discussion, sympathetic understanding and unfailing support are necessary, if a source of future disaster is to be avoided at the moment when the few volunteer innovators are joined by the body of conscript imitators; and this is bound to be a long process, spread over several months and terms, or even years. Far more changes fail from lack of adequate discussion, preparation and training than from a failure to generate initial enthusiasm and professional zeal.

Eventually, however, it will be possible to survey all the evidence, and to decide whether the proposal should be adopted or not. If the decision is favourable, then appropriate action will have to be taken, resources made available, and consequential administrative decisions reached, in order that the change can be put into effect according to an agreed programme. And this is the moment at which a danger signal must be hoisted! After months of deliberation and discussion, it is temptingly easy to sit back and relax, supported by a sense of satisfaction, and the achievement of a job well done. But the job is still far from done, and there is imperative need to begin the process of monitoring the change: *How will you know when you have got there?* Continuous observation must be made, evidence collected, opinions weighed, enthusiasm or despair assayed; those results which are measurable must be measured, and professional judgements must be reached on effects and consequences which are of the utmost importance even though they cannot be quantified. Only by such means can we hope to be able to decide whether the change is working out satisfactorily, whether it calls for a further injection of professional skill and enthusiasm or of resources, whether it needs a new sense of direction, or a reaffirmation of faith and purpose, or whether it should be abandoned.

From the outset, in fact, all major changes of policy or practice should embody a healthy element of flexibility and an escape route. For it may be necessary to summon up the courage to press the 'abort button', just before the moment when it is too late to put the whole process into reverse. For this reason, it may be prudent to agree upon an initial period of terms or years, after which the project will be subject to thorough reexamination and reassessment. Such a precaution would avoid many of the most serious traps into which such innovatory processes often fall; either because particular consequences were not foreseen, or because the resources available proved to be inadequate. Perhaps, too, the initial head of steam generated to get the project under way, could prove unable to sustain its momentum against the inertia, simple weariness, passive resistance or overt opposition which all new educational ideas succeed in arousing!

By way of demonstrating all these stages and factors in operation, let us consider a specific proposal to introduce Russian into the curriculum, as the second modern language; and let us begin by identifying some of the major questions which would have to be answered, under five main headings:

Reasons for making the change

1 What are presumed to be the advantages and disadvantages of introducing Russian?

2 If Russian were adopted, what other subject(s) might have to be dropped from the curriculum?

3 At what stage should Russian be introduced: in the 2nd, 3rd, 4th or 6th year?

4 What is the value of Russian in academic, vocational and career terms?

Staff

1 Is a teacher available who can teach Russian?

2 What would be the chances of recruiting a successor, if he

leaves, or of appointing additional teachers, if this were found to be necessary?

3 Will any members of staff be adversely affected by the introduction of Russian? For example, will their subject be crowded out of the curriculum, or will it attract fewer pupils?

4 Will it be possible to secure the appointment of Russian students or young teachers as conversational 'assistants', as with French and German?

5 How many teachers of Russian will be required, if the subject eventually becomes established?

Pupils

1 What are the minimum and maximum numbers of pupils who should be allowed to choose Russian?

2 How should they be selected?

3 What criteria for making the choice should be established?

4 What other subject(s) would they have to give up?

Resources

1 Can the necessary funds be made available for text-books, for audio-visual teaching materials and for language laboratory facilities, not only in the first year, but as the subject becomes established?

2 Will a typewriter with Cyrillic characters be required, in order to produce teaching material and to set internal examination papers?

External interests to be consulted or informed

1 The Governors of the School.

2 The Local Education Authority.

3 Parents.

4 Examining Bodies: Which external examinations, at 16 and 18, would it be appropriate to adopt?

5 Can educational visits or exchanges of pupils be arranged, as with France and Germany? If so, what will be the cost, and will some pupils learning Russian have to be subsidised, because their parents cannot bear the cost of such visits?

6 Can colleges of education, polytechnics and universities which offer courses in Russian at different levels be identified?

7 Will there be political objections from any quarter, whether justified or not?

Now this is a comparatively short and simple 'check list'. The introduction of a second modern language, in fact, raises far fewer difficulties than a proposal to abandon some existing arrangement, method or technique and to replace it by another, such as the substitution of mixed-ability grouping for streaming, setting or broad-banding. The introduction of Russian is likely to affect only one teacher, apart from the head of the modern languages department, although the history, geography and English (literature) departments may eventually be confronted with the need for some modification of the content, timing and balance of their work. No one will be expected to abandon established attitudes or teaching methods and to replace them by others less familiar and more demanding. No prolonged period of staff preparation, training or re-training will be necessary. And all this is in striking contrast with many changes which have actually been introduced into secondary schools in recent years. These have affected every single member of staff, from the youngest and least experienced, to those holding senior and responsible positions. There is certainly the possibility of a bandwagon element in the Russian proposal, when it first reaches the head. But there is little chance, in this case, that decisions will be taken, at two different levels, which are found to be contradictory. This would occur, for example, if the head (after full consultation) decided to include history among the options available in the middle school, at the same time as the head of the history department decided that history should be taught chronologically. The effect of such a conflict would be that for some children their study of history would be abruptly sawn off at some arbitrary date such as 1485, 1603, 1685 or 1715 (which is, alas, still a common disadvantage in many secondary schools today).

But if the 'check list' in the case of the Russian proposal is short and straightforward, it illustrates the basic innovatory principle that a head must confront himself with the question: 'Whom do I need to consult or inform?' Quite often, of course, he will be able to reject particular items on his list, provided that the list itself is comprehensive in its scope. And, even if the introduction of Russian is an innovation which can be accepted as comparatively uncomplicated and free from embarrassment, it still involves the head in the exercise of all those skills and techniques which headship demands of him: the identification of aims and objectives, the definition of priorities, the processes of communication, consultation, delegation and administration, the provision of resources and the deployment of manpower, plus the capacity to subject himself and the school, (including the operation of particular features within it), to continuous, critical and realistic assessment.

Yet there will be occasions when the head will not be able to follow these orderly sequences in a series of measured steps. For not only may actual changes in the process of adoption run out of steam (as we have seen), but schools may be suddenly confronted by circumstances which not only demand a major modification of existing practice but, at the same time, allow no time for leisurely investigation. Decisions by examining boards may have to be implemented, for example, whether we like them or not; sudden financial restrictions may adversely influence the whole pattern of a year's work; the attainment of adult status at 18 has affected the whole post-16 pupil-teacher relationship; the sudden and drastic modification of a plan to extend a school building, because the lowest tender grossly exceeds the sum available, may undermine the purposes for which the extension was designed; or changes in the likes, dislikes and attitudes of children can alter the whole pattern of the school meals service. These are all changes in which schools are overtaken by events beyond their control. But, if decisions have to be taken quickly, as in these cases, it is even more essential that there should be well-established patterns of communication and consultation, so that the problems to be solved can be fed into the system, in an emergency, and still lead to an orderly and thorough examination of the issues involved. Even though it may well be a characteristic of skilful headship that crises can be foreseen, and their impact thus greatly diminished, most heads are likely to find themselves in such situations during the course of their careers. Sudden demands upon a school's decision-making machinery are likely to occur, however skilfully the education service is planned, organised and administered. The crucial test then becomes whether the normal school processes can continue to operate efficiently, under pressure, or whether hunch and 'ad hoc-ery', or even sheer exasperation, will determine the quality of the decision.

The successful mediation and adoption of change is only one respect in which much is expected of heads. They are concerned with the daily exercise of authority, responsibility and control. They derive their ultimate inspiration and strength from the realm of ideas, attitudes and convictions. Yet schools are not run by philosophers alone; they are run by men and women steeped in the practice of human affairs and relationships, and motivated by a lively sense of purpose. The quality of their resourcefulness, enthusiasm, patience and example, their sensitivity and integrity, their capacity for concern, compassion and insight, the cogency and adaptability of their powers of judgement, their firm grasp of abiding values and standards and (last, but by no means least) their capacity to laugh at themselves — all these go far to determine the quality of a school's life and work. For it is given to them, as it is given to few other men and women, greatly to influence the extent to which the needs and interests of the nation's children are recognised, satisfied and protected.

Their task is exacting; their difficulties are formidable. Yet there are, surely, few careers in the whole field of human endeavour, which offer a greater intellectual and practical challenge, a wider opportunity of service to the community, or a greater reward.

Bibliography

THE SOCIOLOGY OF EDUCATION

Banks, O.   *The sociology of education* (Batsford 1968)

Banton, M.   *Roles* (Tavistock Publications 1965)

Baron, G. and Taylor, W. (ed)   *Educational administration and the social sciences* (Athlone Press 1969)

Carver, F. and Sergiovani, T. (ed)   *Organisations and human behaviour: focus on schools* (McGraw-Hill 1969)

Eggleston, S. J.   *The social context of the school* (Routledge & Kegan Paul 1967)

Floud, J. E., Halsey, A. H. and Martin, F. M. (ed)   *Social class and educational opportunity* (Heinemann 1957)

Halsey, A. H., Floud, J. E. and Arnold, C. (ed)   *Education, economy and society* (Collier-Macmillan 1961)

Hargreaves, D. H.   *Social relations in a secondary school* (Routledge & Kegan Paul 1967)

Hoyle, E.   *The role of the teacher* (Routledge & Kegan Paul 1969)

Jackson, B. and Marsden, D.   *Education and the working class* (Routledge & Kegan Paul 1962)

Lacey, C.   *Hightown Grammar: the school as a social system* (Manchester University Press 1970)

Mays, J. B.   *The school in its social setting* (Longmans 1967)

Musgrave, P. W.   *The sociology of education* (Methuen 1965)
The school as an organisation (Macmillan 1968)

Musgrove, F.   *Patterns of power and authority in English education* (Methuen 1971)
Family, education and society (Routledge & Kegan Paul 1966)
Youth and the social order (Routledge & Kegan Paul 1968)

Musgrove, F. and Taylor, P. H.   *Society and the teacher's role* (Routledge & Kegan Paul 1969)

Richardson, E.   *The environment of learning: conflict and understanding in the secondary school* (Nelson 1967)

Shipman, M. D.   *Sociology of the school* (Longmans 1968)
Education and modernisation (Faber 1971)
Childhood: a sociological perspective (NFER 1972)

Swift, D. F. *The sociology of education* (Routledge & Kegan Paul 1969)

Taylor, W. *Society and the education of teachers* (Faber 1969)

Wedge, P. and Prosser, H. *Born to fail?* (Arrow Books/National Children's Bureau 1973)

THE ECONOMICS OF EDUCATION

Blaug, M. *The economics of education* 2 vols (Penguin 1968-9)

Coombs, P. H. and Hallak, J. *Managing educational costs* (Oxford University Press 1972)

Correa, H. *The economics of human resources* (Humanities Press 1963)

Maclure, S. *Learning beyond our means?* (Councils and Education Press 1968)

Peacock, A. et al *Educational finance: its sources and uses in the UK* (Oliver & Boyd 1968)

Robinson, E. A. G. and Vaizey, J. (ed) *The economics of education* (Macmillan 1966)

Vaizey, J. *The economics of education* (Faber 1962)

Vaizey, J. and Sheehan, J. *The resources for education* (Allen & Unwin 1965).

THE PRINCIPLES AND SKILLS OF MANAGEMENT

Abercrombie, M. L. J. *The anatomy of judgement* (Pelican 1969)

Bains, M. A. *The new local authorities: management and structure* (HMSO 1972)

Banks, A. L. and Hislop, J. A. *The art of administration* (University Tutorial Press 1968)

Barker, R. G. and Gump, P. V. *Big school, small school: high school size and student behaviour* (Stanford University Press 1964)

Bennis, W.G. *Changing organisations* (McGraw-Hill 1966)

Birley, D. *Planning and education* (Routledge & Kegan Paul 1972)

Blau, P. M. and Scott, W. R. *Formal organisations* (Routledge & Kegan Paul 1963)

Boyce, R. O. and Eisen, H. *Management diagnosis: a practical guide* (Longmans 1972)

Brech, E. F. L. *Management: its nature and significance* (Pitman 1967) *The principles and practice of management* (Longmans 1963)

Brieve, F. J., Johnston, A. P. and Young, K. M. *Educational planning* (Wadsworth Publishing Company 1973)

Brown, J. A. C. *The social psychology of industry* (Penguin 1970)

Burns, T. and Stalker, G. M.　*The management of innovation* (Tavistock Publications 1971)

Drucker, P.　*The practice of management* (Pan 1968)
Drucker on management (Management Publications Ltd 1970)
Management: tasks, responsibilities, practices (Heinemann 1974)

Etzioni, A.　*A comparative analysis of complex organisations* (Collier-Macmillan 1961)

Fowler, G., Morris, V. and Ozga, J.　*Decision-making in British education* (Heinemann 1973).

Gorden, R. L.　*Interviewing: strategy, techniques and tactics* (Dorsey Press 1969)

Griffiths, D. E. et al　*Organising schools for effective education* (Interstate Publishers, Illinois 1962)

Halpin, A. and Croft, D. B.　*The organisational climate of schools* (US Office of Education 1962)

Halpin, A. W.　*Administrative theory in education* (Collier-Macmillan 1967)

Hansen, D. A. and Gerstl, J. E.　*On education: sociological perspective* (Wiley 1967)

Hughes, M. G. (ed)　*Secondary school administration: a management approach* (Pergamon 1970)

Humble, J.　*Management by objectives* (British Institute of Management 1972)

Jackson, M. J.　*Recruiting, interviewing and selecting* (McGraw-Hill 1972)

Kogan, M., Van der Eyken, W. et al　*County Hall: the role of the Chief Education Officer* (Penguin 1973)

Lazarfield, P. F. et al (ed)　*The uses of sociology* (Weidenfeld & Nicolson 1968)

Lessinger, L. M. and Tyler, R. W.　*Accountability in education* (C. A. Jones, Ohio 1971)

Lewis, L. J. and Loveridge, A. J.　*The management of education* (Pall Mall Press 1965)

Liston, D. J.,　*The purpose and practice of management* (Hutchinson Educational 1971)

March, J. G. (ed)　*Handbook of organisations* (Rand McNally 1966)

March, J. G. and Simon, H. A.　*Organisations* (Chapman & Hall 1959)

McGregor, D.　*The human side of enterprise* (McGraw-Hill 1960)

Pollard, H. R.　*Developments in management thought* (Heinemann 1974)

Richardson, E.　*The teacher, the school and the task of management* (Heinemann 1973)

Sidney, E. and Brown, M.　*The skills of interviewing* (Tavistock Publications 1961)

Sofer, C.   *Organisations in theory and practice* (Heinemann 1973)
Stewart, R.   *Managers and their jobs* (Macmillan 1967)
   Reality of management (Pan 1967)
Taylor, G. (ed)   *The teacher as manager* (National Council for Educational Technology 1970)
Thomas, H.   *Decision theory and the manager* (Pitman 1972)
Vickers, Sir Geoffrey   *The art of judgment* (Methuen 1968)
   Towards a sociology of management (Chapman & Hall 1967)
Walker, W. G. (ed)   *The principal at work* (University of Queensland Press 1968)
Walton, J.   *Administration and policy making* (Johns Hopkins Press 1959)

BOOKS OF GENERAL RELEVANCE, WITH IMPLICATIONS
FOR THE RUNNING OF SCHOOLS

Allan, B. (ed)   *Headship in the seventies* (Blackwell 1968)
Anderson, R. H.   *Teaching in a world of change* (Harcourt Brace Jovanovich 1966)
Banks, O. and Finlayson, D.   *Success and failure in the secondary school: an inter-disciplinary approach to school achievement* (Methuen 1973)
Baron, G. and Howell, D. A.   *The government and management of schools* (University of London Press 1974)
Barrell, G. R.   *Teachers and the law* (Methuen 1966)
Bassett, G. W. et al   *Headmasters for better schools* (University of Queensland Press 1967)
Bell, R. and Jones, K.   *Education, economy and politics: case-studies parts 3 and 4* (Open University 1973)
Bennis, W. G. et al   *The planning of change* (Holt, Rinehart & Winston 1961)
Biddle, B. J. and Ellena, W. J. (ed)   *Contemporary research on teacher effectiveness* (Holt, Rinehart & Winston 1964)
Birley, D.   *The Education Officer and his world* (Routledge & Kegan Paul 1970)
Bishop, A. S.   *The rise of a central authority for English education* (Cambridge University Press 1971)
Blishen, E.   *This right soft lot* (Thames & Hudson 1969)
   The school that I'd like (Penguin 1973)
Bloom, B. S. et al   *Taxonomy of educational objectives* (Longmans 1965)
Boyson, R.   *Oversubscribed: the story of Highbury Grove* (Ward Lock 1974)
Bradshaw, K. D.   *Counselling in schools* (H M A and the National Association of Educational Counsellors 1973)

Breese, J. *Freedom and choice in education* (Hutchinson 1973)

Brown, G. H. and Eggleston, S. J. *Towards an education for the 21st century* (University of Keele 1970)

Brown, M. *Introduction to social administration in Britain* (Hutchinson University Library 1969)

Bruner, J. S. *The process of education* (Harvard University Press 1969)
The relevance of education (Allen & Unwin 1972)

Buck, V. E. *Working under pressure* (Staples Press 1972)

Buckman, P. (ed) *Education without schools* (Souvenir Press 1973)

Burgess, T. *Inside comprehensive schools* (HMSO 1970)
Home and school (Penguin 1973)

Cave, R. G. *Partnership for change: parents and schools* (Ward Lock 1972)

Cave, R. G. and O'Malley, R. *Education for personal responsibility* (Ward Lock 1967)

C E R I *Case-studies of educational innovation: III—At the school level* (Centre for Educational Research and Innovation. OECD 1973)

C E R I *The nature of the curriculum for the eighties and onwards* (Centre for Educational Research and Innovation, OECD 1972)

Clegg, Sir A. and Megson, B. *Children in distress* (Penguin 1970)

Conway, E. S. *Going comprehensive* (Harrap 1970)

Creber, J. W. P. *Lost for words* (Penguin 1972)

Croft, M., Raynor, J. and Cohen, L. *Linking home and school* (Longmans 1967)

Dale, R. R. *Mixed or single-sex school? Vol III* (Routledge & Kegan Paul 1974)

Davie, R., Butler, N. and Goldstein, H. *From birth to seven* (Longmans 1972)

Davies, T. I. *School organisation* (Pergamon 1969)

Delacour, A. W. *Logical time-tabling* (Pulin Publishing Co, Porthcawl, S. Wales 1971)

Donnison, D. (ed) *A pattern of disadvantage* (National Children's Bureau 1972)

Douglas, J. W. B. *Home and the school* (Panther 1969)

Douglas, J. W. B., Ross, J. M. and Simpson, H. R. *All our future* (Peter Davies 1968)

Dreeben, R. *On what is learned in school* (Addison-Wesley 1968)

Edmonds, E. L. *The first headship* (Basil Blackwell 1968)

Elgin, H. *The law and the teacher* (Ward Lock 1967)

Exeter University *Headship today and tomorrow* (Exeter University, Institute of Education 1967)

Freeman, J. *Team teaching in Britain* (Ward Lock 1969)

Garner, N. et al *Teaching in the urban community school* (Ward Lock 1973)

Gibson, T. *Teachers talking: aims, methods, attitudes to change* (Allen Lane 1973)

Goodacre, E. *Home and school relationships* (Home and School Council 1968)
School and home (Pergamon 1970)

Gowers, Sir E. and Fraser, Sir B. *The complete plain words* (HMSO 1973)

Green, L. *Parents and teachers: partners or rivals?* (Allen & Unwin 1968)

Griffiths, D. E. *Human relations in school administration* (Appleton-Century-Crofts 1956)

Gronlund, N. E. *Measurements and evaluation in teaching* (Collier-Macmillan 1971)

Halsall, E. *Becoming comprehensive: case histories* (Pergamon 1970)
The comprehensive school: guidelines for the reorganisation of secondary education (Pergamon 1973)

Halsey, A. H. (ed) *Educational priority Vol. I EPAs: problems and policies* (HMSO 1972)

Herndon, J. *The way it spozed to be* (Pitman 1970)

Hewitson, J. N. *The grammar school tradition in a comprehensive world* (Routledge & Kegan Paul 1969)

Heycock, C. *A comprehensive education study: organisation, aims, management* (Sceptre Publishing Co., Port Talbot, Glam 1970)

Hilsum, S. *The teacher at work* (NFER 1972)

Hirst, P. H. and Peters, R. S. *The logic of education* (Routledge & Kegan Paul 1970)

HMSO *Parent-teacher relations in primary schools* (HMSO 1968).

Holden, A. *Teachers as counsellors* (Constable 1969)

Hooper, R. (ed) *The curriculum: context, design and development* (Oliver & Boyd 1972)

Hoyle, E. and Bell, R. *Problems of curriculum innovation I* (Open University 1972)

Hoyle, E. *Problems of curriculum innovation II: a theoretical overview* (Open University 1973)

Hughes, P. *Guidance and counselling in schools* (Pergamon 1971)

Ilich, I. *De-schooling society* (Penguin 1973)
Tools for conviviality (Calder & Boyars 1973)

Jackson, P. W. *Life in classrooms* (Holt, Rinehart & Winston 1968)

James, C. *Young lives at stake* (Collins 1968)

Jenkins, D., Pring, R. and Harris, A. *Curriculum philosophy and design* (Open University 1972)

Jones, A. *School counselling in practice* (Ward Lock 1970)

Judge, H. G. *School is not yet dead* (Longmans 1974)

Keating, L. *The school report* (Kenneth Mason 1969)

Kelsall, R. K. and H. M. *Social disadvantage and educational opportunity* (Holt, Rinehart & Winston 1972)

King, R. *School organisation and pupil involvement: a study of secondary schools* (Routledge & Kegan Paul 1973)

King, S. *Ten years all in* (John Baker 1969)

Koerner, J. D. *Reform in education* (Weidenfeld & Nicolson 1968)

Lawton, D. *Social change, educational theory and curriculum planning* (University of London Press 1973)

Lindsay, C. *School and community* (Pergamon 1970)

Lingard, A. and Allard, J. *Parent/Teacher relations in secondary schools* (Pergamon 1970)

Lister, I. (ed) *De-schooling* (Cambridge University Press 1974)

Lovell, K. *Team teaching* (Leeds University, Institute of Education 1967)

Lytton, H. and Craft, M. *Guidance and counselling in British schools* (Edward Arnold 1969)

Maclure, J. S. *Curriculum innovation in practice* (HMSO 1968)

Marland, M. *Head of department* (Heinemann 1971)
Pastoral care (Heinemann 1974)

Mason, E. *Collaborative learning* (Ward Lock 1970)

Mays, J., Quine, W. and Pickett, K. *School of tomorrow* (Longmans 1968)

McGeeney, P. *Parents are welcome* (Longmans 1969)

Merritt, J. and Cohen, A. *Priorities in education* (Ward Lock 1972)

Merritt, J and Harris, A. *Curriculum design and implementation* (Open University 1972)

Midwinter, E. *Social environment and the urban school* (Ward Lock 1972)
Projections (Ward Lock 1972)

Miles, M. *Comprehensive schooling: problems and perspectives* (Longmans 1968)

Miller, D. *The age between: adolescents in a disturbed society* (Cornmarket — Hutchinson 1969)

Miller, G. W. *Educational opportunity and the home* (Longmans 1971)

Monks, T. G. *Comprehensive education in England and Wales: a survey of schools and their organisation* (NFER 1968)

Moore, B. M. *Guidance in comprehensive schools: a study of five systems* (NFER 1972)

Musgrave, P. W. *Knowledge, curriculum and change* (New Educational Press)

Nicholls, A. and H. *Developing a curriculum: a practical guide* (Allen & Unwin 1972)

OECD *List of social concerns common to most OECD countries: OECD social indicator development programme I* (OECD 1973)

Orring, J. *Comprehensive schools and continuation schools in Sweden* (Kungl, Ecklesiastik Departementet, Stockholm)

Owen, J. G. *The management of curriculum development* (Cambridge University Press 1973)

Peterson, A. D. C. (ed) *Techniques of teaching* (3 vols) (Pergamon 1965)

Pidgeon, D. A. *Expectation and pupil performance* (NFER 1970)

Pines, M. *Revolution in learning* (Penguin 1967)

Raynor, J. and Grant, N. *Patterns of curriculum* (Open University 1972)

Raynor, J. and Harden, J. (ed) *Cities, communities and the young: Readings in urban education* Vol I (Open University 1973)
Equality and city schools: readings in urban education Vol II (Open University 1973)

Rich, J. *Interviewing children and adolescents* (Macmillan 1969)

Richardson, K. *Do it the hard way* (Weidenfeld & Nicolson 1972)

Richardson, W. K. *The teaching revolution* (Methuen 1967)
The school curriculum (Methuen 1971)
The free school (Methuen 1973)

Ross, J. M. et al *A critical appraisal of comprehensive education* (NFER 1972)

Ross, J. M. and Channan, G. *Comprehensive schools in focus* (NFER 1972)

Saran, R. *Policy-making in secondary education: a case study* (Clarendon Press 1973)

Shaplin, J. T. and Olds, H. F. (ed) *Team teaching* (Harper & Row 1964)

Sharp, J. *Open school,* (Dent 1973)

Sharrock, A. *Home/School relations* (Macmillan 1970)
Home and school (NFER 1971)

Shipman, M. and Raynor, J. *Perspectives on the curriculum* (Open University 1972)

Spolton, L. *The upper secondary school: a comparative study* (Pergamon 1967)

Stefflre, B. *Theories of counseling* (McGraw-Hill 1965)

Stewart, W. A. C. and McCann, W. P. *The educational innovators* (Macmillan 1967)

Sumner, R. and Warburton, F. W. *Achievement in secondary schools: attitudes, personality and school success* (NFER 1972)

Swift, D., Williamson, B and Byrne, D. *Education, economy and politics: case studies, Parts I and II* (Open University 1973)

Taylor, G and Saunders, J. B. *The new law of education* (Butterworth 1971)

Taylor, W. *Heading for change: the management of innovation in the large secondary school* (Routledge & Kegan Paul 1973)

UNESCO *World trends in secondary education* (UNESCO 1962) *Educational planning: a world survey of problems and prospects* (UNESCO 1970)

Vaizey, J. *Britain in the sixties: education for tomorrow* (Penguin 1962)

Walton, J. (ed) *Curriculum organisation and design* (Ward Lock 1972) *The secondary school time-table* (Ward Lock 1972)

Wardle, D. *The rise of the schooled society* (Routledge & Kegan Paul 1974)

Warters, J. *Techniques of counseling* (McGraw-Hill 1964)

Warwick, D. *Team teaching* (University of London Press 1971) (ed) *Integrated studies in the secondary school* (University of London Press 1973)

Whisler, T. L. and Harper, S. F. *Performance appraisal: research and practice* (Holt, Rinehart & Winston 1962)

White, J. P. *Towards a compulsory curriculum* (Routledge & Kegan Paul 1973)

Williams, K. *The school counsellor* (Methuen 1973)

Williams, P. *Behaviour problems in schools* (University of London Press 1974)

Wiseman, S. and Pidgeon, D. *Curriculum evaluation* (NFER 1970)

Worrall, P., et al *Teaching from strength: an introduction to team teaching* (Hamish Hamilton 1970)

Young, M. *Innovation and research in education* (Routledge & Kegan Paul 1965)

Young, M. and McGeeney, P. *Learning begins at home* (Routledge & Kegan Paul 1968)